Constructing a Mediating Theology

STUDIES IN THE DOCTRINE OF GOD
Exploring Classical and Relational Theism

Studies in the Doctrine of God: Exploring Classical and Relational Theism is a series of books that explore the nature and attributes of God in the context of current debates over classical theism and relational models of God. This series includes volumes that advance the discussion of the doctrine of God, with particular focus on advancing the discussion of conceptions of God that affirm the Creator-creature distinction while also affirming that God is freely and genuinely related to the world in a way that makes a difference to God. Such conceptions of God are sometimes referred to as modified or moderate classical theism or neoclassical theism. These conceptions of God are classical in that they affirm some core tenets of classical theism (divine perfection, necessity, aseity, self-sufficiency, unity, eternity, immutability, omnipotence, omniscience with foreknowledge, and omnipresence). At the same time, such conceptions are also relational in that they affirm God is genuinely related to the world and depart from one or more attributes of (strict) classical theism such as divine timelessness, strict simplicity, strict immutability, and/or strict impassibility. Each volume in this series will address some aspect or aspects of the nature and attributes of God and the God-world relation in a way that advances the discussion of approaches that are both classical and relational in these respects.

Series Editors:

R. T. Mullins
John C. Peckham

Editorial Board:

David Baggett
Daniel Castelo
Paul Copan
Jeanine Diller
Scott Harrower
William Hasker

Veli-Matti Kärkkäinen
Kevin Kinghorn
Andrew Loke
Roger Olson
Anastasia Scrutton
Jordan Wessling

Constructing a Mediating Theology

Affirming the Impassibility
and the Passibility of the Triune God

J. D. KIM

Foreword by
PAUL T. NIMMO

CASCADE *Books* • Eugene, Oregon

CONSTRUCTING A MEDIATING THEOLOGY
Affirming the Impassibility and the Passibility of the Triune God

Studies in the Doctrine of God

Copyright © 2022 J. D. Kim. All rights reserved. Except for brief quotations in critical publications or reviews, no part of this book may be reproduced in any manner without prior written permission from the publisher. Write: Permissions, Wipf and Stock Publishers, 199 W. 8th Ave., Suite 3, Eugene, OR 97401.

Cascade Books
An Imprint of Wipf and Stock Publishers
199 W. 8th Ave., Suite 3
Eugene, OR 97401

www.wipfandstock.com

PAPERBACK ISBN: 978-1-6667-3385-3
HARDCOVER ISBN: 978-1-6667-2882-8
EBOOK ISBN: 978-1-6667-2883-5

Cataloguing-in-Publication data:

Names: Kim, J. D., author. | Paul T. Nimmo, foreword.

Title: Constructing a mediating theology : affirming the impassibility and the passibility of the triune God / J. D. Kim.

Description: Eugene, OR: Cascade Books, 2022 | Series: Studies in the Doctrine of God | Includes bibliographical references.

Identifiers: ISBN 978-1-6667-3385-3 (paperback) | ISBN 978-1-6667-2882-8 (hardcover) | ISBN 978-1-6667-2883-5 (ebook)

Subjects: LCSH: God (Christianity)—Immutability. | Theology, Doctrinal—History. | Suffering of God.

Classification: BT153.I47 K60 2022 (print) | BT153 (ebook)

Table of Contents

Foreword vii
Acknowledgments xi
Chapter 1: Approaching the Doctrine of the (Im)Passibility of God 1
    What is the Doctrine of the (Im)Passibility of God? 1
    The Debate Concerning Divine Impassibility and Passibility 2
    Mediating Positions 5
    The Premise of This Work 8
    Definitions 10
    Exploring Divine (Im)Passibility 12
    Book Outline 14

Chapter 2: The Doctrines of Divine Impassibility and Passibility 15
    Historical Developments in the Debates 16
    Factors in the Rise of Passibilism 20
    Thematic Discussion of Impassibility and Passibility 25
    Constructive Lessons from Weinandy and Moltmann 53

Chapter 3: Mediating Theologians of the Nineteenth
  and Twentieth Centuries 58
    Theological Background of Strong, Martensen, and Clarke 59
    Thematic Discussion of Impassibility and Passibility 66
    Constructive Lessons from Strong, Martensen, and Clarke 94

Chapter 4: Mediating Theologians within Evangelical Theology 96
    Theological Background of Pinnock and Frame 97
    Thematic Discussion of Impassibility and Passibility 103
    Constructive Lessons from Pinnock and Frame 134

Chapter 5: The Immanent Trinity Is Impassible 136
    The Self-Movement of the Immanent Trinity 136
    The Characteristics of the Reciprocity of the Immanent Trinity 142
    The Impassibility of the Immanent Trinity 150

Chapter 6: The Economic Trinity Is Passible 162
    The Self-Movement of the Economic Trinity 163
    The Characteristics of the Operations of the Economic Trinity 166
    The Passibility of the Economic Trinity 173

Chapter 7: Concluding Thoughts on God's (Im)Passibility 200
    Answering Mozley's Six Necessary Questions 200

Bibliography 207

Foreword

Paul T. Nimmo

Does God suffer?

The question of divine passibility has been a topic of ongoing reflection and debate in the church since the earliest days of Christian witness. It arises straightforwardly out of the complex testimony of Scripture in its description of the history of God with creation, and finds its focal point in the desire to affirm both the suffering of Jesus Christ on the cross and the divinity of this Crucified One simultaneously. In the unfolding of church history, there have been esteemed voices raised on both sides of the debate. At times, as in the early and mediaeval church, the pendulum largely swung towards favoring the trope of divine impassibility; more recently, in the modern and contemporary church, it has broadly inclined towards affirming the idea of divine passibility. To add to the positions available, there have also been more or less prominent voices that have sought to mediate between the two positions, desiring to hold the predicates together in a sophisticated, sometimes even paradoxical fashion.

It is into the ongoing and contested dialogue around divine impassibility that the present work of J. D. Kim makes an important and creative intervention. Kim, a talented scholar with wide experience of both academy and ministry, presents here a generative line of argument that merits the attention not only of scholars reflecting upon this debate in particular but also of Christian academics and ministers more widely. It is not simply the fact that Kim here advances a fresh and provocative iteration of a mediating position in this debate, according to which the immanent Trinity is impassible and the economic Trinity is passible. It is also the fact that Kim takes the contemporary dialogue forward in three significant ways.

First, at a historical level, and by way of preparing the foundation of his constructive position, Kim sets forth an insightful example of theological *ressourcement*. The resources to which he turns, however, are not the vaunted riches of the patristic or mediaeval period. Instead, Kim turns to the nineteenth- and early twentieth-century legacy of the esteemed Christian writers Augustus H. Strong, Hans L. Martensen, and William N. Clarke. Theologians such as these have all too easily and all too readily been dismissed as "liberal theologians," discarded without proper reading or genuine consideration in the haste to return to something of greater age that is purported to be more worthy of investigation. Yet such indecent haste to pass over theological works from more recent history risks missing the genuine wrestling with the gospel and important insights for current thinking that may be found within them. It is the labor of Kim to retrieve and reread the works of these three figures in particular as exemplars of the genre of mediating theology that he seeks to advance, gleaning building blocks for constructing and supporting his own argument. It is these sources, among others, that he brings into conversation with more contemporary mediating positions such as those advanced by John M. Frame and Clark H. Pinnock.

Second, at a theological level, Kim sets out a detailed consideration of the eternal way in which God moves. Specifically, Kim suggests in respect of the immanent Trinity not only that God moves, but that God is moved by Godself. There are thus active and passive dimensions of the eternal self-movement of God, a core reciprocity that can also be considered at the level of the divine persons: the three divine persons both move themselves and each other, and are moved by each other. It is at this point that Kim introduces what he refers to as the "dynamic reciprocity model." With this model, he advances the idea that, in eternity, it is as valid to speak of an action causing a passion as of a passion causing an action: the two are simultaneous, co-conditioning and co-constitutive. This suggestion is challenging, even provocative. But it allows Kim to illuminate the full eternal relationality of the divine persons, the way in which they exist freely yet necessarily in a dynamic and reciprocal impassible blessedness. Without denying the *taxis* of the Trinity, each of the three persons is thus both Lover and Beloved here—each one moving to and moved to love the other persons, willing to and willed to love the other persons. It is this rich conception of the inner divine life that funds the next step of Kim's argument—the conception of God in the economy.

Third, then, and again at a theological level, Kim presents a careful account of how God operates in the economy. For Kim, as in eternity, so in the economy, God both moves and is moved by Godself. Yet as God moves towards and in the creation, Kim suggests, God additionally wills in the divine love and in the divine freedom to be moved by the world. This introduces an additional dimension into the "dynamic reciprocity" model introduced previously. The effect of this willed activity and its opening up of mutual relational engagement between God and creation is not to compromise the eternal blessedness of God; for Kim, the divine perfection remains entirely untarnished by this economic action and passion. Its effect, rather, is to render God *ad extra* susceptible to being in relationships of reciprocal love with created beings, and to moving and being moved in relation to the world generally. In the sphere of creation, the actions and passions of God are entirely free, bound by no necessity other than the divine will. Kim tracks how this conception of the divine being and action in the economy plays out over a range of themes of theological enquiry, culminating in a treatment of the cross. Here, at the culmination of the argument, Kim writes suggestively of the suffering of all three divine persons on Golgotha.

These specific contributions to the contemporary debate regarding divine passibility may not persuade everyone to move to a mediating position. But the light that they—and Kim's volume as a whole—shed on themes within that debate is instructive. Kim draws the reader to revisit their own presuppositions and conclusions in this conversation, and challenges them to reassess and to reconceive their ideas. His work is thus a welcome addition to the literature on this subject, providing fresh material for consideration and reflection. I commend it to you warmly.

Paul T. Nimmo
Aberdeen
October 2021

Acknowledgments

Just as raising a child takes a village, completing this book has taken an entire village to come alongside me, and I want to mention many individuals who have made this project possible.

I thank my brothers—Caleb Chung, Sean Baek, James Choi, and Inho Choi—who have been part of my life before and after the snowboarding accident in 2004 and strengthened me to endure many challenges that I experienced related to my spinal cord injury.

I express my gratitude for my friends from the Evangelical Presbyterian Church, Cherry Hills Community Church, Uphold, International Section Community, Craig Hospital, Denver Seminary, WHOOT, and Parker Evangelical Presbyterian Church.

I have been encouraged especially by Xio Castelo, In-Kyung Chung, E. S. Han, Jihoon Park, Min Kyu Park, Jihye Yu, Deirdre Harlow, Lucy Hong, Yuri Hong, Andrus Yoon, Shao Kim, Dick Elliot, and Sung Yoon, and I extend my sincere appreciation to my mentors, Stephanie Percival, Sharon Beekmann, Jae Son, Myung S. Lee, and Rich Sweeney, whose love, support, and wisdom have been nothing but inspiration. I am simply grateful for them.

The supporters of J. D. Kim Ministries have been a blessing to my theological and ministry callings with their prayer, help, and friendship. Particular thanks go to Mike Gardener, Karin Gardener, Carol Bullis, Rosa Frazel, Niki Hyde, Tony Hyun, and Dennis Russo for their encouragement and friendship.

Countless teachers have helped in shaping my theological understanding, including my professors at Iliff School of Theology and Denver Seminary and Sung Wook Chung, my mentor who has motivated me to pursue doctoral work and aided me throughout the process as a valuable source of advice and encouragement. He has impacted my life and ministry tremendously.

I owe a great debt of gratitude to my doctoral supervisor, Paul T. Nimmo, for his perceptive insight and thoughtful annotation that he offered during my studies. He was actively and passionately engaged with my doctoral work and was humble and sincere in his effort to challenge and shape my thought and argument. I would not have been able to cross the finish line without his gracious support.

I want to express my deep gratitude to my mom and dad, Grace and Seung, for loving me with a Christlike love and for sacrificing their lives for their only son, who has a physical disability. They have been my greatest supporters, friends, ministry partners, and role models of faith. I love them very much. I am grateful for my family living in Colorado, Hyun Kim and Kathie Kim, and South Korea, for their prayer, help, and thoughtfulness.

My debts to God are too innumerable to be written in this limited space. To say the least, I am so thankful for his unconditional and unceasing love and his gracious sovereignty over my life. *Soli Deo gloria!*

I

Approaching the Doctrine of the (Im)Passibility of God

What Is the Doctrine of the (Im)Passibility of God?

The theological task of the doctrine of the (im)passibility of God considers whether God is capable of being associated with suffering and of being moved by the world.[1] More specifically, it is concerned with exploring *whether* and—if so—*how* the triune God of Scripture, who is both almighty and all love, responds to his beloved human creatures who were made in his image and yet who are now implicated in sin and suffering. Exploring God's response should be of interest to all people, not only to certain theologians, for we have been observing and experiencing the impact of the coronavirus in all corners of the world since its breakout in early 2020. The questions about the capability of God's suffering and being moved by human sin and suffering may only seem appropriate in these post-coronavirus days. But in reality, these questions have been reflected, debated, and answered for much of the history of Christian theology.

Two major views have been advanced in the course of describing God's response: divine impassibility and divine passibility. More recently, a third, mediating position between impassibilism and passibilism has arisen: the view that the triune God is impassible *in se* (in himself) and

---

1. The term "(im)passibility" is used in contemporary theological discussion to refer to God's impassibility and/or passibility.

passible *ad extra* (in his relationship with the world). According to this position, God, who is impassible in himself, is capable of relating to human suffering and of being moved by the world and responds *through* his own suffering to the conditions and choices of humanity. This publication follows this third position.

The Debate Concerning Divine Impassibility and Passibility

A careful and thorough exposition of the doctrine of divine (im)passibility first requires describing the terms "divine impassibility" and "divine passibility." First, divine impassibility means that "God is not passible or subject to passion (im = not, and passible = having passion). God cannot undergo passion or suffering."[2] In this view, God is infinitely perfect and does not suffer. Suffering is seen to be related to negative emotion, imperfection, sin, and evil; therefore, suffering cannot be an experience of the triune God.

Second, divine impassibility indicates that God is not capable of being affected or acted upon: "Hence, impassibility is imperviousness to causal influence from external factors."[3] God who is eternal and immutable can experience neither time nor change, both of which are crucial aspects pertaining to being acted upon. God is pure act without passion and has no need to change, being fully actualized within himself. Therefore, he does not undergo mutable and temporal experiences such as would be involved in being moved by the world: God is impassible *in se* and *ad extra*.

By contrast, divine passibility can be defined in three ways: "(1) external passibility or the capacity to be acted upon from without, (2) internal passibility or the capacity for changing the emotions from within, and (3) sensational passibility or the liability to feelings of pleasure and pain caused by the action of another being."[4] In this view, God can be passible in his nature and therefore is capable of suffering *ad extra*. Suffering is not necessarily in conflict with God's eternal happiness and perfection so that God can experience both happiness and suffering *in se* and *ad extra*. God is capable of being affected or acted upon. He interacts with

---

2. Geisler, *Systematic Theology*, 462.
3. Creel, *Divine Impassibility*, 11.
4. Cross and Livingstone, eds., "Impassibility of God," 828.

human beings mutably and reciprocally, and through that interaction can be moved by creatures and their miseries.[5]

Discussions of divine (im)passibility are robust in contemporary theological conversation.[6] The doctrine of the impassibility of God has been the dominant theological view in the tradition, at least from the writings of the patristic theologians to the post-Reformation theologians.[7] In the early church, there was evidence of belief in divine passibility in the forms of patripassianism and theopaschitism. Patripassianism was treated as a trinitarian heresy, as a version of Sabellianism, with its endorsement of the view that the Father suffered the same suffering as the Son because the Father and Son were considered as mere manifestations and modes of one God, without any distinctions.[8] Theopaschitism was another way of indicating divine suffering, particularly the suffering of the Son in relationship to the hypostatic union of the divine and human natures of the incarnate Jesus.[9] There are possible traces of openings to passibilist thinking in the works of such figures as Origen and his disciple, Gregory Thaumaturgus, during the patristic era[10] and Martin Luther during the Reformation era.[11] Divine passibility has become a significant voice in the debates concerning divine (im)passibility particularly since

---

5. The term "passibilists" will be used to refer to those who affirm that God suffers in response to human suffering and sin, as well as the person of Jesus on the cross in his divine nature and/or his human nature.

6. For some of the most recent works on divine (im)passibility, see Peckham, *Doctrine of God*; Matz and Thornhill, eds., *Divine Impassibility*; Mullins, *End of the Timeless God*; Powell, *Impassioned Life*.

7. A non-exhaustive list of key theologians from this period of Christian history who support the doctrine of the impassibility of God might include Anselm, "Proslogium," 56–64; Aquinas, *Summa Theologica*, 1:14–46; Augustine, "Concerning the Nature of God, Against the Manichaeans," 4:351–65; Calvin, *Institutes of the Christian Religion*, 1:226–28; Charnock, *Existence and Attributes of God*, 98–143; Clement of Alexandria, "Book Two," 206–8; Justin Martyr, "First Apology," 39–42; Tertullian, *Tertullian's Treatise Against Praxeas*, 175–79.

8. Kelly, *Early Christian Doctrines*, 119–23.

9. Sarot, "Patripassianism, Theopaschitism."

10. Thaumaturgus, *St. Gregory Thaumaturgus*, 156–59; Origen, "Homily 6," 92–93.

11. Luther, *Word and Sacrament III*, 151–250.

the beginning of the nineteenth century.[12] Ronald Goetz even goes as far as to say that passibilism has become "the new orthodoxy."[13]

In much of the current theological dialogue, divine impassibility and divine passibility are construed as opposing conceptions of the Christian God. Impassibilist theologians are committed to maintaining what they consider to be a biblical view of the transcendent God and accept the broad tenets of classical theism to defend their understanding of the perfections of God.[14] In this line of thinking, the affirmation of God's passibility implies a direct rebuttal of the undisturbed transcendence of God represented by the classical divine attributes of immutability, impassibility, eternity, simplicity, and aseity.

It is customary for modern passibilists to view this doctrine of divine impassibility as constructed with the aid of Hellenistic philosophies and as perfected in the scholastic metaphysics associated with, among others, Thomas Aquinas.[15] The Hellenistic philosophies that are considered as the precursors of impassibilism include Stoicism, middle Platonism, and Neoplatonism.[16] Ohlrich considers that Platonism and Aristotelianism had the most impact on Christian doctrines of impassibilism and notes that "early [Christian] theologians simply carried over Plato's argument that the gods are exalted above pleasure and pain and Aristotle's description of God as the 'first cause' or 'unmoved mover.'"[17] Adolf von Harnack offers support for such a view in his claim that impassibility "in its conception and development is a work of the Greek spirit on the soil of the

---

12. Possible reasons for this rise in the popularity of passibilism will be explained in chapter 2. For other scholars who affirm the suffering of God whether *in se* and/or *ad extra* and are not introduced in this work, see Bauckham, "In Defense of the Crucified God"; Bonhoeffer, *Cost of Discipleship*; Pool, *God's Wounds*; and Sarot, *God, Passibility and Corporeality*.

13. Goetz, "Suffering of God," 385.

14. Impassibilist theologians will be outlined in the next chapter, but to name a few impassibilists, see Dolezal, "Still Impassible"; Renihan, *God Without Passions*; Dodds, *Unchanging God of Love*.

15. Many passibilists hold deeply negative perceptions of divine impassibility. For instance, Fairbairn writes, "Theology has no falser idea than that of the impassibility of God." Fairbairn, *Place of Christ in Modern Theology*, 483. Recently, many impassibilists have refuted such perceptions as unfair and unbalanced and have in turn expressed grave concerns regarding the doctrine of the passibility of God.

16. Kearsley, "Faith and Philosophy in the Early Church," 81–82.

17. Ohlrich, *Suffering God*, 39.

Gospel."[18] E. Pollard agrees with von Harnack's assessment: "Among the many Greek philosophic ideas supported into Christian theology, and into Alexandrine Jewish theology before it, is the idea of the *impassible* God (*apathes theos*), and this idea furnishes us with a particularly striking illustration of the damage done by the assumption of alien philosophical presuppositions when they are applied to Christian theology."[19]

In opposition to the impassibilist view, passibilist theologians therefore replace the emphasis on the classical divine attributes with a foregrounding of God's love, relationality, and faithfulness, construing them as accurate descriptions of the God of the Bible. In the terms that will be used in this work, passibilist theologians not only affirm the suffering of God in the economy but also the suffering of God *in se*. This often involves the drawing of a necessary connection between God as love and his suffering. In this line of thinking, accepting the idea of divine impassibility means violating the integrity and relationality of the love of the triune God. It is customary for modern impassibilists to consider that the affirmation of divine passibility tends to undermine the perfection of God and to portray him as pathetic, inconsistent, and vulnerable.[20] Against the passibilists' agenda of dismissing divine impassibility, Vanhoozer complains, "By so dismissing the alleged *apatheia* [impassibility] of God as to be left with a 'pathetic' God who exists in a dependency-relation with the world, a God who is so affected by the world that he ceases to be worthy of worship."[21]

Mediating Positions

Recognizing the crucial theological insights present in the arguments of both impassibilists and passibilists, a number of theologians have

18. von Harnack, *History of Dogma*, 1:17.

19. Pollard, "Impassibility of God," 356, emphasis original. Likewise, Moltmann complains that "Christian theology acquired Greek philosophy's ways of thinking in the Hellenistic world; and since that time most theologians have simultaneously maintained the passion of Christ, God's Son, and the deity's essential incapacity for suffering." Moltmann, *Trinity and the Kingdom*, 22.

20. Thomas, "Frame on the Attributes of God," 367. Thomas claims that "the implications of a doctrine of divine passibility . . . are catastrophic. We are left with a God who is crippled with pain and whose ability to engage in more than just empathy is severely curtailed as a consequence."

21. Vanhoozer, *Remythologizing Theology*, 404.

proposed a third option—or mediating position—within the debate between impassibilists and passibilists.[22] These "mediating" theologians seek to recognize both God's eternal blessedness[23] and his perfection—the major tenets of the classical accounts of God's eternity, aseity, omniscience, omnipresence, immutability, and sovereignty—and simultaneously to affirm God's suffering in his relationship with his creatures.[24] This type of account of classical theism is described as modified or moderate classical theism or neoclassical theism.[25] Three identifiable views within mediating theology have been advanced at this point: each view affirms God's passibility in a slightly different way.

Mediating theologians who hold the first view affirm God's capacity to suffer *ad extra*, proposing that God is not moved by anything external to himself but chooses in eternity to suffer with human creatures without being moved by them. J. I. Packer writes in this vein that divine impassibility means

> not impassivity, unconcern, and impersonal detachment in the face of creation; not insensitivity and indifference to the distresses of a fallen world; not inability or unwillingness to empathize with human pain and grief; but simply that God's experiences do not come upon him as ours come upon us, for his are foreknown, willed and chosen by himself, and are not involuntary surprises forced on him from outside, apart from his own decision, in the way that ours regularly are.[26]

In his affirmation of the classical doctrine of God's attributes, John Cooper makes a similar argument to support this aspect of God's suffering: "God's feelings are *affections*—intentional affective attitudes that

---

22. Castelo, *Apathetic God*, 14. In this context, Castelo uses the term a "middle way" because he finds merits in both impassibilism and passibilism.

23. Blessedness means to be happy and joyous in the fullest degree and expresses "a life which is complete in itself . . . the eternal *peace* of love, which is higher than all reason . . . the sabbath of love in its state of eternal perfection." Martensen, *Christian Dogmatics*, 101, emphasis original. Terms such as "blessedness," "happiness," and "joy" will be used interchangeably.

24. "A mediating position" describes the arguments of those theologians who attempt to grasp both the dynamics of God's perfections and blessedness *in se* and his passibility *ad extra*.

25. Not all mediating theologians will identify their position as modified classical theism, but the mediating position that we propose in this volume can be referred to as modified classical theism.

26. Packer, "Theism for Our Time," 17.

he eternally chooses to take toward his creatures. One need not abandon classical theism in order to affirm that 'God feels our pain.'"[27] Such theologians stress that the doctrine of divine impassibility is necessary as an apophatic qualifier to sustain the distinctions between the Creator and creation and between divine emotions and human emotions and the ways in which they are respectively experienced.[28] Using the term that will be developed later on, these theologians affirm only the *active* dimension of the suffering of God.

Second, a group of mediating theologians affirms that God, in his impassibleness, not only suffers in this first, active way, but is also moved by his human creatures and suffers mutably and temporally in his personal relationship with them. For example, Michael Horton suggests that divine impassibility is "incapacity for being overwhelmed by suffering, not inability to enter into it,"[29] and adds that "we must avoid the conclusion that God is untouched or unmoved by creaturely suffering."[30]

Daniel Castelo affirms this position and holds that God "cannot be affected against God's will by an outside force,"[31] yet at the same time acknowledges God's ability to be moved by the world willingly and experience temporal suffering. Rob Lister argues that God is *both* impassible and impassioned and explains his argument in this way:

> God is *impassible* in the sense that he cannot be manipulated, overwhelmed, or surprised into an emotional interaction that he does not desire to have or allow to happen.... God is *impassioned* (i.e., *perfectly* vibrant in his affections), and he may be affected by his creatures, but as God, he is so in ways that accord rather than conflict with his will to be so affected by those whom, in love, he has made.[32]

Likewise, John Frame—whose work will be discussed extensively in chapter 4—affirms that God decrees that he will suffer in eternity and that God experiences the mutable, temporal, and passive aspects of passibility in the economy. Using the terms that will be developed later, these

---

27. Cooper, *Panentheism*, 332, emphasis original.
28. Gavrilyuk, *Suffering of the Impassible God*, 48; Lister, *God Is Impassible*, 102.
29. Horton, *Lord and Servant*, 195.
30. Horton, *Christian Faith*, 247.
31. Castelo, "Qualified Impassibility," 66.
32. Lister, *God Is Impassible*, 36, emphasis original.

theologians uphold both the *active and passive* dimensions of the suffering of God.

Third, there are other mediating theologians who affirm that God chooses to suffer with the world in response to the conditions and choices of human beings and hold the mutable, temporal, and passive aspects of God's suffering. However, unlike the first and second views, they do not agree that God is impassible or cannot be moved by the world and that God decrees his suffering in eternity. In his rejection of such an understanding of divine impassibility,[33] John Peckham argues that "God is voluntarily passible in relation to the world, meaning he freely chose to create this world and freely opened himself up to being affected by it in a way that does not diminish or collapse the Creator-creature distinction."[34] In this way, God experiences emotions and suffering as the result of his free response to the choices and actions of his creatures.

In a similar way, Clark Pinnock, whose work will be discussed in chapter 4, stressing God's nature as relationality, is focused more on grasping God's suffering that occurs as the result of his reciprocal relationship with the world rather than the active dimension of divine emotions and suffering noted above. Pinnock writes that "God does not simply rule over creation, he is moved and affected by what happens in history. Events arouse joy or sorrow, pleasure or wrath in him. Our deeds move, grieve, gladden, or please him. His nature is not characterized merely by intelligence but is also characterized by pathos."[35] Likewise, Augustus Strong, Hans Martensen, and William Clarke—whose work will be discussed in chapter 3—affirm that God experiences the passive aspect of suffering in the economy. In the terms that will be introduced later on, these theologians affirm only the *passive* dimension of the suffering of God.

The Premise of This Work

This publication both goes beyond the antithesis of impassibilists and passibilists and addresses the strengths and weaknesses of the mediating

---

33. Peckham, "Qualified Passibility," 107. Peckham offers two reasons for his rejection of divine impassibility: (1) the insufficient biblical affirmation of divine impassibility (semantically or conceptually) and (2) "the confusion and diversity of meanings associated with this term in past and present theology."

34. Peckham, "Qualified Passibility," 98.

35. Pinnock, *Most Moved Mover*, 55.

positions by articulating a mediating position according to which the triune God is both impassible and passible—the immanent Trinity is impassible but is also passible when acting for the benefit of world in the economy. The three divine persons of the immanent Trinity, who move themselves and are moved by the other divine persons only, are not moved by the world. They exist in eternal blessedness, as the result of the infinite perfections of the three divine persons and of the inner communion of sharing their endless blessedness and glory, and as the expression of their reciprocal love for the divine persons.

This construal of divine impassibility relates to the immanent movements of the three divine persons and prevents suffering from intruding upon the peace and blessedness of the inner life of the triune persons. The three divine persons of the economic Trinity freely move themselves to move *toward* the world (actively) and to be moved *by* the world (passively). They thus chose to suffer with human creatures as the expression of their love for them, as their response to human sin and suffering, and as the outcome of their decision to participate in real and actual reciprocal relationship with human creatures that entails mutable and temporal modes of emotions and suffering. This understanding of divine passibility stresses the freedom of the triune persons to engage in reciprocal relationship with the world and sets the divine suffering within the domain of salvation history.

This work has roots in the arguments of the mediating theologians and yet differs from them in two important ways. First, it explores the distinctive characteristics of the immanent reciprocal relations of the Father, Son, and Holy Spirit and considers how these serve as the basis of the relations both between the divine persons of the economic Trinity and between the divine persons and human creatures. It considers how the self-moving God of the Trinity moves himself actively and is moved by himself passively *ad intra* before considering how he is moved by the world. The self-movement of the triune God *in se* by virtue of which the three divine persons are free to move themselves and to be moved by the divine others serves as the principle of the movement of the persons of the economic Trinity, in their relation to each other and to the world.

Second, this work introduces a new way of understanding the way in which the eternal actions (and corresponding passions) of the divine persons condition one another—the "dynamic reciprocity model."[36] This

---

36. The "dynamic reciprocity model" is a constructive insight of this work and will be explained in greater detail in chapter 5.

model illuminates the answers to the questions of *whether* God is moved by the world and, if so, *how* he is moved by it.

By way of an initial sketch, it might be said that the dynamic reciprocity model proposes that the eternal actions and eternal passions of the divine three persons have the ability to condition one another mutually. It is intuitive that, for every action of one trinitarian person upon another, there is a corresponding passion on the part of the trinitarian person acted upon.

The additional insight of the model developed here is that this passion does not have to be considered as a secondary or derivative event only, as merely the result of the first action. Divine actions and passions are not bound by the same logical and chronological sequence as human actions and passions. On this basis, it can also be suggested that the prior passion moves the subsequent action: as the prior active movement conditions the subsequent passive movement, the subsequent passive movement can condition the prior active movement.

This aspect of the model is clearly less intuitive as it goes against the temporal run of cause and effect familiar to everyday life. But this aspect of the model is particular to the unique, eternal life of God. The benefit of this dynamic reciprocity model is that it allows for a reconsideration of the relationship between the actions and the passions of the triune God *ad intra* and *ad extra*, and thus for a reconceptualization of the way in which the immanent and economic Trinity can be distinguished but related.

Definitions

Several important terms that will be used throughout this book require an initial working definition. Regarding terms such as "emotion," "feeling," and "affection," multiple academic disciplines show that each term can convey a different meaning from one another.[37] However, here these terms are used interchangeably to convey the meaning of emotions such as anger, joy, jealousy, and so forth. In the same manner, terms such as "suffering," "pain," "sorrow," "passibility," and "grief" are used interchangeably to convey the meaning of suffering.

---

37. For researches on these subjects, see Beck and Demarest, *Human Person in Theology and Psychology*; Roberts, *Emotions*; Scrutton, *Thinking Through Feeling*.

APPROACHING THE DOCTRINE OF THE (IM)PASSIBILITY OF GOD

When referring to the Trinity, though some recent work—such as that of Gilles Emery—has preferred to use the language of processions and missions to describe the life of the Trinity,[38] this publication retains the language of the immanent and economic Trinity. The immanent Trinity refers here to "the Trinity as it exists necessarily and eternally, apart from creation. It is, like God's attributes, what God necessarily is."[39] The economic Trinity in turn refers to "the Trinity in its relation to creation, including the specific roles . . . that the persons of the Trinity have freely entered into; they are not necessary to their being."[40]

The terms "action," "passion," and related terms also need clarification. An action implies a prior intention and movement to act, and a passion indicates both "a caused state of being into which one is moved by the activity of some agent"[41] and "the reception of change in the being acted upon."[42] When the term "passion" is used, it refers to the above definitions, to passivity only, rather than including the additional possible definition of suffering. In speaking of the divine will, the active will is defined as the prior will to act, and the passive will as the subsequent will to be acted upon by virtue of the prior will. These terms are used to stress that the subjects and objects of action and passion are engaged in reciprocal relationship that includes both action and passion and active and passive will.

To speak of active emotions and suffering or of their active dimension indicates that God chooses his foreknown emotional responses and suffering in relation to his human creatures without undergoing any process of change, of succession of time, and of being moved or conditioned by them. By contrast, to speak of passive emotions and suffering or of their passive dimension indicates God being acted upon in such a way that he is moved by the world and experiences emotions and suffering as mutable and temporal responses to human beings. This publication affirms both dimensions of God's emotions and suffering.

---

38. Emery, *Trinitarian Theology of Aquinas*, 364–67.
39. Frame, *Doctrine of God*, 706.
40. Frame, *Doctrine of God*, 706.
41. Dolezal, "Strong Impassibility," 16.
42. Wuellner, "Passion," 88–89.

Exploring Divine (Im)Passibility

This work explores divine (im)passibility with a view to the domain of theology proper, not from the event of the cross, which has been the conventional way to explore divine passibilism. This approach demonstrates that divine suffering can be upheld without compromising and limiting God's infinite perfections. This present work adopts a relational or social trinitarian model that posits that each of the three divine persons is its own center of consciousness, will, and feeling.[43] The divine three persons are united in an eternal and immutable communion of love and glory: they are united in their wills and in both the absolute or immanent attributes that "are involved in God's relations to himself" and in the relative or transitive attributes that "are involved in God's relations to the creation."[44] Since the twentieth-century rise of interest in trinitarian theology, numerous works have been published in favor of a social trinitarian model[45] and in opposition to this model,[46] such that a full defense of this position is beyond the scope of this present work. However, the principal reasons why this position is adopted here can be sketched in outline.

This work chooses the relational Trinity model for two reasons. First, Scripture affirms the relational nature of each divine person and of the life of the triune God. Mutual love[47] and mutual glory[48] are considered

---

43. Likewise affirming a social Trinity model, Coppedge notes that "a working definition of *person* is a social being with conscious life who exercises reason, imagination, emotion and will in moral choices, freedom, creativity and responsibility." Coppedge, *God Who Is Triune*, 181, emphasis original.

44. Strong, *Systematic Theology*, 1:247.

45. For a selection of works advocating a social trinitarian view, see: Boff, *Trinity and Society*; Zizioulas, *Being as Communion*; Grenz, *Theology for the Community of God*.

46. For a sample of works critiquing the social trinitarian view, see: Bartel, "Could There Be More Than One Lord?"; Gresham Jr., "Social Model of the Trinity and Its Critics"; Holmes, "Three versus One?"

47. Unless otherwise noted, all biblical passages referenced in this work employ the *New International Version*. The Son loves the Father who is loved by the Son, and the Father loves the Son who receives his Father's love (mutual love). John 3:35; 5:20; 14:31; 15:9; 17:23–26.

48. The Father glorifies the Son, and the Son is glorified by the Father; the Son glorifies the Father, and the Father receives the Son's glory; the Holy Spirit glorifies the Son, and he is glorified by the Holy Spirit (mutual glory). John 8:50, 54; 13:31–32; 14:12; 17:1, 4, 5, 22, 24; 18:19. Even though the Holy Spirit is not explicitly mentioned in the descriptions of mutual love between the Father and Son, Jesus affirms its

to be the results of the activities of the three divine persons in the exercise of their freedom and wills in their modes of life *ad intra* and *ad extra*.[49] Opponents of social trinitarianism such as Carl Mosser are skeptical of exploring the inner being and life of God and object to any reading of the historical activity of the three divine persons into their immanent life, on the basis that it collapses the distinction between the economic and the immanent Trinity.[50] However, this work maintains a clear distinction between the economic and immanent Trinity without historicizing the eternal life of the Trinity. Second, relational trinitarianism offers space for creative theological reflection on the inner life of the triune God. In the consideration of the divine nature of each person of the Trinity, mutual love and mutual glory are seen to be the most appropriate ways to explore the eternal life of the Father, Son, and Holy Spirit who deserve nothing but holy love and perfect glory. In fact, an unwillingness to reflect scripturally upon the life of the triune God *in se* might itself cause problems in the doctrine of the Trinity. Such an approach risks unintentionally encouraging agnostic thinking and pure speculation regarding the inner life of the three divine persons.[51]

Concerning the scope of this research, it will be helpful at this point to draw attention to two intentional restrictions of the scope of this present work. First, this work excludes the approaches to the doctrine of the (im)passibility of God of the process philosophy of Alfred Whitehead.[52] Second, it leaves aside direct conversations with patristic, medieval, and Reformed theologians on this theme, though the principles of classical theism that are central to the work of these periods are clearly inherited

---

relationships are also mutual glory: "He [the Holy Spirit] will glorify me because it is from me that he will receive what he will make known to you" (16:14).

49. The direct words of Jesus in the following verses affirm two modes of the eternal life of the inner trinitarian persons: Jesus asks the Father to glorify him with the glory he had with him *before* the existence of creation (John 17:5) and says that the Father glorifies the Son because he loved him *before* the foundation of the world (John 17:24). Insufficient scriptural references respective of this triune fellowship in the Old Testament is a weakness of the relational Trinity model. However, the notion of the oneness of God in the *Shema* (Deut 6:4), which implies the uniqueness and unity of the God of Israel, supports the argument of the relational Trinity model of this present work as the three divine persons are one in their eternal fellowship of love and glory and their essence and attributes.

50. Mosser, "Fully Social Trinitarianism," 147.

51. Van den Brink, "Social Trinitarianism," 345.

52. Whitehead, *Process and Reality*. For more on options related to process theism, see also Cobb Jr., *God and the World*; Hartshorne, *Man's Vision of God*.

by the more recent impassibilists who have been indicated above, such as James Dolezal, Paul Gavrilyuk, Norman Geisler, and Thomas Weinandy.

Book Outline

This book unfolds as follows: chapter 2 briefly sketches the recent history of the doctrine of divine (im)passibility from the early nineteenth century to the contemporary era and outlines the central arguments of the impassibilists and passibilists during this period. The third and fourth chapters attend in detail to the arguments of a select sample of mediating theologians and consider how they exposit divine (im)passibility. The third chapter converses with mid-nineteenth and early twentieth century Protestant theologians, particularly Augustus H. Strong, Hans L. Martensen, and William N. Clarke. The fourth chapter turns to the positions of late-twentieth and early twenty-first century evangelical theologians, particularly those of John M. Frame and Clark H. Pinnock. The fifth and sixth chapters move to the constructive aspect of this work by considering the characteristics of the reciprocal relationship between the immanent Trinity and the economic Trinity as these are illuminated by the dynamic reciprocity model. Chapter 5 explores the way in which necessity and freedom are the two distinctive characteristics of the immanent Trinity and describes how the inner triune persons are not moved by the world but exist in an eternal fellowship of blessedness with one another. The sixth chapter explores the way in which God's freedom and his creative, redemptive, and sanctifying love for the world are the distinctive characteristics of the economic Trinity and describes how the three divine persons choose to experience the active and passive dimensions of emotions and suffering in the economy. The conclusion recalls the key contours of the book and sets out some of the constructive prospects for future research on this theme of divine (im)passibility.

2

The Doctrines of Divine Impassibility and Passibility

The debates surrounding the (im)passibility of God have been consistently contentious in contemporary theology. The impassibility and passibility theologians can reach agreement that God loves his created beings, has a personal relationship with them, and desires to overcome the existence of evil and suffering in the world so as to have an eternal and blissful fellowship with them, a fellowship without any suffering and fear.

With regard to examining how God responds to the human situation, however, the impassibilists and passibilists arrive at different conclusions.[1] The former group, attending to the classical divine attributes and stressing the transcendence of God, argues that God has compassion for and mercy upon his people in their pain and travails, without undergoing any hint of emotional and relational mutability or being moved by them. This is the disposition that is here referred to as exercising the "active dimension of emotions." The latter group, reading the crucifixion and suffering of the Son as a revelation both of God's ability to suffer in time and of his divine nature in eternity, asserts that God changes in his emotional and relational responses to creation and even suffers along with the creation that he loves, being moved by it. This is the disposition that is referred to as undergoing the "passive dimension of emotions and suffering."

1. The approaches to impassibilism and passibilism that are outlined in this chapter are those of strong impassibility and strong passibility that were noted in the chapter 1.

Each group challenges whether the approach of the other group can be justified according to its own respective biblical and theological standards of qualification. Impassibilists accuse the passibilists of minimizing the transcendence of the God of the Bible and of interpreting divine emotions in too close a parallel with human emotions. Passibilists respond that impassibilists use classical theologies that are based on Hellenistic philosophies to portray the relational and loving God who suffered and died on the cross as cold and impersonal.

Historical Developments in the Debates

This section sketches the major historical developments in debates concerning the impassibility or passibility of God since the nineteenth century and considers what provoked these developments. In particular, it outlines the rise of the passibility movement during the early to mid-nineteenth century, in an effort to understand how passibilism developed into an influential position in contemporary debates on the doctrine of divine (im)passibility.

From the early to mid-nineteenth century, the discussion of the passibility of the person of Jesus Christ in particular gave rise to consideration of the passibility of God in general. This latter current of thought went beyond the long-standing traditional account, in which the Son was said to experience suffering in his human nature only, and began to reject the long-standing tradition of divine impassibility. Passibilists began to attend to the suffering of Jesus Christ in both his human *and* his divine natures and were driven by new perspectives on theories of the atonement and on the interconnection between the crucifixion and suffering of Jesus Christ and the eternal nature of God.[2]

This new trajectory of passibilist thought was evident as early as the 1850s in British and German theological circles. Michael Brierley has identified fifty British passibilists who were implicitly or explicitly engaged in discourse concerning the passibility of God in the English context.[3] At this same time, German theologians such as Gottfried Thomasius, who was influenced by the German Lutheran theologians of the sixteenth and seventeenth centuries, reconstructed Christology

---

2. Campbell, *Nature of the Atonement*; Morgan, *Bible and the Cross*; Brent, *Mount of Vision*.

3. Brierley, "Introducing the Early British Passibilists," 228.

focusing on the doctrine of the self-limitation of the Son and in so doing attended to the passibility of the Son.[4] Such active engagements among British and German theologians contributed to a reinvigoration of the hitherto largely neglected notion of divine passibility.

This trajectory of passibilism has continued into the twentieth century. Since the early twentieth century, many scholars have published robust and thought-provoking work on passibilism, among them the Russian theologian Nicolas Berdyaev,[5] the Spanish philosopher Miguel de Unamuno,[6] the Japanese Lutheran theologian Kazoh Kitamori,[7] the German theologian Jürgen Moltmann,[8] the North Korean theologian Jung Y. Lee,[9] the African American theologian James Cone,[10] the English process philosopher A. N. Whitehead,[11] and the American process theologian D. D. Williams.[12] Moltmann and Lee in particular have elevated the issue of divine passibility to the status of a major doctrinal theme with wide-reaching import, such that it is no longer merely a side note or a minor topic within their Christian theology in particular, or indeed within the discipline in general.

Impassibilists have reacted to this growing wave of passibilism in different ways. Marshall Randles published a monograph on divine impassibility in 1900, seeking to examine whether suffering can be attributed to the almighty and blessed God. Concluding his theological investigation, he wrote: "Believing the advocacy of the doctrine of God's passibility by Christian men is a new departure in a wrong direction, and fraught with peril to practical Christianity, all the more so because of the ability and sincerity of its advocates, the present writer feels constrained

---

4. This debate on the doctrine of the self-limitation of the Son was reprised in a different key in German theological circles during the mid-nineteenth century and inspired German theologians such as Thomasius and Gess to engage in the theological treatment of the kenosis. Welch, *God and Incarnation*; Gess, *Die Lehre von der Person Christi*.

5. Berdyaev, *Meaning of History*.
6. Unamuno, *Tragic Sense of Life*.
7. Kitamori, *Theology of the Pain of God*.
8. Moltmann, *Crucified God*.
9. Lee, *God Suffers for Us*.
10. Cone, *God of the Oppressed*.
11. Whitehead, *Process and Reality*.
12. Williams, "Suffering and Being."

to raise the signal of danger."[13] Robert Mackintosh, in his survey of views on atonement in 1920, criticized the passibilist agenda that eternalized the cross and suffering of the Son: "An unhappy God would mean a bankrupt universe, a demonstrated pessimism, a doomed faith."[14]

As the passibilist movement spread within British theological circles, in September 1924 the Archbishops' Doctrinal Commission of the Church of England assigned John Mozley to examine the issue.[15] He subsequently published a balanced work on the doctrine of divine (im)passibility, a work that outlines his view of the impassibility doctrine from the patristic period and of the passibility movement of his time. Mozley criticizes his contemporaries for simply rejecting the doctrine of God's impassibility without any theological and historical engagement with the tradition of divine impassibility.[16] But he also poses "six necessary questions" with respect to any attempt to develop a theologically and historically balanced theology of passibilism.[17]

Many Reformed theologians of the nineteenth and twentieth centuries, such as William Shedd,[18] Herman Bavinck,[19] Louis Berkhof,[20] and Charles Hodge,[21] accepted the traditional Reformed presupposition of divine impassibility uncritically, often dismissing any discussion directly connected to divine impassibility.[22] This was because the idea of God's impassibility was already assumed in their understandings of the doctrine of God.

In the late twentieth century, impassibilists began paying more systematic attention to and engaging in more theological debate with the passibility movement—rather than simply dismissing the position as untenable. Richard Creel, for example, proposed a strong sense of divine impassibility in his work *Divine Impassibility*,[23] and was driven to do so

---

13. Randles, *Blessed God*, vi.
14. Mackintosh, *Historic Theories of Atonement*, 254.
15. Mozley, *Impassibility of God*, viii.
16. Mozley, *Impassibility of God*, 46.
17. Mozley, *Impassibility of God*, 177–83.
18. Shedd, *Dogmatic Theology*, 1:337–92.
19. Bavinck, *Doctrine of God*, 145–52.
20. Berkhof, *Systematic Theology*, 57–81.
21. Hodge, *Systematic Theology*, 1:376–441.
22. Kuyper, "Suffering and the Repentance of God," 267.
23. Creel, *Divine Impassibility*, 2.

by the arguments of passibilists who perceived the notion of God's impassibility as being incompatible with his love.

In addition, Weinandy published a detailed defense of the doctrine of divine impassibility. Observing the negative portrayal of Aquinas's theology among passibilists, Weinandy nevertheless drew on Aquinas to expound the impassibility of God theologically and philosophically with two purposes in view: first, "to demonstrate not that *despite* God's impassibility he is nonetheless loving and kind, but rather precisely *because* he is impassible that he is loving and kind,"[24] and second, to defend the doctrine of the impassibility of God from "the frequent criticism that the God of traditional Christian philosophy differs from, and often is in conflict with, the God of Christian revelation."[25]

Gavrilyuk, meanwhile, summarized the accusations of the passibilists to be that patristic theology represents the church fathers being defeated by or compromising with Hellenistic philosophies. He refers to the accusation as the "Theory of Theology's Fall into Hellenistic Philosophy" and, in addition to rejecting this theory, he in turn defends the theology of impassibility in order "to show that this widely accepted view [divine passibility] is a misinterpretation that stands in need of a thorough revision."[26]

Against the theory of theology's fall into Hellenistic philosophy, Norman Geisler similarly asserts that "the early fathers of the church offered biblical support, not just philosophical arguments, for their views. The New Testament alone was quoted by the Fathers of the first few centuries over 36,000 times, including all verses except eleven."[27] Other theologians as well continue to defend the doctrine of divine impassibility. In light of this ongoing support for impassibilism, the expectation of thinkers such as Charles Taliaferro and Marcel Sarot—that the doctrine of divine impassibility would fade away—is being proved wrong.[28]

---

24. Weinandy, *Does God Suffer?*, 37–38, emphasis original.

25. Weinandy, *Does God Suffer?*, 113.

26. Gavrilyuk, *Suffering of Impassible God*, 5.

27. Geisler, *Systematic Theology*, 450. The theory of theology's fall into Hellenistic philosophy has received significant critiques in recent times. For further recent defenses of the doctrine of divine impassibility against the theory, see Bray, "Christian Doctrine of God," 112; Grillmeier, *Christ in Christian Tradition*, 1:555–56.

28. Taliaferro, "Passibility of God," 217; Sarot, "Suffering of Christ," 113.

Factors in the Rise of Passibilism

There are various accounts offered as to why the rise to prominence of passibilism has occurred in a relatively short period of time, theologically speaking. Weinandy, for example, notes the cultural factors that have influenced the movement, including "the demise of nineteenth-century optimism" and "the social suffering caused by the Industrial Revolution and the agony of World War I."[29]

Marc Steen, meanwhile, considers three factors as contributing to the growth of interest in passibilism: (1) developments in biblical and christological interpretation, (2) the emergence of process philosophy, and (3) concerns about theodicy.[30] Paul Fiddes, on the other hand, focuses on four explanatory theological perspectives: (1) the love of God, (2) the theology of the cross, (3) the issue of human suffering, and (4) the contemporary worldview.[31] While each of these causes of explanation has some merit, there are three in particular that might usefully be considered further at this point in the chapter: a theological transition of attention and emphasis from God's transcendence to his immanence, issues arising out of modern theodicy, and developments in the interpretation of the Scriptures.[32]

The first factor is a swing of theological focus from God's transcendence to his immanence that brought significant challenges to and sometimes revision of the classical system of theology. The late nineteenth and early twentieth centuries observed the rise of a number of modern movements highlighting ideas such as natural evolution,[33] human progress,[34] religious liberalism,[35] social gospel,[36] and pantheism paired with natural-

---

29. Weinandy, *Does God Suffer?*, 2.

30. Steen, "'Suffering' God," 71–78.

31. Fiddes, *Creative Suffering of God*, 16–45.

32. The further factors of the love of God and the theology of the cross will be explored later in this chapter.

33. Crerar, "Hermeneutics of Augustus Hopkins Strong," 71; Reist, "Augustus Hopkins Strong and William Newton Clarke," 31; Olson, *Journey of Modern Theology*, 149.

34. Crerar, "Hermeneutics of Augustus Strong," 71; Smyth, *Progressive Orthodoxy*, 7, 13; Van Dusen, *Vindication of Liberal Theology*, 36.

35. Moore, "Academic Freedom," 64; Reist, "Augustus Hopkins Strong and William Newton Clarke," 27; Olson, *Journey of Modern Theology*, 17–98.

36. Reist, "Augustus Hopkins Strong and William Newton Clarke," 27; Handy, ed., *Social Gospel in America, 1870–1920*, 4–6.

ism.[37] In particular, the growing acceptance of evolution posed an immediate threat to Christian doctrines such as cosmology, anthropology, teleology, and eschatology.[38]

In theological circles, increasing attention to the immanence of God began to challenge traditional ideas regarding the metaphysical attributes of God such as omnipotence, immutability, impassibility, sovereignty, eternity, and omniscience. Charles Hopkins observes that the doctrine of the immanence of God "assumed the divine presence in nature and in human society, broke down traditional distinctions between sacred and secular, and regarded Christianity as a natural religion."[39] Arthur McGiffert correspondingly writes that "[t]he old chasms between the divine and the human, God and the world, this life and another, have been bridged by it [immanence], and the result has been a profound modification of the old doctrines of salvation, eternal life, the incarnation, the person and work of Christ, the sacraments, religious authority, and the like."[40] The emphasis on God's immanence and the revision of these doctrines paved the way to challenging the traditional notion of divine impassibility and to accepting suffering as an appropriate view of the Christian God.

The second factor is the challenge of modern theodicy, most notably in the form of the problem of human suffering, particularly as it swept the world during the period of the two world wars. In the face of the tragic outcomes of the world wars, the theodicy question began posing more questions and demanding more answers regarding the relationship between a morally perfect God and the suffering of the world that he himself created.

In this trajectory of thought, some modern theologians have found the doctrine of divine impassibility to be unsuited, and even unable to explain God's apparently impassive response to human suffering.[41] Richard Bauckham, for example, remarks that an impassible God cannot be justified in the world of human suffering.[42] Castelo perceives that the great pressure of human suffering has encouraged modern theologians

---

37. Pelikan, *Christian Doctrine*, 200.

38. White, *Warfare of Science with Theology*, 2:393; Pelikan, *Christian Doctrine*, 216.

39. Hopkins, *Social Gospel*, 123–24.

40. McGiffert, "Immanence," 171.

41. Keating and White, "Impassibility in Contemporary Theology," 20.

42. Bauckham, "In Defence of the Crucified God," 96.

towards the notion of God's passibility as part of an attempt to link the divide between God and human suffering, allowing him thereby to be engaged in it, and seeing this as the only qualified and moral response to the suffering of humanity.[43]

Frances Young concurs with this position that "only a suffering God is morally credible."[44] The event of the Holocaust, above all, raises the most challenging questions with respect to the relationship between God and human suffering, because the horrific and evil genocide of millions of Jews occurred within God's covenantal relationship with his chosen people.[45] With this tragic history in view, Kenneth Surin asserts that "the only credible theodicy for Auschwitz is one that makes God an inmate of the place, one that acknowledges the possibility that he too hung on the gallows."[46]

Moltmann, himself a prisoner during the Second World War, provides an even stronger reflection on Auschwitz: "Any other answer would be blasphemy. There cannot be any other Christian answer to the question of this torment. To speak here of a God who could not suffer would make God a demon."[47] For many theologians, the passibility of God has become the only possible answer to the theodicy question.

The third factor is the growing trend in biblical studies towards interpreting scriptural references to God's emotional life in a more ontologically meaningful way, rather than seeing them as mere anthropopathism and metaphors that are irrelevant to the actual being of God. In the view of some scholars, the Hebrew texts concerning God have been studied from the beginning of Christianity in the context of Hellenistic philosophical perspectives regarding immutability and impassibility, leading to a correspondingly negative reception of the possibility of divine emotions.[48]

---

43. Castelo, *Apathetic God*, 6–7. For others holding similar views, see Brasnett, *Suffering of the Impassible God*, 131; Jantzen, *God's World, God's Body*, 84–85; Jenkins, *Glory of Man*, 106–7.

44. Young, "Incarnation and Atonement," 101.

45. Castelo, *Apathetic God*, 5; Rubenstein, *After Auschwitz*, 161.

46. Surin, "Impassibility of God," 105; Jantzen agrees and writes, "Only a God who can suffer could command respect after Auschwitz." Jantzen, *God's World, God's Body*, 84.

47. Moltmann, *Crucified God*, 274.

48. For the advocates of this view, see Bauckham, "'Suffering God Can Help,'" 7; Edwards, "Pagan Dogma"; von Harnack, *History of Dogma*, 1:17; House, "Barrier of Impassibility," 414.

For passibilists, this Hellenistic view of God's nature, and his relation to emotions and suffering, has dictated the ways in which the church developed the Christian doctrine of God to an excessive extent, resulting in the view that to speak of God with reference to emotions is an inappropriate rendering of the immutable and impassible God.[49] Such a process would have ancient predecessors; according to C. Fritsch, historical evidence shows that "the translators [of the Septuagint] sought to remove or moderate many of the human qualities and emotions attributed to God in the Hebrew Old Testament."[50] For instance, whereas in Genesis 6:6 it is said that God repented and was grieved, the translators of the Septuagint, committed to upholding God's immutability, translate "repented" as God "reflected" or "was concerned,"[51] and was grieved as "he thought it over."[52]

This suspicion of the concept of divine emotions and of the doctrine of divine passibility continued throughout the patristic, medieval, and Reformation eras. Some modern impassibilists such as Geisler similarly consider that scriptural references to God's emotions do not literally describe God's true identity and inner being, and thus interpret them as metaphors that describe God "in an *indirect* and *nonliteral* way."[53] Robert Dabney agrees that those biblical passages portray "the outward manifestations of his [God's] active principles."[54] Gilles Emery correspondingly warns that to assign human attributes to God's nature would be to succumb to anthropomorphism.[55]

The modern passibilists, however, find there to be an inconsistency between the biblical descriptions of God and philosophical descriptions of an immutable and impassible God.[56] Passibilists consider the God of the Bible to be personal and relational and fully involved in the affairs of human beings. Steen complains that "a static concept of God [of

---

49. Rice, "Biblical Support for a New Perspective," 35.
50. Fritsch, *Anti-Anthropomorphisms*, 3.
51. Fritsch, *Anti-Anthropomorphisms*, 17.
52. Fritsch, *Anti-Anthropomorphisms*, 18.
53. Geisler, *Systematic Theology*, 414, emphasis original. Hodge and Emery support such a way to interpret the biblical languages. Hodge, *Outlines of Theology*, 132; Emery, "Immutability of the God of Love," 68.
54. Dabney, *Systematic Theology*, 153.
55. Emery, "Immutability of the God of Love," 68.
56. Lee, *God Suffers for Us*, 46. Lee asserts boldly that "the traditional idea of divine impassibility is largely based on a metaphysical notion of deity rather than the biblical idea of God."

philosophy] has been exchanged for a dynamic perspective in which God is conceived as personal, loving, and history-making."[57]

According to Colin Grant, passibilist reflection on Scripture "exposed the inadequacy of the immutable and impassible model of God" and disentangled "the God and Father of our Lord Jesus Christ from the impassible God."[58] In recent passibility literature, the doctrine of divine impassibility thus continues to be linked to a theory of theology's fall into Hellenistic philosophies. As such, passibilists consider divine impassibility to be a non-Christian teaching, rooted in non-biblical resources.

Passibilists, therefore, consider the scriptural references to God's emotions to portray his true emotional life. Abraham Heschel explains the reason for this positive attitude towards divine emotions, observing that the Bible does not "share the view that passions are disturbances or weaknesses of the soul, and much less the premise that passion itself is evil, that passion as such is incompatible with right thinking or right living."[59]

Charles Ohlrich finds in the scriptural portrayal of divine and human emotions a similarity between the Creator and his creatures, and thus favors a positive reading of the divine emotions, unlike the impassibilists who—in Ohlrich's view—emphasize dissimilarity and discontinuity between God's emotions and human emotions.[60] The result is that divine feelings are not to be dismissed as mere metaphors that denote God's nonemotional attributes but in fact describe the actual emotions that God has in response to various human experiences.[61] Similarly, Thomas Tymms suggests that "as a person most resembles God, it follows that He [God] can best reveal His heart in the language which expresses human affections."[62] This argument is a direct challenge to the metaphor argument noted above, for according to this view God *directly* and *truly* reveals himself through his feelings.

The description of God in the personal and dynamic language of the Bible, as opposed to the philosophical reasoning of immutability or impassibility, is therefore the passibilists' guiding principle for interpreting

---

57. Steen, "'Suffering' God," 71–72.
58. Grant, "Possibilities for Divine Passibility," 9.
59. Heschel, *Prophets*, 331.
60. Ohlrich, *Suffering God*, 52.
61. Ohlrich, *Suffering God*, 52.
62. Tymms, *Christian Idea of Atonement*, 312.

scriptural language. While some, such as John Goldingay, go so far as to collapse the distinction between God's feelings and human feelings, interpreting them as fundamentally alike,[63] other passibilists perceive the relation as analogous, pointing out the need to postulate that there is both continuity and discontinuity between their respective emotions. Thus Terence Fretheim, for example, explicates that while the passibility of God "does have some basic points of continuity with the way God actually relates to the world," nevertheless "God does not suffer in exactly the same way as humans do; . . . to try to get at that is important."[64]

Thematic Discussion of Impassibility and Passibility

We turn to the work of Thomas G. Weinandy, a Catholic defender of the impassibility model of God, and Jürgen Moltmann, a Protestant supporter of the possibility model of God, in order to consider more closely how both divine impassibility and passibility are presented thematically in contemporary theological literature, though the voices of other passibilists and impassibilists will be introduced at various points to illustrate and supplement their views. These two theologians have been chosen as focal voices since they represent widely held positions within their respective groups and have engaged in thorough and thoughtful investigations of the doctrine of the (im)passibility of God. Their respective theological arguments will be explored with reference to the following themes in turn: the starting points in considering the doctrine of God, the mode of God's experience of love and emotions, the nature of God's impassibility and passibility, and the immutability and mutability of God.

Starting Points in Considering the Doctrine of God

The differences between impassibilist and passibilist theologies are immediately evident from their divergent starting points, as exemplified by the doctrine of God in the work of Weinandy and Moltmann; each will be explored in turn.

Weinandy's theological project starts by identifying three essential pillars of the perfection of God. The first pillar is the biblical revelation of Yahweh, who is wholly other. This pillar sets the ground for a clear

63. Goldingay, *Old Testament Theology*, 1:168.
64. Fretheim, *Suffering of God*, 8.

ontological distinction between the Creator and his created beings and thus for the transcendence and immanence of God's interactions. Weinandy is committed to upholding that Yahweh is both transcendent and immanent and posits that the absolute otherness of Yahweh (his transcendence) is the driving force behind his immanence and his intimate and active relationship with his covenant community.

The transcendence of God, Weinandy writes, "is not then a description of how God exists in himself as isolated from the created order, but rather how he exists in relation to the created order."[65] Weinandy thus strongly affirms that not only does God have a personal relationship with his people, being present and active in the historical realm, but he does so "as the Wholly Other without jeopardizing his total otherness in so doing."[66] The corollary of this is that the name of God as Yahweh reveals the sovereignty and independence of God who cannot be separated from his covenant.[67] Martin Henry concurs, stating, "It is his transcendence that allows him to overcome and not be restricted by the world's differences, and to be present to, or immanent in, creation in a unique way."[68] In the same way, impassibilists such as Berkhof support the contention that the sufficiency and infinite perfection of Yahweh is the basis of his immanence and cannot be compromised for the sake of his relationship to the world.[69]

Next, Weinandy's engagement with the theology of Thomas Aquinas leads him to identify the second pillar of the perfection of God as God's essence as *ipsum esse* (to be) and *purus actus* (pure act). No passion related to change, time, or potentiality exists in God. He does not go through any process to actualize his inner potential or to complete his incompleteness, because he is already fully actualized and complete eternally. Weinandy states, "Being pure act (pure verb) as *ipsum esse* does not mean that God is *something* fully in act, such as a creature might actualize its full potential, but rather that God is act pure and simple."[70] This means that all of his inner actions and his external actions towards the creation

---

65. Weinandy, *Does God Suffer?*, 56–57.
66. Weinandy, *Does God Suffer?*, 53.
67. Highfield, *Great Is the Lord*, 159.
68. Henry, *On Not Understanding God*, 91.
69. Berkhof, *Systematic Theology*, 61.
70. Weinandy, *Does God Suffer?*, 122, emphasis original.

are completely actualized. If God were to be moved by the world, it would imply that he was not already actualized before.

It is in this sense that God cannot be affected by anything. Ron Highfield agrees that since God lacks any sense of being not yet perfect within himself, "God is unchangeably full, rich, active, present, attentive, compassionate, and loving."[71] In the same way, Thomas Aquinas's doctrine of pure act also provides the conceptual background for the perfection of God in the works of Emery and Michael Dodds.[72] This concept of the pure activity of God identifies the perfections of God.

The last pillar of the perfection of God that Weinandy describes is the relational nature of the operation of the triune persons. The three persons of the Trinity subsist in their particular identities as the Father, Son, and Holy Spirit, and are defined by their interrelated acts. Weinandy considers the triune life of God to be relational and active to the highest degree: the divine persons "are fully, completely, and absolutely relational"; indeed, "because the persons of the Trinity subsist only in relation to one another, they are relations in act and only relations in act."[73]

For Weinandy, the triune God has no relational potentiality, cannot be more or less relational within himself, and likewise cannot be more or less relational in his interaction with his creatures.[74] God is always fully active and fully relational, both within the inner triune life and in relation to creation. Dodds agrees with Weinandy's assessment that the activities of the triune persons are completely dynamic and immutably relational: "the three divine persons are not a static triad but a dynamic life, a never-ceasing yet ever-unchanging activity of knowledge and love."[75] Thus, Weinandy's understanding of God's nature starts out from the three pillars of the wholly otherness of Yahweh, the pure activity of God, and the complete relationality of the three persons.

Turning to Moltmann, one finds a very different starting point: the theology of the cross. The immanence of God is thus the starting point of his reflection on the Christian God, with the cross in particular as the primary source for understanding the nature of God. Moltmann makes

71. Highfield, *Great Is the Lord*, 366; Rogers likewise supports that the full actualization of God means exclusion of any potentiality. Rogers, *Perfect Being Theology*, 46.

72. Dodds, *Unchanging God of Love*; Emery, "Immutability of the God of Love," 99–116.

73. Weinandy, *Does God Suffer?*, 118.

74. Weinandy, *Does God Suffer?*, 119.

75. Dodds, *Unchanging God of Love*, 163.

the point that the event of Christ is the event of God, so that the revelation of Jesus is the true revelation of God. In this way, he can confidently state that "*this* [Jesus] is God, and God is like *this*. . . . The nucleus of everything that Christian theology says about 'God' is to be found in this Christ event."[76]

Thus, since the cross reveals the nature of God, Moltmann urges that the dogmatic investigation of the Christian doctrine of God should be launched "from the event of the suffering and death of the Son of God."[77] Similar to Moltmann's focus on the theology of the cross, S. Schilling writes that the life, teaching, and ministry of Jesus Christ reveals the truths of the character of God.[78] A. Fairbairn goes so far as to see the incarnation as the complete manuscript of Christian theology and estimates that the incarnation is "the externalization of what was innermost in God, the secret of the eternal manifested in time."[79] As such, for Fairbairn as for Moltmann, the cross provides the material principle and primary source of Christian theology.

In Moltmann's theological system, the trinitarian love is the essence of God. Moltmann asserts that in classical theism, the central idea of God is "the image of the imperial ruler," "the image of the personification of moral energy," and "the image of the final principle of philosophy."[80] In contrast, Moltmann presents divine love as the main theme of the Christian belief system, for it is love that defines the essence of the triune God and identifies his operations *ad intra* and *ad extra*. As the triune persons of the Father, Son, and Holy Spirit are love ontologically, they give themselves to one another and exist in the communion of love.

Moltmann notes that "in eternity and out of the very necessity of his being the Father loves the only begotten Son. . . . In eternity and out of the very necessity of his being the Son responds to the Father's love."[81] He adds that "the triune God reveals himself as love in the fellowship of the Father, the Son, and the Holy Spirit."[82] The triune God loves his creatures with the same love that is exercised reciprocally between the

---

76. Moltmann, *Crucified God*, 205, emphasis original.

77. Moltmann, *Crucified God*, 215.

78. Schilling, *God and Human Anguish*, 253; likewise, Douglas Hall starts his theological works from the theology of the cross. Hall, *God & Human Suffering*.

79. Fairbairn, *Christ in Modern Theology*, 483.

80. Moltmann, *Crucified God*, 250.

81. Moltmann, *Trinity and the Kingdom*, 58.

82. Moltmann, *Trinity and the Kingdom*, 56.

divine persons and in turn God desires to receive and be moved by the free love of creatures.[83] In this way, Moltmann prioritizes God's love over God's omnipotence, using the former to reconceive the latter: "It is not God's power that is almighty. What is almighty is his love."[84] Similarly, Lee, rejecting the classical attributes that are involved with divine impassibility, asserts that "God as the Ultimate reality is essentially love."[85] These theologians construe love as the fundamental attribute of the God who revealed himself on the cross.[86]

Here, it is illuminating to note Moltmann's understanding of the diverse facets of God's love, since these directly inform his doctrine of divine passibility: God's love is self-communicating, creative, responsive, necessary, and suffering. First, God's love is a self-communicating love. This love communicates its goodness both between the divine persons and between God and his creatures.[87] Moltmann describes this self-communicating love in this way: "It is the power of good to go out of itself, to enter into other being, to participate in other being, and to give itself for other being."[88]

Second, God's love is a creative love. Moltmann recognizes that God's love in its essence must go out of itself, such that "not to reveal himself and to be contented with his untouched glory would be a contradiction of himself."[89] In this sense, Moltmann is convinced that God's act of creating non-divine others is in some way *necessary* to fulfill the nature of love, and contends that "God 'needs' the world and man. If God is love, then he neither will nor can be without the one who is his beloved."[90]

Third, God's love is a responsive love. As noted earlier in this section, the three divine persons simply *are* love ontologically and thus

---

83. Moltmann, *Trinity and the Kingdom*, 59.

84. Moltmann, "God's Kenosis," 149.

85. Lee, *God Suffers for Us*, 3; Hall, meanwhile, focuses on the power of love as the true power of God for suffering humanity: "The only power that can address suffering humanity is the power of love, and that is a power 'made perfect in weakness' (2 Cor 12:9)." Hall, *God & Human Suffering*, 106.

86. Brunner, *Christian Doctrine of God*, 1:191. Brunner believes that the influence of philosophy led to the prioritization of the metaphysical attributes of God over the treatment of the love of God that he claims is the cardinal theme of Christian faith.

87. Moltmann, *Trinity and the Kingdom*, 58.

88. Moltmann, *Trinity and the Kingdom*, 57.

89. Moltmann, *Trinity and the Kingdom*, 53.

90. Moltmann, *Trinity and the Kingdom*, 58.

participate together in a reciprocal communion of love. Moltmann writes that God "is responsive love, both in essence *and* freely."[91] Correspondingly, the triune God desires to enjoy a relationship of reciprocal love with his human creatures.

Fourth, God's love is a necessary love. The God of love, who exists in love and whose existence is constituted in the event of love, cannot choose not to love the world, and cannot deny himself, for "he does not have the choice between being love and *not* being love."[92] Last, God's love is a suffering love. As the theology of the cross reveals, the love and suffering of God cannot be separated from each other.[93]

Weinandy and Moltmann present two different models of God. Weinandy and the impassibilists base their theological understanding of God on a description of God as completely actualized, relational, and transcendent, and are committed to maintaining an infinite distinction between the Creator and his creatures. Since the fundamental otherness of Yahweh is the foundation of God's presence in, and relationship with, the world, his perfections cannot be—and are not—reduced or minimized even in his relationship with human beings. Moltmann and the passibilists, meanwhile, offer a different theological approach, and consider the revelation of the cross to be the true foundation of Christian faith and theology. They therefore reinterpret love to be itself the omnipotence of God and do not draw upon classical theism to resource their projects. It is the event of the cross and the love of the triune God, *in se* and *ad extra*, that determine the trajectory of their work.

God's Emotions and Love

With these divergent starting points in view, the way in which Weinandy and Moltmann deal with the emotions of God, especially love, will now be considered. Both impassibility and passibility theologians concur that God has a personal relationship with his creatures and is capable of certain emotions, such as joy and love, but they disagree in how they describe God's emotional responses to human conditions—in the terms of this publication, the difference lies in whether these responses are

---

91. Moltmann, *Trinity and the Kingdom*, 59, emphasis original.
92. Moltmann, *Trinity and the Kingdom*, 54–55.
93. Moltmann, *Trinity and the Kingdom*, 53, emphasis original. God's necessary love and suffering love will be further explored in the next section.

considered as essentially active or essentially passive. The concepts of love and suffering contain too much theological depth and complexity to be categorized simply as emotions, and certain other emotions of God may be no less significant than love and suffering. Nevertheless, God's love and suffering are explored here by way of example in order to explore the different proposals regarding the mode of God's personal interaction with his creatures.

Weinandy explains that the ontological distinction between the Creator and his creatures demands a unique paradigm of relationship. With reference to the biblical passages on God's feelings, he complains that on the one hand, some impassibilists simply disregard references to God's emotions as anthropomorphic language and as mere metaphors, while on the other hand passibilists jeopardize God's infinite perfections in the process of approving a literal interpretation of divine feelings.[94] For Weinandy, understanding God as the Wholly Other is the first rule in investigating the divine emotions: "Yahweh is passionate but it is the passion of the Wholly Other, and he is able to express such depth of passion only because he is the Wholly Other."[95] Drawing here on Aquinas's teaching on real relations and logical relations, Weinandy voices the need for and explains God's unique relationship with his creatures.[96]

There are three types of relations. The first relation is logical; the second relation is real; the third relation is a mix of logical and real. The Creator and his human creatures are located in different orders. Weinandy assigns logical relations to the Creator, which cannot be changed, and real relations to his human creatures, which can be changed. God's relationship with human beings belongs to the third type of relation, as a mixed relation: the relation is real from the human side, meaning that the human creature can change in it, but logical from the divine side, meaning that God does not change in it.

In this way, human beings in the *same* ontological order can move themselves and can be moved by one another; however, although God can move the world and its creatures, creatures—as ontologically limited beings—cannot move God, who is in a different ontological order.[97] For God to be moved by the world, after the manner of human reciprocity,

---

94. Weinandy, *Does God Suffer?*, 59.
95. Weinandy, *Does God Suffer?*, 59.
96. Weinandy, *Does God Suffer?*, 130.
97. Weinandy, *Does God Suffer?*, 130.

would imply that he is in the same ontological order as his creatures. Consequently, the mode of Yahweh's feelings is not to be understood in the same way as human feelings.

To examine further the details of God's wholly other emotional state, Weinandy turns to his understanding of the pure act of God. Unlike created beings who must go through a process of change to experience various feelings, God feels emotions without any process of change. The divine emotions therefore only have an active dimension; they are not passive emotions that he experiences at specific points in history,[98] for he is fully and eternally realized within himself. If God were to be moved by the conditions of human creatures so as to feel various emotions in the present that he did not experience in the past, then this would suggest that God's actions and emotions were not fully actualized before and that he possessed within himself a potential that had not previously been realized—as is the case with human beings.

In this line of thinking, Weinandy thus affirms a very different view of divine emotions. He posits that what appear as emotions such as compassion, sorrow, and grief are actually the expressions of God's love: "God's love possesses, as does human love, many different facets and expressions.... God's love, as does human love, also embraces mercy, compassion, patience, forgiveness and even sorrow and grief."[99]

However, God's love is fully actualized, so that God loves without going through any processes of passion or change, the very processes that cause suffering for human beings. Weinandy notes, "While some facets of love within human beings entail suffering, such as compassion and grief, they are [in God] subsumed and contained within the perfectly actualized love of God, but now devoid of the suffering."[100] In this way, Weinandy affirms the active dimension of God's emotions. Tying together these two threads of the pure act of God and the Wholly Otherness of Yahweh, he argues that God cannot be moved by the world and that the divine emotions are not the result of being moved by the world.

In a similar way, other impassibilists who advocate that God's emotions operate differently from those of human beings propose that divine emotions are active emotions without passion. Emery posits that passion is involved with corporeality and sensible affection and makes a

98. Weinandy, *Does God Suffer?*, 162.
99. Weinandy, *Does God Suffer?*, 162.
100. Weinandy, *Does God Suffer?*, 164.

distinction between intellectual or spiritual and sensible affections. On this basis, the former affections such as love and joy are without passion and "are employed in proper discourse concerning God," whereas the latter affections such as suffering and pity are involved with passion and cannot be ascribed to God who is spirit.[101]

To underscore the divine nature of God's emotional life, Highfield contends that divine emotions are not "caused or conditioned by anything outside of God" and "are his own freely self-enacted being."[102] In a similar way, Helm argues that to avoid assigning passions to God, "we may think of God's 'feelings' as simply his attitudes to what he knows."[103] Hence, when God expresses his wrath against the disobedience of sinners and his joy over the righteous deeds of his people, the expressions are not a change from wrath to joy but rather God's eternal attitudes towards the sinful and righteous state of human beings.

Passibilists accuse impassibilists of describing God as incapable of true emotions and as having no feeling at all.[104] Yet Geisler argues that such a criticism is the result of a misunderstanding of impassibilism, since God's impassibility "affirms that God is without changing *passions*, but it does not deny that He has different *feelings*."[105] Impassibilists are thus committed to preserving a balance between the view that God is not affected by the world and the fact that Scripture refers to God's emotions. They seek to ascribe to God an appropriate modality of emotions without simultaneously ascribing temporal passion to him. God's feelings are thus unmoved feelings, and not the outcome of moved feelings.

Passibilists also often accuse impassibilists of portraying God as uncaring and unloving, claiming that a God of love must suffer along with his human creatures.[106] Against such an allegation, as noted

101. Emery, "Immutability of the God of Love," 67. Geisler also conceives of God as pure act and thus concurs that "God has no potentiality to be actualized; therefore, it follows that God, as Pure Actuality, cannot undergo passion or suffering." Geisler, *Systematic Theology*, 464.

102. Highfield, *Great Is the Lord*, 375. Vanhoozer defines God's active feelings as affections to exclude any nuance of passion that involves temporal changes. Vanhoozer, *Remythologizing Theology*, 404.

103. Helm, "Warfield on Divine Passion," 101. Similar to Helm, Piper holds that God's emotion, such as repentance, is "his expression of a different attitude and action about something past or future." Piper, *Godward Life*, 191.

104. Ngien, "God Who Suffers," 40.

105. Geisler, *Systematic Theology*, 462, emphasis original.

106. White, *Forgiveness and Suffering*, 84; Schilling, *God and Human Anguish*,

above, Weinandy responds that, whereas human forms of compassion and mercy entail suffering, the perfect expressions of joy, compassion, mercy, kindness, grief, and anger present in God's love do not entail suffering.[107] Instead, he writes, these expressions "are subsumed and contained within the perfectly actualized love of God, but now devoid of the suffering which would render his love less than perfectly actualized."[108] God acts in response to his creatures with fully actualized expressions of love, such that "God's love as fully actualized is 'ready made' to meet any situation."[109] In that sense, God does not go through a temporal process of responding to human beings, re-responding to their responses and conditions, and so forth.

For impassibilists, therefore, to refer to God's reaction to the suffering of the world is to indicate divine compassion, yet without suffering. Hence impassibilists avoid conceiving the divine response to creaturely suffering along the same lines as human compassion since the latter necessitates passion (suffering). For instance, Dodds feels no need to include suffering as part of divine compassion, especially as "it is love rather than suffering that we truly admire in the compassionate person, and it is love rather than suffering that brings healing and comfort to the person for whom we have compassion."[110]

Highfield, meanwhile, indicates two characteristics of God's compassion for the world. First, as God's compassion is nothing less than his triune love, there cannot be any form of suffering in his compassion.[111] Second, God's compassion is related to his foreknowledge of the cause, remedy, and degree of human suffering, so that his compassion, experienced without suffering or fluctuation, is able to meet any need and condition of human beings.[112] On the basis of this account, Highfield argues

---

253–54. Support for this passibilist perspective led White and Schilling to label impassibility a heresy. Owen remarks that impassibility "is the most questionable aspect of classical theism." Owen, *Concepts of Deity*, 24.

107. Weinandy, *Does God Suffer?*, 164.
108. Weinandy, *Does God Suffer?*, 164.
109. Weinandy, *Does God Suffer?*, 164.
110. Dodds, *Unchanging God of Love*, 300.
111. Highfield, *Great Is the Lord*, 204.
112. Highfield, *Great Is the Lord*, 205. In a similar way, Vanhoozer underscores that God's "compassion is kyriotic . . . not a commiserating but a commanding, effectual compassion that does not share but transforms the sufferer's situation." Vanhoozer, *Remythologizing Theology*, 446.

that the accusation "that God cannot be compassionate without himself suffering is as cruel as it is shallow."[113] As such, these scholars propose that the compassion of God contains no suffering, yet is nevertheless affective with respect to meeting the needs of those in suffering.

A very different view is encountered in the way in which Moltmann describes the mode of God's actualizing and experiencing emotions. In Moltmann's theology, God's suffering is constituted by his suffering love. He explains the logic that underpins the close connection between the concepts of divine love and divine suffering as follows: "God is love; love makes a person capable of suffering; and love's capacity for suffering is fulfilled in the self-giving and the self-sacrifice of the lover."[114] In other words, the ability to love is the capacity to suffer, and if God is love, he is capable of suffering.

Still, Moltmann's understanding of divine suffering goes further because he interprets God's self-sacrifice as "God's very nature and essence."[115] It is God's suffering love which moves him to participate in the travails of human beings, and through which he "lays himself open to the suffering which love for another brings him."[116] God experiences suffering along with his human creatures in his love for them. In making this connection between God's love and God's suffering, Moltmann criticizes those who reject the passibility of God and who base their work on Aristotelian philosophical positions. He writes, "a God who cannot suffer is poorer than any man. For a God who is incapable of suffering is a being who cannot be involved . . . he is so completely insensitive, [that] he cannot be affected or shaken by anything. . . . But the one who cannot suffer cannot love either. So he is a loveless being. Aristotle's God cannot love."[117] Since Moltmann treats the event of the cross as the cardinal foundation of the Christian faith, the denial of the passibility of God jeopardizes "the fundamental Christian assertion that God is love."[118]

This claim that to love is to suffer is the determinative presupposition of many modern accounts of the passibility of God, and is centrally

---

113. Highfield, *Great Is the Lord*, 205.
114. Moltmann, *Trinity and the Kingdom*, 32.
115. Moltmann, *Trinity and the Kingdom*, 32.
116. Moltmann, *Trinity and the Kingdom*, 23.
117. Moltmann, *Crucified God*, 222.
118. Moltmann, *Crucified God*, 230.

motivated by the revelation of the Son on the cross.[119] For instance, Horace Bushnell reads God's love as a vicarious sacrifice and posits that the principle of love is "a principle essentially vicarious in its own nature, identifying the subject with others, so as to suffer their adversities and pains, and taking on itself the burden of their evils."[120] The relationship between God's love and suffering is extended in Douglas White's work to the relationship between God's forgiveness and suffering, when he stresses that divine forgiveness is the essence of God's love and entails divine suffering: "without suffering there is no forgiveness."[121] Therefore, for these passibilists, God's love and his suffering are so intimately connected with each other that if God is love, he cannot not suffer.[122]

In connecting divine love with divine suffering, Moltmann and other passibilists posit that God has the capacity to respond to human beings emotionally and passively. For Moltmann, this capacity for reciprocity is grounded in God's love and freedom. First, God who is a responsive love ontologically cannot *not* have reciprocal relationships with human beings. Moltmann holds that "God is love. That means he is responsive love, both in essence *and* freely."[123] That is, if God is love, he responds to them necessarily. Second, Moltmann rails against the tradition that sees God as having absolute freedom of choice and asserts that true freedom "is by no means a matter of power and domination over a piece of property."[124]

---

119. Sarot, "Auschwitz, Morality," 148. Providing an exhaustive list of passibilists, Sarot estimates that "almost all contemporary theologians" acknowledge that "divine suffering is entailed by the divine love." Among other passibilists who agree that divine suffering is entailed by divine love, see Oord, *Defining Love*, 178–95; Placher, *Narratives of a Vulnerable God*, 192.

120. Bushnell, *Vicarious Sacrifice*, 42. Lee's theological construal of the possibility of God is also oriented to this theme of God's love and empathy. Lee, *God Suffers for Us*, 3.

121. White, *Forgiveness and Suffering*, 94. Ohlrich concurs that the receiving of God's forgiveness by sinners causes joy while the granting of forgiveness by God causes suffering. Ohlrich, *Suffering of God*, 49. Interestingly, Kitamori relates his discussion of divine passibility to the inner divine conflict between God's love for his human creatures and his anger regarding their failure: "God who must sentence sinners to death fought with God who wishes to love them. The fact that this fighting God is not two different gods but the same God causes his pain." Kitamori, *Pain of God*, 21.

122. Jüngel, *God as the Mystery*, 373. Jüngel notes, "The God who is love must be able to suffer and does suffer beyond all limits in the giving up of what is most authentically his for the sake of mortal man."

123. Moltmann, *Trinity and the Kingdom*, 59, emphasis original.

124. Moltmann, *Trinity and the Kingdom*, 55.

Instead, Moltmann adopts a model of freedom centered on friendship, which promotes community and fellowship and is founded on love, not on control and dominion. This model of freedom along with the responsive character of God's love strengthen Moltmann's view of God's capacity for reciprocal relation with the world and of God's nature as the most moving Being. This freedom centered on friendship "consists of the mutual and common participation in life, and a communication in which there is neither lordship nor servitude."[125] This type of freedom not only defines the fellowship of the triune God but is also given to human beings in their analogous friendship with God. It follows from this that the triune God cannot choose not to engage reciprocally with human beings and to involve himself in their lives. Still, within this necessity, God experiences passive emotions freely.

Subsequent passibilists also stress that God as person has the capacity to be moved by human beings and experience passive emotions. H. Robinson argues that "the personality of God is capable of emotion as well as of thought and will. . . . The moral evil of the world moves God to anger, even though his love for men moves him to costly sacrifice."[126] In the same manner, focusing on reciprocity as the essence of human conception of personal relationship, Surin asserts that divine suffering "is the corollary of responsiveness, for we cannot respond to someone without relating to that person, and we cannot relate to that person without being affected by him. A God who loves his creation must be a God who is affected by its travails."[127] For Lee, the essence of God's interaction with his creatures is an empathic relationship. As God creates to participate in their lives, they "are [also] called to participate in his participation."[128] Thus, there is mutual reciprocity and participation between the Creator and his human creatures. Heschel stresses that God is present with human beings afflicted with pain and sorrow and is moved by them: "God does not stand outside the range of human suffering and sorrow. He is personally involved in, even stirred by, the conduct and fate of man."[129] The capacity for this response indicates that God's nature is reciprocal and therefore able to engage in reciprocal relations with the world.

125. Moltmann, *Trinity and the Kingdom*, 56.
126. Robinson, *Suffering*, 143.
127. Surin, "Impassibility of God," 113–14.
128. Lee, *God Suffers for Us*, 48.
129. Heschel, *Prophets*, 224.

Another common claim of passibilists is that human sins cause grief to God's heart.[130] Fairbairn, for example, claims that the suffering of Jesus on the cross not only shows God's love for the world, but also reveals God's grief in respect of the sins of his human creatures.[131] Fretheim contends that the biblical references in the Old Testament concerning God's grief at sin are an authentic description of divine suffering.[132] In this view, God's grief over human sin can even be described as the result of God's sin-bearing nature. George Stevens argues that "they [human sins] mean that God is, by his very nature, a sin bearer—that sin grieves and wounds his heart, and that he sorrows and suffers in consequence of it."[133]

Other passibilists such as Wilfrid Harrington posit that the suffering of the Old Testament prophets offers an embodied vision of the passibility of God. Pointing to Jeremiah the prophet, Harrington argues that "a prophet's life reflects the divine life. If to hear the word of a prophet is to hear God, to see a suffering prophet is to look upon a suffering God. For a prophet not only speaks the word of God, he embodies it."[134]

The impassibilists and passibilists, therefore, offer very different ways to describe how God experiences emotions. Weinandy and the impassibilists engage in the discussion of God's active emotions by capturing the radical distinction between the Creator and creation. God communicates his feelings without any process of change or passion, since his emotions are already actualized to their richest extent and are expressed as his dispositions and attitudes towards certain conditions of humanity. Moltmann and the passibilists, meanwhile, confirm God's capacity to experience passive emotions. This view is driven by a vigorous reinterpretation of the personhood and love of God, and the attribution to God of the capability for genuinely reciprocal relations with the world,

---

130. Tymms, *Christian Idea of Atonement*, 312; Robinson, *Suffering*, 182–83; Dinsmore, *Atonement*, 231. Tymms, Robinson, and Dinsmore are passibilists who offer similar thoughts about the relationship between God's suffering and sin.

131. Fairbairn, *Place of Christ*, 483.

132. Fretheim, *Suffering of God*, 140.

133. Stevens, *Christian Doctrine of Salvation*, 442.

134. Harrington, *Tears of God*, 28. Fretheim make the same observation: "In and through the suffering of the prophet, the people both hear and see God immersed in human experience. Through the prophet, Israel relates not only to a God who speaks, but also to a God who appears." Fretheim, *Suffering of God*, 165. Heschel provides a detailed explanation of the suffering of God in reference to the suffering of the Old Testament prophets. Heschel, *Prophets*, 32–201.

including their passive dimensions. Thus, God experiences emotions in a passive way analogous to human beings.

God's Impassibility and Passibility

Building on the above discussions of starting points in considering the doctrine of God and God's emotions and love, what follows here considers further God's impassibility and passibility, and the way in which Weinandy and Moltmann further develop their theological arguments. First, there is an exploration of Weinandy's view of God's impassibility, which is constructed on biblical, philosophical, and theological bases, together with his reasons for rejecting the passibility of God; second, the way in which Moltmann and the passibilists divinize suffering as the eternal nature and life of the triune God and exposit the suffering of the Son on the cross will be explored.

Weinandy's theology of impassibility is founded on grasping the utmost passion (not passive action) and love that spring from the interaction of the three eternal persons of the Trinity. Positively speaking, the triune God is the most passionate Being of all, because of the fullness of action and completeness of love present in the subsistent triune relationships.[135] Dodds depicts the positive interaction of the trinitarian persons as follows: "The Trinity involves the perfect reflection of the divine knowledge of the Father in the procession of the Son, the impulse of divine love of Father and Son in the procession of the Spirit, and the complete and continuous self-communication and interpenetration of Father, of Son and Spirit."[136]

Negatively speaking, the triune God cannot be more or less passionate or affectionate, and thus cannot experience any new, changing, or passive emotions, because he cannot be moved by the world and does not relate reciprocally to human beings as they relate reciprocally to one another.[137] Emery concurs that the triune hypostases, who are in this full and complete relationship with each other, cannot be affected or modified by anything external.[138] In this account, divine impassibility serves as the demonstration of the fully dynamic and relational nature of the inner life

---

135. Weinandy, *Does God Suffer?*, 123.
136. Dodds, *Unchanging God of Love*, 163.
137. Weinandy, *Does God Suffer?*, 119–20.
138. Emery, "Immutability of the God of Love," 74.

of the Trinity.[139] Drawing on his understanding of God as wholly other and pure act, Weinandy proposes that the relationships between the three divine persons of the Trinity are fully actualized within their subsisting relationship, and that these relationships operate differently from the way in which human beings relate to one another, in that the divine emotions are immutably and unconditionally pure and wholly other. The triune God is therefore impassible.

Weinandy's views on suffering lead him to reject the passibility of God for two reasons. The first reason is related to the ontological location of suffering. Evil, sin, and suffering are located in the created order, and their existence is the outcome of human misuse of the freedom given to creatures to practice goodness. Sin is the cause of the existence of suffering. Weinandy holds that "evil, for it to exist, must be caused by sin, a free misuse of what is good, and so evil is a deprivation of good. It is this deprivation which causes suffering."[140] While sin, evil, and suffering are on the same side of the created order, the Creator is on the side of the uncreated order. God can relate to and influence the created order, but sin, evil, and suffering cannot move and penetrate the uncreated order because of the ontological distinction between God and his creatures. The Creator, Weinandy posits, "is related to the created order as the one who is not of the created order. Thus evil does not and cannot reverberate back into the uncreated order where God alone exists as absolutely good."[141] Correspondingly, God cannot be "infected by the evil that takes place within the created order" and is therefore "immune to suffering."[142] Weinandy thus endeavors to sustain the distinction between the uncreated and created orders without either polluting the uncreated order with sin and suffering or divinizing the created order.

The second reason for Weinandy's denunciation of assigning passibility to God is the perfection of the goodness of the triune God. Since God is actualized and completed goodness, his goodness is impassible, being unable to be moved by anything; and immutable, being unable to be or to become more or less good. Suffering, which is defined as the

---

139. Weinandy, *Does God Suffer?*, 119.

140. Weinandy, *Does God Suffer?*, 153. Moltmann, however, rejects the view that sin is the cause of human suffering and argues instead that human beings are created to experience suffering even without the fall of humanity. Moltmann, *Trinity and the Kingdom*, 51.

141. Weinandy, *Does God Suffer?*, 153.

142. Weinandy, *Does God Suffer?*, 154.

deprivation of goodness, cannot however deprive the ontological goodness of the triune God. Weinandy posits that "nothing can impair God's goodness so as to inflict a loss of some good which would then entail God suffering."[143] If the triune God were to be moved by the condition of the world and to experience the suffering that is the effect of transgression and evil, it would imply that he is in need of achieving some unfulfilled goodness within himself on the basis of his external works in relation to his human creatures. Weinandy correspondingly states that if "the Trinity were infected with suffering, it would mean that they were deprived of some good, and so enmeshed in sin and evil."[144] By contrast, however, God's perfect goodness is directed against the lack of goodness in human beings. In a similar way, Randles posits that the eternal blessedness of God is founded in his goodness and perfection while suffering is founded in evil and imperfection.[145] This negative understanding of suffering and positive view of the goodness of God drives impassibilists to reject passibilism.[146]

From the passibilist perspective, meanwhile, it was noted earlier that a number of scholars considered the historical suffering of Jesus on the cross as demonstrating the nature of God's suffering. Unlike impassibilists, who affirm that the triune God exists in perfect blessedness and holiness,[147] certain passibilists see the cross of the Son as the direct scene of the eternal *activity* and *life* of the triune God. This argument can be found, for example, in Bushnell's work when he introduces the concept of the cross in God before the actual cross in history. He writes that "there is a cross in God before the wood is seen upon Calvary; hid in God's own virtue itself, struggling on heavily in burdened feeling through all the previous ages, and struggling as heavily now even in the throne of the worlds."[148] In this trajectory of reading, the cross as a reflection of the

---

143. Weinandy, *Does God Suffer?*, 157.

144. Weinandy, *Does God Suffer?*, 158.

145. Randles, *Blessed God*, 27–35.

146. Geisler refuses to assign to God anything short of God's glorious nature, declaring "God cannot undergo passion or suffering; nothing in the created universe can make God feel pain or inflict misery on him." Geisler, *Systematic Theology*, 112.

147. Randles, *Blessed God*, 43. Randles particularly disavows that anything contrary to happiness cannot be part of the eternal blessedness of God: "Perfect blessedness excludes everything contrary to happiness.... But that, though real, is not perfect happiness such as the blessedness of God must be, seeing He is absolutely perfect in all His attributes. A God of imperfect blessedness were an imperfect God."

148. Bushnell, *Vicarious Sacrifice*, 73. Other passibilists, following Bushnell, began

eternal passibility of God is further described as the *activity* of the life of the eternal Trinity[149] and as the "*transcripts* of eternal fact."[150] As Fiddes observes, eternalizing the event of the cross "has been a characteristic theme of Anglo-Saxon theology since the end of the last century."[151] Following this pattern, Lee concurs that the cross represents "the eternal *reality*, that is, the eternal suffering and death of God on the eternal Cross."[152] For Lee, in this mode of thinking, a kind of ahistorical, atemporal event of the cross is prior to and necessary for the historical event of the cross: "The Cross as the depth of divine empathy denies any assertion that the Cross is the event which has happened once upon a time in history. It means more than the mere event on Calvary."[153]

Certain passibilists claim that the eternal suffering of the Son is a biblical revelation,[154] citing Revelation 13:8: "All inhabitants of the earth will worship the beast—all whose names have not been written in the Lamb's book of life, the Lamb who was slain from the creation of the world." After observing that the eternal Son of God exists with the Father before the foundation of the world (John 1:1), Dinsmore posits that the eternal Son of God is none other than "the Lamb that hath been slain from the foundation of the world."[155] In this trajectory of thought, the revelation of the cross serves to affirm the suffering of the triune God and to expose that suffering as the eternal reality, life, transcript, and activity of God *in se*.

---

construing the cross of the Son as the eternal event of God. Fairbairn, for example, argues that the cross is "the externalization of what was innermost in God, the *secret* of the eternal manifested in time." Fairbairn, *Place of Christ*, 483, emphasis added.

149. Kennedy, *Hardest Part*, 62, emphasis added; Kennedy posits that the cross "is the act in time which reveals to us the eternal *activity* of suffering and redeeming love all down the age." Moltmann likewise interprets the event of the cross as the eternal experience of the triune God: "If we follow through the idea that the historical passion of Christ reveals the eternal passion of God, then the self-sacrifice of love is God's eternal nature." Moltmann, *Trinity and the Kingdom*, 32.

150. Stevens, *Christian Doctrine of Salvation*, 450, emphasis added.

151. Fiddes, *Creative Suffering*, 29.

152. Lee, *God Suffers for Us*, 59, emphasis added.

153. Lee, *God Suffers for Us*, 58. Lee adds that "divine passibility was not the consequence of incarnation but the incarnation was the consequence of divine passibility... not the beginning of divine passibility but the continuation of it with an intensification in time and space." Lee, *God Suffers for Us*, 56.

154. White, *Forgiveness and Suffering*, 90; Ohlrich, *Suffering of God*, 50; Morgan, *Bible and the Cross*, 58.

155. Dinsmore, *Atonement*, 228.

Another question arises as to how this suffering of God relates to the different persons of the Trinity. Impassibilists argue that the person of Jesus Christ, who is fully God and fully human, suffered only in his human nature on the cross, because Jesus cannot suffer in his divine nature.[156] The traditional approach to the crucifixion underscores the role of the Father as the One who receives the self-sacrifice of the Son but often remains silent with respect to the Father's decision not to spare the Son and thus his emotional response to the agony of the Son. This is so because of the perceived insufficient scriptural warrant for expounding upon the grief of the Father, the thoroughgoing emphasis on the Father's love, joy, and satisfaction with respect to the work of the Son, and the persistent upholding of the impassible nature of the Father.[157]

Moltmann and the passibilists, however, expand the scope of the discussion of the suffering of God from considering the Son on the cross alone to reflecting upon the impact of the cross on the Father and Holy Spirit who are in eternal fellowship with the Son.[158] Moltmann's view of passibility is interwoven with the fabric of his trinitarian theology and explores in detail the way all three divine persons experience suffering in distinct ways. For Moltmann, the suffering of the Father is the pain of abandoning the Son who loves him with his self-surrendering love; the Son suffers the pain of being forsaken by the Father who loves him with fatherly love; and the Holy Spirit suffers the pain of accompanying the Son from his birth to the crucifixion.[159] Fairbairn similarly recognizes

---

156. Weinandy, *Does God Suffer?*, 213. See Marshall and Vanhoozer for other impassibilists who affirm the suffering of the human nature of the person of Jesus only. Marshall, "Dereliction of Christ and the Impassibility of God," 273; Vanhoozer, *Remythologizing Theology*, 424.

157. Weinandy, *Does God Suffer?*, 228. Interestingly, after outlining the fully actualized and relational nature of the triune God, Weinandy asserts that the Father, in his fully actualized love, nevertheless grieves over the suffering of the Son—though without undergoing any emotional changes. He explains, "While grief and sorrow are predicated of the Father metaphorically, in that such emotions do not imply that the Father underwent emotional changes of state or that he suffered some form of divine mental and emotional distress comparable to human beings, yet what is expressed within these metaphors is nonetheless absolutely true." Weinandy, *Does God Suffer?*, 228.

158. This affirmation of the suffering of the Father is thus very different from that advanced by the patripassian understanding that stresses that the Father suffers exactly the same suffering as the Son because they are united as one mode and essence of being.

159. Moltmann, *Spirit of Life*, 62.

the sorrow that is involved in the Father's surrendering of the Son on the cross and describes it as the Father's invisible sacrifice.[160] Lee, concentrating on the communion of love and empathy of the three divine persons, argues that "the Father, Son and the Holy Spirit are so completely and perfectly participating in one another as to be one in experience," so that "the suffering of Christ ought to be the suffering of the Father and the Holy Spirit as well."[161] In this way, passibilists seek to connect the suffering of the Son to the suffering of the other triune persons and thereby affirm the passibility of the Father, Son, and Holy Spirit.

Weinandy and the impassibilists posit that the source of all types of suffering is sin and evil and that suffering, sin, and evil lie on the creaturely side of the Creator–creature divide. They therefore oppose assigning to God any form of defect or imperfection such as suffering. For passibilists, however, such an understanding contradicts the revelation of the cross, for divine suffering is rooted in God's love and his attitude towards sins that is revealed on the cross. Thus, the suffering of God is no longer defined as an imperfection or defect but is seen as the nature and eternal reality, activity, and life of God *in se*. Such a view of the eternal suffering of God leads them to a position that divine suffering has a necessary characteristic: if suffering is God's nature, he must suffer to fulfill his nature. This expanded understanding of suffering that is part of God's eternal life is both the purest vision of the passibilists and the worst nightmare of the impassibilists.

God's Suffering and Immutability

One further aspect of the disagreement between the impassibility and passibility perspectives on the suffering of God is worthy of exploration at this point: the doctrine of the immutability of God, especially in relation to concepts of eternity and time. The impassibilists and passibilists debate whether the relation that God has with human creatures is immutable and eternal or mutable and temporal, and thus whether or not God can undergo suffering, which both sides agree is a mutable and temporal experience.

On the one hand, impassibilists take a strong view of divine immutability, which can be labeled "strong immutability" and indicates that

---

160. Fairbairn, *Place of Christ*, 484.
161. Lee, *God Suffers for Us*, 75.

THE DOCTRINES OF DIVINE IMPASSIBILITY AND PASSIBILITY 45

neither God *in se* nor God *ad extra* can be changed at all.[162] On the other hand, passibilists reject this view of divine immutability and take a different view, which can be labeled "weak immutability" and indicates that God is immutable in or faithful to his character, but that he can change in the external expressions of that character and in his relationship with the world.[163]

It is important to outline the positions on both sides in greater detail. The impassibilist position on the strong immutability of God and its relationship to suffering can be summarized in the following ways.

First, God is immutable in his perfection, which is demonstrated through his attributes such as omnipotence, love, eternity, omniscience, sovereignty, holiness, and omnipresence. Because the degree of God's perfection cannot increase or decrease in any way, he cannot experience suffering.[164]

Second, God who is pure act and fully actualized within himself cannot undergo any change. Because suffering is not his nature, it would represent a potential for God. If God were to go through a process of suffering, it would suggest that God was not fully actualized and completed within himself.[165] Therefore, God cannot undergo suffering.

Third, God's eternal blessedness *in se* cannot be changed. He exists in eternal blessedness that is grounded in his goodness, love, and perfection. However, suffering is related to evil, imperfection, and sin; therefore, it cannot either be part of or impact the state of God's blessedness in any way.[166]

Fourth, God's emotional responses to humanity *ad extra* are immutable. God has positive[167] and immutable[168] emotions; by contrast, suffering is related to negative feelings and mutability. Thus, suffering cannot be included among God's positive and immutable emotions.

Fifth, God cannot be moved by anything external to himself and therefore cannot be changed by the world. To be moved by the world

---

162. Swinburne, *Coherence of Theism*, 212. Swinburne uses the term "strong immutability."

163. Swinburne, *Coherence of Theism*, 212. Swinburne introduces the term "weak immutability."

164. Geisler, *Systematic Theology*, 446.

165. Weinandy, *Does God Suffer?*, 162–64.

166. Randles, *Blessed God*, 44.

167. Rogers, *Perfect Being Theology*, 51.

168. Weinandy, *Does God Suffer?*, 126.

means to be changed by it.¹⁶⁹ However, God is immutable *in se* and *ad extra*. Therefore, as God is not moved by the world, he does not change by experiencing any passive form of suffering in response to the choices and conditions of humanity.

Criticizing this view of the strong immutability of God as a by-product of Hellenic philosophy, a number of theologians affirm instead that there are both immutable and mutable dimensions of the being of God.¹⁷⁰ In Moltmann's view, the rendering of God's strong immutability as existing in tandem with God's love is a fundamental contradiction, since a God who cannot be changed and affected by the world is merely Aristotle's God who cannot love. He therefore refers to strong immutability as deriving from "the philosophical theism of indirect knowledge of God from the world."¹⁷¹

Moltmann offers a particularly clear example of this position from a passibilist perspective, justifying his view by a number of interconnected arguments.¹⁷² First, God's love remains the same because God is love.¹⁷³ For Moltmann, love is the essence of God and therefore, cannot be changed by anything. Second, God cannot *not* have reciprocal relationships with the world. Moltmann argues that "God is love. That means he is responsive love, both in essence *and* freely."¹⁷⁴ That is, if God is love, he cannot *not* respond to the conditions and choices of humanity. Third, God cannot *not* suffer with human beings. Suffering is the eternal nature of God, so that as he is faithful to himself, he suffers with the world necessarily. Fourth, God's being *in se* is mutable, because God's suffering, which is viewed as his nature, changes to eternal bliss in the eschaton.¹⁷⁵ For Moltmann, the eternal suffering that shapes the inner life of the triune

---

169. Helm, "Impossibility of Divine Passibility," 120.

170. Weinandy, *Does God Suffer?*, 62. According to Weinandy, Dorner is the first theologian to argue that God, who is immutable ontologically, changes in his relationship with the world, and many theologians have followed this approach. Dorner, *Divine Immutability*. For other theologians who adopted Dorner's view of God's immutability, see Barth, *Church Dogmatics*, II/1, 490–512; Edwards, "Pagan Dogma," 306; Pannenberg, *Basic Questions in Theology*, 2:161–62, 180.

171. Moltmann, *Crucified God*, 214.

172. Moltmann would prefer the term "God's faithfulness" instead of "God's immutability and mutability."

173. Moltmann, *Trinity and the Kingdom*, 59.

174. Moltmann, *Trinity and the Kingdom*, 59, emphasis original.

175. The details of Moltmann's view with respect to God's eternal suffering and his future bliss that eventually overcomes his suffering will be examined in chapter 5.

God reaches "its fulfilment in the love that is bliss"[176] that is accomplished when human beings are liberated from their affliction. As God's suffering that is his eternal nature changes to eternal bliss, his nature *in se* is mutable. Lastly, God changes in his relationship with the world. Since the nature of love is relational and reciprocal, God changes in his emotional responses to the various conditions and choices of human beings and through the course of his interactions with them in history.

Other passibilists likewise reject the view of strong divine immutability and support instead the view of the weak immutability of God. Passibilists are not satisfied with what they see as the philosophical model of the immutability of God that excludes any possibility of considering changes in God's emotions in his relationship with the world.[177] White, for example, supports certain aspects of divine immutability, such as God's immutable purpose, but opposes the notion of God's strong immutability: "Yes, he is unchangeable; but his is not the unchangeableness of a stone. We do not mean that his expression does not change."[178] Similarly, complaining that Aquinas's pure act of God is static and inert, Lee posits that God's attitude, personality, empathy, and will are immutable, but that God changes in his relationship with human beings. God changes not because of his own need to actualize his imperfection or incompleteness, "but because [of] the active potentiality to give Himself in His empathy in spite of men's unwillingness to accept him."[179]

Important to the affirmation of the weak immutability of God is the desire to recognize that God is free to undergo emotional changes and suffering in personal relationships. For instance, the immutability of Aristotle's unmoved mover, Ronald Nash holds, is in truth an impersonal immutability, for it deprives God of the freedom and capability for interpersonal interaction with his creation.[180] This in turn diminishes the perfection of God, Nash argues, for "a personal God would lack perfection if He were incapable of such relations."[181] W. Clarke complains that Aquinas's version of God portrays God as an "indifferent metaphysical

---

176. Moltmann, *Trinity and the Kingdom*, 60.

177. Schilling, *God and Human Anguish*, 252. Schilling finds no biblical warrant for—and no relational and personal God in—Aristotle's ideas of immutability and unchanging emotions.

178. White, *Forgiveness and Suffering*, 85.

179. Lee, *God Suffers for Us*, 41.

180. Nash, *Concept of God*, 101.

181. Nash, *Concept of God*, 101.

iceberg"[182] and suggests the need to reformulate the traditional model of the strong immutability of God. He argues that "the immutability attributed to God must be that proper to a perfect personal being—i.e., an *immutable intention* to love and save us, which intention then includes all the adaptations and responses necessary to carry this intention through in personal dialogue with us."[183] God's relational mutability in this weak immutability view therefore is a necessary aspect of a personal and perfect God.

The second discussion here relates to how each side defends its position from criticism. Impassibilists defend their doctrine from the accusations of passibilists by pointing to how God's immutability and impassibility illuminate the perfection of God. Weinandy asserts that, despite the negative nuance of the attribute of divine immutability, it is actually structured on a *positive* aspect that describes the perfect *movement* of God. Weinandy writes that "God is immutable not because he is static, inert, or inactive, but precisely because he, as pure act, is supremely active and dynamic and cannot ontologically become more in act."[184] Dodds similarly contends that the concept of immutability serves as an important hermeneutical lens through which to perceive the distinction between perfection and imperfection. He holds that immutability "seems to signify divine being (*esse*) more appropriately since it more clearly indicates the distinction of divine being from all other things and the transcendence of divine being above all our human concepts and knowledge."[185] For Highfield, again, divine immutability has a positive effect: it "guarantees [God's] ability to be absolutely present as our totally reliable Creator."[186] If God's divine attributes that warrant human joy and peace are conditional and can change, there can be no reliability or assurance of eternal felicity for human beings.

In this positive reading of divine immutability, impassibilists seek to interpret God's emotions in light of his immutability. In this reading, as Emery comments, the immutability of God does not contradict the

---

182. Clarke, "New Look at the Immutability of God," 45.

183. Clarke, *Philosophical Approach to God*, 108, emphasis original.

184. Weinandy, *Does God Suffer?*, 123. In the same manner, to highlight the fullness of the movement within the Godhead, Geisler argues that "God can and does act. ... He is the Most Moving Mover." Geisler, *Systematic Theology*, 462. Likewise, Berkhof notes that God "is always in action." Berkhof, *Systematic Theology*, 59.

185. Dodds, *Unchanging God of Love*, 224.

186. Highfield, *Great Is the Lord*, 369.

THE DOCTRINES OF DIVINE IMPASSIBILITY AND PASSIBILITY 49

biblical model of God but plays "a key role in interpreting integrally the biblical teaching concerning the activity of God and his profound engagement with our world."[187] Impassibilists thus attempt to preserve the perfection of God by embracing God's immutability along with his impassibility, and assert that God responds to the conditions of the world without any process of undergoing change or of being conditioned by the world.

As for the passibilists, they defend their position against the impassibilist criticism that the notion of mutability and suffering creates an unreliable and unstable God and "pagan god" by adopting a different yet related argument.[188] Moltmann defends God's passibility and mutable reciprocity as the expression of God's freedom and faithfulness and does so in two ways.

First, Moltmann contends that God's suffering is exercised freely. Divine suffering is the eternal nature and activity of the Trinity, so that when God suffers for his human creatures, he suffers according to his nature. Moltmann describes this form of suffering as "active suffering—the voluntary laying oneself open to another and allowing oneself to be intimately affected by him."[189] Also, since Moltmann uses the "friendship model of freedom" explored above,[190] God is passible along with his creatures according to his eternal nature and in this way is moved by the affairs and suffering of human beings freely.

Second, Moltmann considers that God's suffering is the manifestation of his faithfulness. Moltmann's understanding of divine love is that it shares its goodness even with non-divine beings, being moved by their conditions and situations. When God changes in his relationship to the world, expressing various emotions, this mutability is founded in his love. Indeed, if God does not change and suffer in this way, he would be contradicting his nature, for "God is the God of truth, whose nature is eternal faithfulness and reliability."[191] In this respect, the suffering of God

---

187. Emery, "Immutability of the God of Love," 32.

188. Mackintosh, *Historic Theories of Atonement*, 255. Ware considers that the immutability of God is jeopardized in Moltmann's uncritical theology of the cross and of the mutable love of God. Ware, "Evangelical Reexamination of the Doctrine of the Immutability of God," 236–37.

189. Moltmann, *Trinity and the Kingdom*, 23.

190. Moltmann, *Trinity and the Kingdom*, 56.

191. Moltmann, *Trinity and the Kingdom*, 154.

is not a random or uncontrolled experience, but an affirmation of the divine faithfulness and freedom in act.

As noted above, because both impassibilists and passibilists concur that suffering is a temporal and mutable experience, the third discussion requiring further attention is the relationship between God's eternity and time. There are two broad views on construing God's eternity: (1) God's timeless or atemporal eternity and (2) his temporally everlasting eternity.

The adherents of the timeless eternity view of God argue that God is "time-free"[192] and that his eternity contains no time. He exists outside of time in a timelessly eternal realm without beginning or end and without temporal or chronological duration and succession.[193] Thomas Williams posits that "God is eternal, not in the sense that he exists at every moment of time, but in the sense that his life is not characterized by succession at all."[194] As God does not experience the duration and succession of time, he sees the past, present, and future as one. Rogers explains, "All of time is 'present' to God."[195] God in this timeless eternity interacts with the world without becoming a temporal Being or having the capacity to be influenced or moved by time.

In this perspective, the God who is timelessly eternal is immutable. Time is connected to change, and God cannot be changed at all. Helm notes that "God is timelessly eternal. Whatever is timelessly eternal is unchangeable."[196] Indeed, Rogers avers that eternity is the foundation of God's immutability: "It is only by postulating divine eternity that God's immutability can be preserved,"[197] although Edward Feser contrastingly argues that God's immutability is the basis of God's "strict *timelessness.*"[198] Either way, if God is immutable, he must be timelessly eternal and vice versa. This eternally timeless God cannot be changed by any conditions

---

192. Helm, *Eternal God*, 39.

193. Nash, *Concept of God*, 73. For others who support the view of God's timeless eternity, see Sonderegger, *Systematic Theology*, 493; Cooper, *Panentheism*, 102–9.

194. Williams, "Introduction to Classical Theism," 96.

195. Rogers, *Perfect Being Theology*, 59.

196. Helm, "Impossibility of Divine Passibility," 119.

197. Rogers, *Perfect Being Theology*, 55–56. Williams concurs with Rogers's evaluation of divine eternity and immutability and writes, "Because there is no before and after in God, God cannot undergo change, and so the doctrine of divine [timeless] eternity leads directly to the claim that God is immutable." Williams, "Introduction to Classical Theism," 96.

198. Feser, *Five Proofs of God*, 200, emphasis original.

and circumstances relating to temporal matters and does not undergo any emotional changes or experiences, such as suffering, that require time.[199] God has personal relationships with human creatures, but does so as a timeless and immutable God, not as a temporal and mutable creature, so that he cannot experience any temporal, mutable experience such as suffering.[200]

By contrast, the advocates of the second view of God's eternity propose that God is eternally everlasting, being without beginning or end, but that he is not completely disconnected from the processes of time.[201] The emphasis of this temporally everlasting view is that God is not free from temporal duration or succession but has everlasting duration or succession.[202] Thomas Morris describes the divine eternity in this perspective as follows: "God's existence is temporally infinite in duration, unbounded in the past and future. On this conception, there is in the life of God a past, present and future, as in the life of his creatures."[203] Therefore, the central argument here is that God is capable of having real temporal relationship with his creatures. This in turn holds open the possibility that God can be moved by his creatures.

A series of scholars who argue that God is temporally everlasting thus also argue that God can experience temporally mutable experiences.[204] They consider God's personhood to be of the essence of God and argue that if God is a person, certain conditions need to be assigned to him. These conditions include speaking, expressing different emotions, and being affected by others.[205] They observe that a timeless God, by con-

---

199. Dolezal, "Still Impassible," 131.

200. Creel, *Divine Impassibility*, 102–12; Helm, "Impossibility of Divine Passibility," 119–40. Impassibilists such as Helm and Creel stress God's timeless eternity and reach this conclusion in their theological works.

201. Nash, *Concept of God*, 73. Some call this view temporal eternity, sempiternity, or everlasting. Feinberg, *No One Like Him*, 378.

202. Wolterstorff, "God Everlasting," 77–98.

203. Morris, *Our Idea of God*, 120.

204. For other advocates of this view of God's eternity, see Kenny, *God of the Philosophers*; Pike, *God and Timelessness*; Rowe, *Philosophy of Religion*.

205. Sturch, "Problem of Divine Eternity," 489–90. For Robert Coburn, such conditions include "remembering, anticipating, reflecting, deliberating, deciding, intending, and acting intentionally." Coburn, "Professor Malcolm on God," 155. Similarly, Gale points out that a timeless God cannot engage in intentional action and reciprocal relationship with the world. Gale, "Omniscience-Immutability Arguments," 333.

trast, could not participate in these activities because they require God to be in time and act as a temporal God.[206]

Nicholas Wolterstorff asserts that certain actions require God to be temporal: "If God were eternal, he could not be aware, concerning any temporal event, whether it was occurring, nor aware that it will be occurring, nor could he remember that it had occurred, nor could he plan to bring it about."[207] More than that, for Nelson Pike, God must experience temporal succession in order to be able to engage in personal relationship with human beings and in other temporal activities.[208] Wolterstorff insists that Scripture warrants affirmation of God's temporal and mutable interactions with his creatures, rather than being left merely with timeless and immutable interactions.[209] For these advocates of the everlasting eternity view, God's personal relationship with human persons requires him to be capable of experiencing temporal succession.[210] In this line of thinking of God's eternity, God can be temporally mutable and correspondingly experience temporal experiences such as suffering.

The disagreement between impassibilism and passibilism with regard to the immutability and mutability of God relates to their different interpretations of the mode of God's emotions and suffering. For the impassibilists, the strong immutability of God represents a positive picture of God's full actualization and completeness, so that suffering cannot be associated with the perfection of God either *in se* or *ad extra*. God's emotional responses to the plight and activities of human beings occur without God going through any process of change.

Temporal change and reciprocal relation in time relate to the imperfections of human beings, and to ascribe reciprocal relations with creatures in time to God would not make God more relational but would actually divest him of his divine and uncreated status and of his very capacity for true relationality. On the other hand, Moltmann and other passibilist theologians affirm both immutable and mutable aspects of God. God's love, personhood, and will are the foundation of the divine being, and these permit attributing passibility and mutability to God's nature.

206. Coburn, "Professor Malcolm on God," 155.
207. Wolterstorff, "God Everlasting," 200.
208. Pike, *God and Timelessness*, 94–95.
209. Wolterstorff, "God Everlasting," 193.
210. Pike, *God and Timelessness*, 128.

For the advocates of the temporally everlasting eternity view such as Wolterstorff, indeed, truly reciprocal relations in time are the "only" legitimate indicator and biblical description of God's dynamic and interpersonal relationship with created persons; by contrast, the timeless eternal God cannot entertain such genuine and personal relationships. God's suffering is thus the outcome of God's mutable and temporal interaction with human beings.

Constructive Lessons from Weinandy and Moltmann

There are strengths and weaknesses of the positions on both sides of the (im)passibility debate. The aim is not to dissect all of the arguments but to make a few helpful observations that will move toward the mediating position that attempts to do justice both to the impassibility and passibility of the triune God.

Starting Points in Considering the Doctrine of God

The strength of the impassibilists lies in highlighting the perfections and otherness of the God of Scripture and prioritizing God's transcendence as the ground of his immanence. Their endeavors to begin from the otherness of God in considering his relationship with his creatures is an important theological move. The transcendence of God might, however, instead be considered as the basis of a more dynamic form of reciprocal relation with the creature in time without jeopardizing the otherness of Yahweh. Yahweh is the Lord of not only that which is beyond history, but also of the process of history of which he is in full control, so that he is above the rules of space and time.

As the passibilists advocate, it is crucial to understand the event of the cross as the true revelation of the triune God and to consider how the triune love that was demonstrated through the suffering of the Son might become the starting point for a wider discussion of Christian theology proper and, more narrowly, God's passibility. However, when God's omnipotence, the very divine trait underpinning the creation of the world and the resurrection of Jesus from the dead, is simply replaced by love in an unqualified manner, the danger is that God becomes a pathetic God who no longer deserves the worship of his creatures who are equally pathetic and impotent.[211] Neither God's love nor his omnipotence should therefore be diminished from the perfection that they bear as God's divine attributes.

The mediating position of this work therefore draws on the insights of both views. It seeks, on the one hand, to recognize appropriately both the divine otherness and the divine love; on the other hand, it seeks to do so without compromising the full temporal relationality of God and the limitless perfections of God.

God's Emotions and Love

To ascribe the appropriate form of emotions to God, impassibilists make a clear distinction between the unchanging and unmoved emotions of God and the changing and moved emotions of human beings—what in this work are referred to as active and passive emotions. This approach highlights God's expression of transcendent and unmoved feelings that are not dependent on the conditions of the world and is motivated by the axiom that God cannot be moved by the world. Still, the weakness of this endeavor is that the biblical descriptions of God's feelings do seem to suggest that the emotional state of God is the outcome of being moved by the world. The people of the covenant understand God as One who is moved by their miseries and wickedness, not as a deity who is without any temporal or responsive emotions. The notion of the unconditioned emotion, by itself, therefore, seems inadequate to understand divine emotions.

Assigning to God the capacity to suffer and to engage in reciprocal relationships with the world is a major strength of the passibilists. God is able to participate in the pains and travails of his creatures and to suffer with them by way of conditioned and immanent feelings. If God is always moved by the world, however, that would remove any distinction between the way in which God experiences various feelings and that of human beings. If God's feelings are shaped by the world only, his identity would become determined by the sinful and imperfect conditions of fallen beings.[212]

The doctrine of divine passibility therefore needs to be revised in order to accommodate the need to sustain an appropriate distinction between divine emotions and human emotions. This work stresses that

211. Vanhoozer, *Remythologizing Theology*, 458.
212. Hart, "No Shadow of Turning," 191.

God's active emotions are not dependent on the conditions of the world and affirms the radical difference between divine and human emotions. At the same time, it also recognizes that God chooses to engage in reciprocal relationship with human creatures and experience passive emotions.

God's Impassibility and Passibility

Impassibilists correctly grasp that sin and evil, caused by the misuse of the freedom of human beings, are the origin of human suffering, in contrast with Moltmann, who argues that suffering is the inevitable experience of human beings despite sin and evil.[213] The weakness of the impassibilist position at this point, however, is its generalizing of all forms of suffering as sinful and evil. A careful exegesis of Scripture, however, shows that there are certain types of suffering that are anchored in God's love and goodness and his special plans for his community. Scripture teaches that not all types of suffering are founded in evil and sin and that voluntary participation in the suffering of Christ is commanded by God as the calling for all believers (Phil 1:29; Col 1:24; 1 Pet 2:21). For instance, Paul writes, "Now if we are children, then we are heirs—heirs of God and co-heirs with Christ, if indeed we share in his sufferings in order that we may also share in his glory" (Rom 8:17). Furthermore, the purely negative understanding of suffering prevents impassibilists from engaging in any discussion of the suffering of the Father and the Holy Spirit who both participate in the event of the cross. Unfortunately, such an approach to the triune event of the cross inevitably transforms the Father and the Holy Spirit into aloof deities who cannot share the agony of the Son.

Passibilists make a discerning observation that all three persons are involved in the event of the cross and in the fellowship of love. Along these lines, the suffering of the Father and the Holy Spirit is affirmed in their personal relationships with the Son, who suffered on the cross in his divine and human natures and also in the Father's receiving the sacrifice of the Son and Holy Spirit's accompanying the Son from his birth to the crucifixion.[214] The argument that the life and crucifixion of the person of Jesus reveals the eternal life of the three divine persons causes theological problems; however, insofar as it risks collapsing the distinction between the economic Trinity and the immanent Trinity. For instance, if

---

213. Moltmann, *Trinity and the Kingdom*, 51.
214. Moltmann, *Spirit of Life*, 62.

this argument is true, the temporal experiences of Jesus, such as hunger, thirst, and temptation, should be part of the eternal experience of the divine persons.[215]

Therefore, this work conceives the relationship between the eternal and blessed life of the triune God and the suffering of God in time in a different way. The eternal blessedness of the triune God is considered as the expression of God's love for himself while the suffering of the trinitarian persons in the divine economy is construed as the expression of their creative, redemptive, and sanctifying love for the world, confirming the suffering of the triune persons on the cross.

God's Suffering and Immutability

Sustaining the immutability and timeless eternity of God is a crucial theological undertaking if one is to avoid ascribing human characteristics such as mutability, and temporal experience such as suffering to God. Driven by this concern, impassibilists correctly reject any claim that serves to violate the boundary of the immutability and eternity of the triune God. In this process of preserving God's infinite perfections, however, the classical idea of strong immutability seems to limit God's freedom to engage in reciprocal relations in time with his creatures. Yet, Scripture affirms both notions of God: that God cannot be associated with change and time within himself, and that God can have mutable and temporal interactions with his human creatures.

Passibilist calls to revise the traditional notion of divine immutability are significant. Scripture does indeed seem to portray God's emotional responses to different human conditions in historical situations as mutable. Nonetheless, some aspects of God's immutability must be preserved. If God's inner life and emotional life is dependent on the conditions of the world, God is no longer a self-sufficient God but rather a deficient Being who wrestles with the struggle of the world and is in need of deliverance as well. A deficient Being who needs cooperation from his creatures to be healed and flourish cannot guarantee the fulfillment of the prophecies and promises that are contained in Scripture. In this respect, God's immutable, intrinsic perfection plays a crucial role in engaging with the doctrine of the (im)passibility of God.

---

215. Torrance, *Christian Doctrine of God*, 108–9.

In this work, instead of construing the ideas that God cannot be associated with change and time within himself and that God can have mutable and temporal interactions with his human creatures as immediately contradictory, the doctrine of divine immutability has been revised. The resultant position affirms a weak sense of divine immutability that permits the possibility of conceiving of God's sovereign freedom as enabling him to engage in reciprocal relations in time without jeopardizing his immutability and eternity.

The positions of divine impassibility and divine passibility are framed by two very different models of God: of a God who is not affected by the world and of a God who is moved by the world. The first model is explained through classical theism and stresses God's transcendence and unconditioned emotions. The second model is presented through the theology of the cross and underlines the immanence of the moved God and his conditioned emotions and suffering. Neither solution seems to be without its major concerns.

This work, therefore, seeks to argue that the triune God is both impassible *in se* and passible *ad extra*. In this way, it hopes to indicate a mediating position that supports both the impassibility and the passibility of God, inheriting the helpful theological contributions of the both groups, while addressing the weaknesses of both positions. More specifically, the argument is guided by the main tenets of the classical attributes of God that the modern passibilists neglected and considered as obstacles to the delivery of their version of the doctrine of divine passibility, while still affirming the notion of the temporal and mutable emotions and passibility of God that impassibilists have interpreted as compromising the limitless perfections of the triune God. In the next chapter, the first steps are taken towards this significant constructive argument, by way of an investigation of the work of those who first paved the way towards the kind of position to be presented in this book—the mediating theologians of the nineteenth and twentieth centuries.

3

Mediating Theologians of the Nineteenth and Twentieth Centuries

Already during the nineteenth and early twentieth centuries, as noted in chapter 2, many theologians began to support the idea of the suffering of God, positing love as the ground of divine suffering and often focusing upon the event of the cross. But there were also theologians, such as Augustus H. Strong, Hans L. Martensen, and William N. Clarke, who wished to present a mediating position located between this passibilist view and the classical view.[1] As mediating theologians, these scholars did not accept either the perfect impassibility or the pure passibility of God but strove to uphold both God's eternal blessedness and infinite perfection *and* his mutable passibility in his relationship with the world.

Such mediating positions thus reinterpreted the traditional concepts of the immutability and impassibility of God thus still upholding—in revised form—some of the tenets of the traditional doctrine of God. What is particular about the work of Strong, Martensen, and Clarke is that they were among the few theologians who located their reflections on passibilism within the domain of the doctrine of God. The view that God suffers—in whatever way and to whatever extent—requires precisely the kind of thorough investigation of dogmatic grounding and theological depth that their work provides.

---

1. Strong, *Systematic Theology*; Martensen, *Christian Dogmatics*; Clarke, *Outline of Christian Theology*. Arthur Mason and Bertrand Brasnett also held a mediating position on the divine (im)passibility. Mason, *Faith of the Gospel*; Brasnett, *Suffering of the Impassible God*.

The voices of these late nineteenth- and early twentieth-century mediating theologians have been generally neglected in recent years, such that they have not received much attention within the contemporary divine (im)passibility discussions.² Investigation of their work is thus desirable within the context of this publication, and in view of its desire to develop a mediating position in the (im)passibility debate. Not only will such an investigation provide valuable background context that illuminates the debate and its issues as a whole, but it will also provide generative insights for the constructive work.

Theological Background of Strong, Martensen, and Clarke

To consider how Strong, Martensen, and Clarke approach the subject matter of divine suffering, this section investigates the theological background of each scholar and particularly the way in which modern influences shaped their theological enterprises. In this way, they were often criticized by other theologians for departing from their traditional background; however, Strong, Martensen, and Clarke all seek to maintain the broad, traditional tenets of theology proper.

Augustus H. Strong

An American Baptist theologian, Augustus H. Strong (1836–1921) received his DD in Germany and wrote the first of eight editions of his *Systematic Theology* in 1886. He had an Arminian mentor, Charles G. Finney, and received a Calvinist theological training at Rochester Theological Seminary. As a Baptist, Strong was engaged in the fundamentalist/modernist controversy, in which the doctrines that had been considered to be the fundamentals of Christianity, such as the "doctrines of salvation, eternal life, the incarnation, the person and work of Christ, the sacraments, religious authority, and the life," were challenged.³

---

2. Mozley, *Impassibility of God*. It should be noted, however, that Mozley's influential book *The Impassibility of God*, which many among both the passibility and impassibility theologians quote regularly, mentions Strong, Martensen, and Clarke. Beyond this rather aged reference, Moltmann mentions Martensen's mediating position and seems to affirm it as a possible option in the (im)passibility conversation. Moltmann, *Trinity and the Kingdom*, 53–54.

3. McGiffert, "Immanence," 171.

Strong described the theological developments of his days in this way: "Under the influence of Ritschl and his Kantian relativism, many of our teachers and preachers have swung off into a practical denial of Christ's deity and of his atonement. We seem upon the verge of a second Unitarian defection, that will break up churches and compel secessions."[4] At the same time, philosophy and science also influenced the process of Strong's intellectual development and his theological program, and some aspects of his teaching reflected a revision of traditional positions.[5] This revisionary trajectory is visible above all in the eighth and final edition of his work, *Systematic Theology*,[6] and in his understanding of ethical monism.

Ethical monism is a philosophically infused system of explaining the universe and includes postulating "an intuitive knowledge of the existence of the external world, of self, and of God."[7] Ethical monism became for Strong a way of "reconciling the view that the universe is of one substance with God (divine immanence) while maintaining the personal (ethical) duality between creatures and the transcendent creator."[8] Ethical monism targeted two philosophies that Strong was also keen to oppose: idealism and pantheism. The doctrine of the Trinity was used to refute idealism, for a God who has consciousness, affection, and will is more than an idea.[9] Against pantheism, ethical monism prioritized divine transcendence over divine immanence—chronologically and ontologically.[10] In this connection, Strong also rejected any evolutionary theory of creation in which creation has no Originator who is above the process and moves towards a specific goal.[11]

---

4. Strong, *Systematic Theology*, 1:ix.

5. Strong, *Systematic Theology*, 1:vii.

6. This work uses the reprinted version of the eighth and final edition of Strong's *Systematic Theology*, which was published in 1907. The content of Strong's "Doctrine of God" in this edition is consistent with his previous editions.

7. Strong, *Systematic Theology*, 1:90. This system of thought, he adds, "holds to a single substance, ground, or principle of being, namely, God, but which also holds to the ethical facts of God's transcendence as well as his immanence, and of God's personality as distinct from, and as guaranteeing, the personality of man." Strong, *Systematic Theology*, 1:105.

8. Richardson, "Augustus Hopkins Strong," 292.

9. Strong, *Ethical Monism*, 3.

10. Strong, *Ethical Monism*, 4.

11. Strong, *Ethical Monism*, 5.

Strong reinterprets Christ's union with creation using the ideas of ethical monism. Positing that Jesus reveals God "in nature, in humanity, in history, in science, in Scripture,"[12] Strong views creation in terms of Christ's presence and unity with creation: "Nature is *not* his body in the sense that he is confined to nature. Nature is his body in the sense that in nature we see him who is above the nature and in whom at the same time all things consist."[13] This view of Christ's union with creation was his theological innovation, for the language of "union with Christ" was generally associated with soteriology, not with creation.

There are two contrasting views with respect to Strong's theological program. On the one hand, some assert that Strong departed from traditional Reformed theology.[14] Tracking the developments in Strong's thought, Timothy Christian asserts that Strong "was an 'immediate' creationist, but he became a 'mediate and immediate' theistic evolutionist. He was an inerrantist; he became a denier of inerrancy. He previously rejected historical criticism; he then embraced its conclusions."[15] In a parallel fashion, prominent Presbyterian theologians such as Charles Hodge and B. B. Warfield criticize Strong's ethical monism for being incompatible with supernaturalism or evangelicalism and as indicating his departure from traditional Reformed theology.[16] On the other hand, scholars have presented Strong as being of a more orthodox inclination. Irwin Reist observes that Strong has been presented as a "classical, progressive, orthodox theologian."[17] In his appraisal, Kenneth Cauthen holds that Strong sought to reconcile the classical doctrines and the modern worldviews of his time, "restating for their own day a perspective which was thought to contain the un-changing essentials of Christian belief."[18]

Thus even though Strong was influenced by the philosophies of his day, he robustly challenged the way modern immanentism abandoned God's perfections and sovereignty, the deity of the Son,

---

12. Strong, preface to *Systematic Theology*, 1:xii.
13. Strong, *Ethical Monism*, 14, emphasis original.
14. Henry, *Personal Idealism and Strong's Theology*, 95; 194–95.
15. Christian, "Experiential Theology of Strong," 184. Concerning Strong's ethical monism, Christian observes Strong's departure from the traditional rendering thus: "Strong moved from a soteriological union with Christ to an organic union with Christ." Christian, "Experiential Theology of Strong," 197.
16. Henry, *Strong's Theology*, 194–95.
17. Reist, "Augustus Hopkins Strong and William Newton Clarke," 31.
18. Cauthen, *Impact of American Religious Liberalism*, 31.

supernaturalism, and the necessity of the atonement, portraying God as a moral teacher and nothing more.[19] However, as will be revisited later, Strong still affirms much of the traditional doctrine of God as demonstrated by his willingness to affirm God's aseity, eternity, omnipotence, immutability, omniscience, and sovereignty.

Hans L. Martensen

Unlike Clarke and Strong, who share a broadly similar theological and cultural milieu, Hans L. Martensen (1808–1884) was born in Flensburg, Denmark, and was a bishop of Zealand and a Lutheran theologian. He authored the first edition of his major work *Christian Dogmatics* in 1849, and this volume later appeared in English in 1878. Martensen, once a tutor of the young Søren Kierkegaard, created controversy as a result of his attempt to connect faith and reason, whereas the adult Kierkegaard insisted on a clear gap between them.[20]

The Hegelian notions that swept through German theological circles in the early years of the nineteenth century significantly inspired Martensen's dogmatic construction. Martensen's 1833 essay "An Attempt at a Response to the Theological Prize Subject," written at an early stage of his academic career, already showed the influence of Hegelian philosophy in his theology, Hegelian philosophy that stresses historical revelation and the relationship between the thesis, antithesis, and synthesis.[21] For Martensen, Hegelian philosophy captured the modern scientific worldview of the day.[22] Indeed, Curtis Thompson suggests that Martensen found intellectual philosophies from Kant to Hegel to be necessary "for comprehending the new speculative approach to theology that he believed was demanded by contemporary situations."[23] However, despite their appeal, Martensen was not ultimately satisfied with such modern philosophies, believing them to be lacking the theonomous standpoint that was a requirement for theology.[24]

---

19. Strong, *Systematic Theology*, 1:viii.
20. Cohn-Sherbok, "Martensen, Hans Lassen (1808–1884)," 198.
21. Thompson, *Following the Cultured Public's Chosen*, 10.
22. Thompson, *Following the Cultured Public's Chosen*, 15.
23. Thompson, *Following the Cultured Public's Chosen*, 16.
24. Thompson, *Following the Cultured Public's Chosen*, 10.

Martensen's theological program works with a model of the absolute personality of God. Thompson notes that, during his stay in Berlin between 1834 and 1836, Martensen encountered the vigorous debate between pantheism and theism. He considered pantheism to involve an impersonal God, and wrote later in his *Christian Dogmatics* of the detrimental consequences of this view:

> In the rough hands of this generation, the wings of the pantheistic butterfly have lost their mystic dust. . . . We hear it now proclaimed without circumlocution . . . that there is no God; the name "God" is now a tedious word. . . . [L]et us therefore speak of "nature," instead of God; of the "forces" and "laws of nature," instead of the divine attributes; of the "course of the world" or the "progress of the age," instead of divine providence; and so forth; for we can understand that.[25]

Martensen grounds the distinction between the pantheistic and theistic ideas in the divine transcendence: "there can be only two religious and two scientific systems—the Pantheistic and the Theistic;—the former having for its highest, the derived absolute, the universe; the latter based on the original absolute; that is, on God as God."[26] In contrast to pantheism, Martensen considers the God of Christianity to be the most free and autonomous Being, the infinite personality. In this way, the absolute personality of God is grounded in his revised form of classical theology proper.

Martensen's approach to connecting revelation and philosophy, drawing on the work of Hegel, Kant, and others, was criticized in his day by Bishop Mynster, who pressured Martensen to take his stand—in Schiørring's words—"between supernaturalism (i.e., an orthodoxy faithful to Church and Bible) and rationalism (an unbounded intellectualism, in this case Hegel's)."[27] Kierkegaard likewise considered that Martensen's approach to linking revelation and philosophy failed to grasp the correct balance between philosophy and revelation.[28] Others such as Frederik Sibbern, meanwhile, described Martensen as a critic of Hegel.[29] Perhaps the most appropriate view of his work is suggested by Schiørring, who

---

25. Martensen, *Christian Dogmatics*, 83.
26. Martensen, *Christian Dogmatics*, 82.
27. Schiørring, "Martensen," 190.
28. Schiørring, "Martensen," 204.
29. Stewart, "Kierkegaard and Hegelianism," 122.

writes that Martensen, rejecting the "either this or that approach," mediates between supernaturalism and naturalism and between "speculative philosophy and a dogmatics which was faithful to Bible and Church."[30] Still, as Martensen sought to reconcile revelation and philosophy, his theological work was oriented on the absolute personality of God.

William N. Clarke

William N. Clarke (1841–1912) was an American theologian who has been called "the empirical, evolutionary, and evangelical liberal"[31] and "the first systematic theologian of theological liberalism in America."[32] Clarke published the first edition of his work *An Outline of Christian Theology* in 1898 and his major monograph *The Christian Doctrine of God* in 1909.[33] Though he grew up in a Baptist family, trained in a Baptist seminary, and practiced his ministry in a Baptist institution, modern ideas, especially evolution, were integrated into his theological construction. Clarke had no hesitation in applying the science and philosophy of his day in and to his theological work.

Claude Howe correspondingly remarks that Clarke "believed that science, in discovering how the universe works, adds to our knowledge of the One who produced it and thus supplements rather than conflicts with theology."[34] At the same time, Clarke consistently acknowledged the authority of Scripture and considered it to be the main source of Christian theology throughout his career.[35] In this way, he endeavored to be faithful to both the traditional teaching of Christian theology and the modern world.[36]

Despite his acceptance of evolution, it is important to note that Clarke's own theological program never descends into pantheism, as if God himself were confined to the processes of evolution and of naturalism. Clarke endorses the view that "the doctrine of evolution declares the

---

30. Schiørring, "Martensen," 191.
31. Reist, "Augustus Hopkins Strong and William Newton Clarke," 31.
32. Howe, *Theology of Clarke*, 2.
33. Clarke, *Outline of Christian Theology*; Clarke, *Christian Doctrine of God*.
34. Howe, *Theology of Clarke*, 36.
35. Clarke, *Use of the Scriptures*, 50–145.
36. Clarke, preface to *Christian Doctrine of God*, vii.

unity and continuity of things,"³⁷ but insists that evolution and its principle of process are a divine method of developing the physical nature of human beings and other creatures. Thus, evolution is construed as God's general way of interacting with the world and of accomplishing his will in creation,³⁸ and God's transcendence is not reduced to an evolutionary process but is what causes his immanence and effects the evolutionary process in the world. This pattern of interaction includes the evolutionary process of transforming human beings into the character of the divine Being. Hence, Howe contends, "For this reason it was easy for Clarke to speak of the evolutionary process as the presence of the indwelling God, who is continually sustaining and directing the progress of his creation."³⁹

There are mixed views concerning Clarke's theological works. On the one hand, Reist asserts that Clarke disavows the traditional understanding of creation by accepting modern views such as evolution theory.⁴⁰ On the other hand, even though Clarke may have sought to humanize and reinterpret theology in the modern context and may have rejected the doctrine of inspiration of Scripture, Shailer Matthews holds that Clarke never abandoned the orthodox root of theology and instead presented Christian ideas of God consistent with the historical and biblical revelations of the past.⁴¹

William Brown similarly stresses that Clarke's view of God is not derived from "an idea of God which we gain through modern science primarily and then baptize with the name Christian for the purpose of convenience."⁴² Clarke's own confession confirms Matthew and Brown's analysis of his theological commitments: "So far as I have the power, I have sought to be faithful both to the ancient light and to the modern, and I have hoped that my presentation might bear reasonably well the tests of the present time."⁴³

One important difference between Clarke's *Outline of Christianity* and *The Christian Doctrine of God* might briefly be noted. When dealing with the presentation of the doctrine of God's attributes, the former

---

37. Clarke, *Can I Believe in God the Father?*, 50.
38. Howe, *Theology of Clarke*, 38.
39. Howe, *Theology of Clarke*, 72.
40. Reist, "William Newton Clarke," 9.
41. Mathews, "In Memoriam," 445.
42. Brown, "Theology of William Newton Clarke," 169.
43. Clarke, *Christian Doctrine of God*, vii.

publication starts with the metaphysical attributes of God, whereas the latter prioritizes Clarke's later principle of theology, i.e., "the ethical concept of the character of God as revealed in Christ."[44] Investigating the *character* of God that is revealed in this way is the first approach to the Christian doctrine of God, before turning to the doctrine through natural scientific, philosophical, and metaphysical approaches. Clarke states:

> The experience in Christ by which God has become vitally known to the Christian people is an ethical experience, expressive of the character of God and realized in the character of men. The Christian salvation is God's characteristic work, and the Christian doctrine is primarily an account of him as a moral Being, in characteristic relations with other moral beings. In other words, the Christian doctrine of God is first of all a doctrine of the divine character.[45]

Reist has suggested that Clarke's emphasis on the ethical concept of God in *The Christian Doctrine of God* is evidence of Clarke's deserting classical theology.[46] In both works on the divine attributes, however, Clarke's affirmation of the infinite perfections of God is preserved, as will be seen in detail below.[47] For the purposes of this publication, then, the difference in order of presentation between *Outline of Christianity* and *The Christian Doctrine of God* does not lead to any significant material difference: both will therefore be used in the exploration of the work of Clarke that follows.

Thematic Discussion of Impassibility and Passibility

Having briefly considered the theological backgrounds of Strong, Martensen, and Clarke, we will now consider their work as mediating theologians who in some way uphold the suffering of God with respect to a series of heuristic topics. Hence, what follows will explore in turn the way in which these thinkers presented their starting points in considering the themes of the doctrine of God, his emotions, his suffering and love, his suffering and human sin, his suffering and immutability, and his self-limitation.

---

44. Howe, *Theology of Clarke*, 17.
45. Clarke, *Christian Doctrine of God*, 57.
46. Reist, "William Newton Clarke," 9.
47. Clarke, *Outline of Christian Theology*, 276–351.

Starting Points in Considering the Doctrine of God

All three mediating theologians adhere in their starting points in considering the doctrine of God's attributes to a traditional approach to the doctrine. They affirm the divine attributes that demonstrate God's perfections such as his omnipotence, aseity, eternity, omniscience, omnipresence, holiness, and love, but differ in their classification of God's attributes.

Strong distinguishes between God's absolute or immanent attributes and relative or transitive attributes, while Martensen disapproves of Strong's approach; meanwhile Clarke chooses a different route to expound God's attributes. Each of their diverse starting points of the doctrine of God is nonetheless grounded in an understanding of God's perfections, especially of God's aseity. In this way, these mediating theologians share an initial approach to the doctrine of God with impassibilist theologians.

The doctrine of aseity drives Strong's doctrine of God. Strong is dedicated to defending the Christian idea of God from pantheism and makes a clear distinction between the Creator and creation, emphasizing the superiority of the Creator over the result of his works. He states: "The whole universe is but a drop of dew upon the fringe of God's garment, or a breath exhaled from his mouth.... Nature is but the symbol of God."[48] This motif is further clarified in Strong's twofold classification of God's attributes: (1) the absolute or immanent attributes that belong to the inner life of God in which he moves himself *in se*, independently of his involvement with the world; (2) the relative or transitive attributes that belong to his relationship with the world and by which God moves non-divine created objects outside of himself, objects dependent upon the Creator.[49]

The absolute or immanent attributes are spirituality (life and personality), infinity (self-existence, immutability, and unity), and perfection (truth, love, and holiness).[50] The relative or transitive attributes are related to time and space (eternity and immensity), to creation (omnipresence, omniscience, and omnipotence), and to moral beings (veracity and faithfulness, or transitive truth; mercy and goodness, or transitive love; justice and righteousness, or transitive holiness).[51] The intention

---

48. Strong, *Systematic Theology*, 1:249.
49. Strong, *Systematic Theology*, 1:248.
50. Strong, *Systematic Theology*, 1:249–75.
51. Strong, *Systematic Theology*, 1:275–95.

of Strong's classification is to demonstrate the self-sufficiency and the complete freedom of God, who created the world out of nothing.[52] Therefore, Strong proposes that "God would be God, if he had never created."[53]

Just as divine aseity drives Strong's doctrine of God, a focus on the absolute personality and aseity of God propels Martensen's approach to the doctrine of God. Martensen first defines God as personal and absolute against the objection of pantheism that God cannot be both absolute and personal. For God to be absolute, according to Martensen, means that God is infinite, unconditioned, and unlimited, and for God to be a person, it means that "he is the *self-centralized* Absolute, the eternal fundamental being, which knows itself as a centre, as the *I am* in the midst of its infinite glory."[54] God's essence as person is omnipotent in wisdom and thus governs the universe and works out the system of the world from eternity; nature and history are the revelation of the will and providence of God.[55] Martensen also stresses that God has his life within himself to the fullest degree and is the eternal One, "the I AM, who is *a se*."[56] On these theological grounds of God's absolute personality and self-existence, Martensen builds his doctrine of God's attributes, including eternity, unchangeableness, omnipresence, omniscience, omnipotence, providence, wisdom, righteousness, goodness, love, holiness, and blessedness.[57]

In formal terms, the concepts of unity and antithesis play a significant role in driving Martensen's way of thinking about God's attributes. Unlike Strong, Martensen rejects the distinction between the absolute (immanent) and relative (transitive) attributes of God. The problem with classifying God's attributes within these two categories, Martensen holds, is that "there are no divine attributes, which, if conceived as living attributes, are not transitive, that is, do not express a relation of God to the world;—nor are there any which are not reflective, that is, which do not

---

52. Strong, *Systematic Theology*, 1:249. Strong writes, "The immanent attributes show us how completely matters of grace are creation and redemption, and how unspeakable is the condescension of him who took our humanity and humbled himself to the death of the cross."

53. Strong, *Systematic Theology*, 1:246.

54. Martensen, *Christian Dogmatics*, 80, emphasis original.

55. Martensen, *Christian Dogmatics*, 80.

56. Martensen, *Christian Dogmatics*, 93.

57. Martensen, *Christian Dogmatics*, 93–101.

go back on God himself."⁵⁸ Instead, Martensen claims that it is better—in classifying the divine attributes—to focus on the two types of relation in which God engages the world: "a relation of unity" and "a relation of antithesis (diversity)."⁵⁹ Of course, God's attributes operate in unity in the life of God. But the relation of unity between his attributes *ad extra* is hindered by sin and therefore becomes a relation of antithesis. Thus, the antithesis between God and human beings is caused by their sins, the violation of divine holiness. Martensen explains that "our religious life . . . moves between these two poles—that of unity and that of diversity [antithesis], that of freedom and that of dependence, that of reconciliation and that of separation."⁶⁰ This dynamic construal of the divine attributes between unity and antithesis shapes Martensen's views on God's emotions, love, and suffering.

God's personal spirit and self-existence are crucial aspects of Clarke's doctrine of God in *Outline of Christian Theology*. For Clarke, personal spirit is the nature of God and one of the four central Christian conceptions of God.⁶¹ Clarke posits that God is personal, having both self-consciousness and self-direction, and that God is spirit: "It means that God is an intelligence; God is a mind. He thinks and feels and wills."⁶² God, whose nature is personal spirit, is a living God and self-existent, being full of life, eternal and sufficient, and possessing both personality and life in unity. Clarke notes, "If there is one divine spirit, the source of all besides, his life must be from ever and for ever, nothing back of it and nothing to outlast it; for as nothing outside caused it, so nothing can bring it to an end."⁶³ After explaining the connection between God's

58. Martensen, *Christian Dogmatics*, 92.
59. Martensen, *Christian Dogmatics*, 93.
60. Martensen, *Christian Dogmatics*, 93.
61. Clarke, *Outline of Christian Theology*, 66. Before outlining the lists of God's attributes, Clarke argues that there are four major Christian conceptions of God and explains them in this order: the nature of God (personal spirit), character of God (perfectly good), relation of God to others (creating, sustaining, and ordering), and motive of God (holy love).
62. Clarke, *Outline of Christian Theology*, 66. In this way, God is personal spirit: God "is a self-conscious and self-directing intelligence . . . who knows himself as himself, and consciously directs his own action." Clarke, *Outline of Christian Theology*, 67.
63. Clarke, *Outline of Christian Theology*, 76. Clarke is cautious of using terms such as "infinite" and "absolute" to reflect the nature of God because they are often ambiguous and indefinite and because they are related to philosophical ideas. Still, he does affirm what these terms denote concerning the perfections of God. God is infinite in the

personal spirit and his self-existence, he discerns two categories of divine attributes: (1) modes of activity or natural attributes including omnipresence, omniscience, omnipotence, and immutability and (2) qualities of character or moral attributes including love and holiness.[64]

With respect to their approaches to the doctrine of God, all three mediating theologians thus begin with a strong affirmation of the aseity of God. Strong, Martensen, and Clarke affirm the tenets of the traditional doctrine of God's attributes, and divine aseity is the fundamental proposition of their theology proper. In this way, as the following section will further indicate, divine aseity and these tenets of traditional theology become a ground for their theological treatment of the doctrine of God's attributes, and for affirming divine emotions and suffering as the result of God's personal relationship with the world.

God's Emotions

As noted in chapter 2, impassibilists hold that God's emotions have only the active aspects that are foreknown, immutable, and unmoved, whereas passibilists argue that suffering is God's eternal nature and his necessary and free reactions to human beings and that God's emotions and suffering also have the passive aspects that are moved, temporal, and mutable. As mediating theologians, Strong, Martensen, and Clarke offer a more nuanced position.

First, Strong and Clarke affirm that God, who is personal spirit and is self-existent, has affections, and construe these affections as an ontological characteristic of personal spirit. Strong, particularly, underscores that God's love is both affectional and rational. Second, the mediating theologians interpret the biblical texts on God's feelings as true descriptions of divine feelings and do not dismiss these texts as mere metaphors and anthropopathism. Third, Strong and Martensen attest that there are clear distinctions between God's interior emotional life and his expressions of emotions towards the world and between divine emotions and human emotions. However, Clarke is more concerned with precluding any distinction between God's emotions and human emotions.

---

sense that "as being free from all such limitations as we find upon all our powers and activities." Clarke, *Outline of Christian Theology*, 73. God is absolute "as independent of the relations in which the existence of anything besides himself places him." Clarke, *Outline of Christian Theology*, 74.

64. Clarke, *Outline of Christian Theology*, 73–102.

Strong's doctrine of God's attributes affirms that God is capable of feeling affection. First, God's affection is closely connected to his life. For Strong, spirituality—observed above to be one of the immanent attributes of God—includes life. God is a living God and has his own life, but his life, according to Strong, is not "[m]ere process [referring to evolution], without a subject for we cannot conceive of a divine life without a God to live it"; nor is it "[m]ere correspondence with outward condition and environment for this would render impossible a life of God before the existence of the universe."[65] Instead, Strong argues that divine life "is rather mental energy, or energy of intellect, affection, and will" and that "God is the living God, as having in his own being a source of being and activity, both for himself and others."[66] God's life, as one of his immanent attributes, belongs to himself only and indicates that as a living God he is capable of experiencing affection.

Second, God's emotional affection is connected to his love. Strong recognizes that God's love is both immanent and transitive, and again he insists that love is ontologically different from the capricious nature of human emotion. Combining the New Testament's definitions of love as *phileo* in John 11:36 (emotional affection) and as *agape* in John 3:16 (a rational choice and benevolent affection), God's immanent love, which is towards himself, and his transitive love, which is towards human beings, have both affectional and rational aspects.[67] More emphatically, Strong holds, "There is an infinite life of sensibility and affection in God. God has feeling, and in an infinite degree. But feeling alone is not love."[68] God's affections infinitely and constantly transpire from the immanent and transitive attributes, in contrast to human emotions, which spring from imperfection, e.g., wild passion and impulse and sinful nature.

Even though Martensen did not connect God's feelings to his spirit, he affirms the reality of the divine emotions *in se* and *ad extra*. For Martensen, the content of God's life *in se* and his life *ad extra* are not the same because of God's relationship with the world is established as a relation of antithesis. Martensen's doctrine of divine blessedness relates to God's feelings *in se* but is not considered as a static elation or joy without motion. Divine blessedness involves eternal life and movement

---

65. Strong, *Systematic Theology*, 1:251.
66. Strong, *Systematic Theology*, 1:252.
67. Strong, *Systematic Theology*, 1:264.
68. Strong, *Systematic Theology*, 1:265.

that is characterized by "eternal *peace* of love,"[69] such that God's inner life and eternal activity is marked by unmixed joy that is preserved eternally without change.

In contrast, in God's life with his creatures, the relation of antithesis that is caused by human sins shapes God's emotional responses to them. In this way, God's emotions that are recorded in Scripture, such as grief and anger, emerge as the outcome of God's interaction with human beings.[70] Maartensen posits that God "submits to the conditions of finitude" and "even allows his power to be limited by the sinful will of man."[71] Thus, two different modes of emotions are expressed in his life *in se* and *ad extra*. Within God's inner life is eternal joy and blessedness, while in relation to sinful creatures, this is not possible.

Clarke also systematically affirms that divine emotions are related to the nature of both the life and the personal spirit of God. First, for Clarke, the life of God is eternal, and includes divine emotions; he writes that the divine life "implies all power of movement, action, thought, emotion, self-direction, communication."[72] That God is a living God means that "his thought is creative, his feeling is intense, his action is infinitely free and powerful."[73] Second, for Clarke, the God who is personal spirit has feeling. Clarke remarks that "God is an intelligence; God is a mind. He thinks and feels and wills."[74] The living God of Scripture is personal spirit and fully capable of undergoing feelings.

Clarke extends this view that feeling is an attribute of personal spirit into a discussion of God making human beings in turn as personal spirit. God is spirit ontologically and thus is immaterial; therefore, feeling is not an attribute of material or flesh. As the fountain of feeling and intellect, God has made human beings as spiritual persons in his image and given them the capacity to feel different emotions. Clarke correspondingly remarks "that God is other than matter in the same way as man, by possessing these powers of thought, affection, and will."[75] At the same time, Clarke draws a clear distinction between the personhood of

---

69. Martensen, *Christian Dogmatics*, 101, emphasis original.
70. Martensen, *Christian Dogmatics*, 101.
71. Martensen, *Christian Dogmatics*, 101.
72. Clarke, *Outline of Christian Theology*, 76.
73. Clarke, *Outline of Christian Theology*, 76.
74. Clarke, *Outline of Christian Theology*, 66.
75. Clarke, *Outline of Christian Theology*, 66.

God and that of human beings: "Personality in God is not an outgrown anthropomorphism. The representation of God as a Father, emphasized by Christ, implies personality as distinctly as any of the early anthropomorphisms, and far more richly. Probably the truth is that complete personality exists in God alone. . . . God alone is fully personal."[76] And on this basis, as the God who has life and is personal spirit, God is fully capable of undergoing various feelings.

All three mediating theologians thus distinguish between God's inner emotional life and his emotions towards the world, although each individual approach is somewhat different. Strong argues that divine love has the characteristics of choice and affection and makes a distinction between God's love for himself and his love for the world. He also claims that God has feeling, but it is not yet clear whether Strong frames divine emotions as active or passive. Martensen makes a distinction between God's life in himself of peace and a life with his creatures of anger and sorrow. His argument that God's anger and grief emerge as he submits to the condition of humankind indicates that God is moved by human conditions and therefore, we can say, experiences passive emotions. Clarke's approach involves assigning feelings to the divine attribute of spirit and of life and interpreting human beings as spiritual beings, a move which seems to preclude any distinction between the way God experiences his emotions in his relation to the world and the way his created spiritual beings experience their emotions. Correspondingly, divine emotions occur through his reciprocal relationship with human beings in the form of passive emotions.

God's Suffering and Love

As noted in chapter 2, passibilists have linked divine suffering with the self-sacrificing and self-giving love of the Son of God that is demonstrated on the cross. The event of the cross is grounded in God's love and reveals both the eternal suffering of the triune God and the principle that to love is to suffer and to be moved by the suffering of others. In this way, passibilists have argued that God suffers eternally *in se* and suffers necessarily with the world that he loves. Strong, Martensen, and Clarke likewise associate divine passibility with God's love but in different ways

---

76. Clarke, *Outline of Christian Theology*, 68.

construe divine passibility as the outcome of God's relationship with the world.

Strong's view of the passibility of God can be recognized by considering further the interplay in his theology between God's immanent love and its expression through blessedness, and his transitive love and its expression through grief. Strong's doctrine of aseity grounds the distinction between God's inner life and his association with the world, and between his immanent love and transitive love. God's immanent love refers to his love within himself and is never an abstract notion.[77] This love is more than a rational and voluntary emotion, for it is self-communicating, self-imparting, and self-giving, representing the self-movement of the triune God *in se*.

As God is the perfect subject of the act of love, the immanent love requires the perfect object as the recipient of the love. Strong notes, "The only sufficient object of his love is the image of his own perfections, for that alone is equal to himself."[78] In this way, God's immanent love, Strong holds, "constitutes a ground of the divine blessedness," for blessedness requires perfect faculties and objects. He continues, "Blessedness is not itself a divine attribute but it is rather a result of the exercise of the divine attributes. . . . Perfect faculties, with perfect objects for their exercise, ensure God's blessedness."[79] The world, both as a subject and object, being ontologically inferior to God cannot give or receive the perfect love that God deserves. Strong observes, "The existence of the universe is not necessary to his serenity and joy."[80]

The immanent love that exists in God's life is translated into transitive love in the form of mercy towards the world. Mercy seeks both temporal and eternal goods for sinners who have disobeyed the divine will, even if mercy requires the self-sacrifice and suffering of God to an infinite degree.[81] Strong warns that God's immanent love must not be confused with God's transitive love, for these categories of love are manifested to two different objects, the immanent love to God himself and the transitive love to human beings.[82]

---

77. Strong, *Systematic Theology*, 1:266.
78. Strong, *Systematic Theology*, 1:266.
79. Strong, *Systematic Theology*, 1:265.
80. Strong, *Systematic Theology*, 1:266.
81. Strong, *Systematic Theology*, 1:289.
82. Strong, *Systematic Theology*, 1:263.

In this trajectory of thinking, Strong explains the passibility of God in the following ways. First, he argues that the God of love has the capacity to suffer: "God is passible, or capable of suffering."[83] He points to the relevant biblical texts to defend his argument and affirms that God's passibility occurs in response to human sin and misery. Second, Strong argues that it is the revelation of Jesus that reveals God's passibility. He posits that "Jesus Christ in his sorrow and sympathy, his tears and agony, is the revealer of God's feelings *toward the [human] race.*"[84] Moltmann and other passibilists argue that Jesus reveals God's feelings towards himself and the human race, while Strong asserts that Jesus reveals God's feelings towards the human race only.

Third, Strong connects the possibility of divine suffering to love. He notes, "The love of God involves also the possibility of divine suffering. . . . We cannot, indeed, conceive of love without self-sacrifice, or of self-sacrifice without suffering."[85] Because God's transitive love is directed towards human beings and their sins and misery, the divine possibility to which Strong refers is the expression of God's love towards the world, not the expression of his immanent love towards himself. Suffering is construed by Strong as God's way of revealing his perfection and mercy in relation to the world.

Even though Strong affirms God's passibility, he seems at the same time to accept the notion that God's nature is impassible—that he is incapable of suffering. In his discussion of the hypostatic union of the divine nature and human nature in the person of Jesus, Strong argues that "the divine nature in itself is incapable of . . . suffering. . . . [S]o the otherwise impassible God can suffer mortal pangs through his union with humanity. He never could suffer if he had not joined himself to human nature."[86] However, he does not attempt to make any connection between this divine impassibility and the divine passibility in his discussion of the doctrine of God's attributes. In light of Strong's emphasis on divine aseity and blessedness, it seems likely that he is using the term "impassible" to argue that God's nature *in se* is not overwhelmed by suffering, and not that God is incapable of undergoing suffering *ad extra*.

---

83. Strong, *Systematic Theology*, 1:266.
84. Strong, *Systematic Theology*, 1:266, emphasis added.
85. Strong, *Systematic Theology*, 1:266.
86. Strong, *Systematic Theology*, 2:697.

Just like Strong, Martensen's notion of love is associated with the suffering of God. His understanding of God's love and suffering begins with interpreting that all God's "attributes are combined in love, as in their centre and vital principle."[87] Because of the ontological and moral inferiority of unrighteous creatures, Martensen draws a distinction between the communication of the love within the inner life of the God and his love towards the world. His approach to God's attributes—unity and antithesis—is important at this point.

In the unity of the divine attributes, God is fully satisfied without interruption and restraint. However, sin disrupts the communication of the unity of the divine attributes to the world, leading to antithesis. The consequence of this disruption, Martensen holds, is that God's "actual relation to it [the world] is not a relation of love, but of holiness and justice, a relation of opposition, because the unity of his attributes is hindered and restrained."[88] He continues, "This restrained manifestation of love, which in one aspect of it may be designated wrath, in another aspect is called *grief*, or *distress*, in the Holy Spirit of love."[89] In this way, God's love is manifested in grief. Martensen observes in the same way as Strong that a love that cannot be wounded by sin is not true love at all.[90] Although wrath, suffering and love may seem to bear conflicting characteristics, for Martensen love is still the common ground of all these divine responses and their various expressions.

Martensen's doctrines of creation and of love can be explored further to examine whether the suffering of God in his view is necessary or free. Martensen's doctrine of creation is grounded in his view of God's love. God's love is the principle divine attribute in Martensen's theological program, however he specifies what it means for this love to be perfect as follows: "[P]erfect love is not merely the love of God to himself, to his own perfection, but must also be conceived as love to what is imperfect; in other words, it must be conceived as the will to create a world, one of whose essential features is the need of God."[91] On this understanding, God creates the world to fulfill the nature of his love necessarily. However, to differentiate his argument from the pantheistic assertion

---

87. Martensen, *Christian Dogmatics*, 99.
88. Martensen, *Christian Dogmatics*, 303.
89. Martensen, *Christian Dogmatics*, 303, emphasis original.
90. Martensen, *Christian Dogmatics*, 305.
91. Martensen, *Christian Dogmatics*, 111.

that God needs creation as much as it needs God,[92] Martensen posits that "this lack [the need to love and create the world] in God is not, as in the God of pantheism, a blind hunger and thirst after existence, but is identical with the inexhaustible riches of that liberty which cannot but will to reveal itself."[93] This suggests that God created the world by the necessity of his love and leads Martensen to deduce that "without the world God is not God,"[94] contradicting Strong's conclusion that God would still be God without creation.[95]

Martensen's understanding of the divine love in relation to the doctrine of creation does not ascribe suffering to God in eternity but does seem to undermine the freedom of God's passibility. On the one hand, in Martensen's view, divine passibility is still categorized as temporal suffering: he maintains the distinction between God's eternal joy and God's suffering caused by human sins without eternalizing the latter as a dimension of the life of God in eternity. Martensen's affirmation that God necessarily wills to reveal his magnificent love and love imperfect human creatures does not violate the eternal blessedness of the inner life of God. On the other hand, however, Martensen renders passibility a necessary feature of God's life with the world. If the God whose essence is love must love what is imperfect, he is not free from manifesting his love through suffering. As God both creates and loves the world necessarily, he has no choice but to experience suffering necessarily.

Connecting love with the divine suffering in a similar way, Clarke articulates that there are two routes to understanding this divine love: (1) "love as it exists among men" or human love and (2) love of God manifested in Christ.[96] Concerning the first source for knowing God's love, Clarke explains that human love in its earliest stages "yearns for its object," "craves possession," and "seems the most selfish—a desire, a craving."[97] However, as this human love matures, it "yearns now for the welfare of its object, and is impelled to do or suffer to promote that welfare."[98] This love grows into and is finally manifested through one's

---

92. Martensen, *Christian Dogmatics*, 100.
93. Martensen, *Christian Dogmatics*, 100.
94. Martensen, *Christian Dogmatics*, 114.
95. Strong, *Systematic Theology*, 1:246.
96. Clarke, *Outline of Christian Theology*, 95.
97. Clarke, *Outline of Christian Theology*, 95.
98. Clarke, *Outline of Christian Theology*, 95.

self-sacrifice. Clarke posits that if the perfect form and practice of human love can lead in this way to self-sacrifice and voluntary suffering, then divine love can in a much deeper way participate in suffering. This approach of relating human love to God's love is a natural movement in Clarke's theology, given that God is a loving personal spirit who made human beings in the form of the likeness of personal spirit with the capability to love.

The mission and work of Jesus Christ, the second way of understanding divine love, is to impart himself and the highest goodness to human beings and to receive human beings into eternal life.[99] This outgoing and self-sacrificial movement of God exhibits how much the eternally sufficient God is willing to sacrifice for sinners, and demonstrates the endless desire of God's love and the actuality of God's passibility.[100] These two sources for understanding God's love affirm the intimacy between God's love and suffering.

According to Clarke, God's love towards the world is demonstrated in two different ways, depending on the moral condition of human beings. Clarke distinguishes between God's "love of complacency, which delights in its object [based on the positive condition of its object], and love of benevolence, which without approving desires to do its object good [regardless of the negative condition of its object]."[101] This distinction exists because God "loves two classes of beings, morally regarded," so that "his love takes different forms accordingly."[102] Nevertheless, God's love of complacency is not radically different from God's love of benevolence, because for Clarke, in both cases, "love is God's desire to give all good and have his love returned."[103] Thus, God can manifest his love for the world in different modes.

In sum, Strong and Clarke both affirm that divine suffering is the voluntary consequence of God's love of fallen creation, whereas Martensen's understanding of divine passibility has a necessary characteristic. Strong argues that the God of love is capable of suffering and suffers in response to human sin and misery in the form of passive suffering. Clarke similarly recognizes that God's love leads to God's suffering in the economy.

---

99. Clarke, *Outline of Christian Theology*, 97.
100. Clarke, *Outline of Christian Theology*, 96–97.
101. Clarke, *Outline of Christian Theology*, 98.
102. Clarke, *Outline of Christian Theology*, 98.
103. Clarke, *Outline of Christian Theology*, 98.

Just like the passibilists, Strong and Clarke affirm the passive dimension of God's passibility, but the difference is that their conception of the suffering of God is guarded by the doctrine of divine aseity and of creation: God, who is fully sufficient and satisfied within himself, created the universe voluntarily and chooses to partake in the pain of his loved human beings freely without any compulsion and need. Meanwhile, Martensen takes a different route in his understanding of the relationship between God's love and God's suffering. As he argues that God must create and love the world necessarily, God cannot but manifest his restrained love for the world through grief.

God's Suffering and Human Sin

Strong, Clarke, and Martensen posit sin as the ultimate cause of God's suffering in the context of Protestant atonement theory. The mediating theologians stress that God is moved by human sins and responds to them through his grief. The discussion of God's passibility within the context of Protestant atonement theory differentiates the mediating theologians from the work of certain passibilists, such as Moltmann and Lee, who largely avoid the issue of sin in their theological programs. The following section demonstrates how these mediating theologians connect God's passibility to human sin and how creatively Strong and Clarke expand the discussion of divine passibility in relation to atonement theory.

A penal substitutionary understanding of the atonement functions as the touchstone of Strong's appraisal of the suffering of God. Divine holiness is expressed to human beings at least in two ways: positively by rewarding righteousness with happiness and negatively by ascribing suffering to sin.[104] In this way, the origin of the existence of suffering in the world is the dire consequence of creatures violating the holiness of God. Without the ability to fulfill the righteousness of God, human beings suffer the consequences of the negative expression of holiness. Sin offends God and his righteousness and entails retribution. Still, God also provides sinners with a way out of this predicament by offering himself as a penal substitutionary atonement for their sins and experiencing suffering and death on the cross.

104. Strong, *Systematic Theology*, 2:714.

Strong relates this conception of the atonement to his proposal that Christ is united with the world from the foundation of the world.[105] He notes, "The life that Christ lived in Palestine and the death that he endured on Calvary were the revelation of a union with mankind, which antedated the Fall. Being thus joined to us from the beginning, he has suffered in all human sin."[106] The direct outcome of Christ's union with the world from the very beginning is that God is able to suffer for human sins by way of substitution: "The imputation of our sins to him is the result of his natural union with us. He has been our substitute from the beginning."[107]

The essence of God's substitution lies at the heart of the union before the event of the cross. Correspondingly, Strong posits, "Sin has cost God more than it has cost man."[108] Strong concludes not only that God is grieved by human sins, but that in the act of substitution God shares the grief and pain caused by sins.[109] Still, he warns that God's suffering is fundamentally different from human suffering. In his absolute perfection, God foreknows that he will overcome the sins of the world, so that it is his blessedness that is the controlling element of his emotional life, not his suffering that occurs in response to human transgressions.[110] Divine suffering then is viewed as a temporal experience in the structure of the redemptive atonement.

Here, it is illuminating to explore Strong's remark that "Cavalry is only the outward manifestation of a sacrifice which was from eternity,"[111] to determine whether he affirms God's eternal passibility, along with theologians such as Moltmann, or only his passibility in his temporal association with the world. It seems at first that Strong considers the divine suffering to be eternal. He turns to Revelation 3:18 as evidence of God's eternal passibility: "All inhabitants of the earth will worship the beast—all whose names have not been written in the Lamb's book of life, the Lamb who was slain [before] from the creation of the world."[112]

---

105. Strong, *Ethical Monism*, 14.
106. Strong, *Systematic Theology*, 2:715.
107. Strong, *Systematic Theology*, 2:716.
108. Strong, *Ethical Monism*, 95.
109. Strong, *Systematic Theology*, 2:716.
110. Strong, *Systematic Theology*, 1:266.
111. Strong, *Ethical Monism*, 95.
112. Strong, *Systematic Theology*, 1:268.

Strong suggests correspondingly that the Son's sacrifice on the cross is a description of the eternal life of the triune God: "Calvary is only the outward manifestation of a sacrifice which was from eternity."[113] More specifically, for Strong, "The suffering of the incarnate Christ is the manifestation in space and time of the eternal suffering of God on account of human sin."[114] However, at this point there seems to arise an inconsistency in Strong's work, between the affirmation of the eternal passibility of God and the affirmation of divine aseity.

The issue that seems to cause the confusion is Strong's usage of the term "eternity" with reference to God's suffering in relation to the atonement accomplished in Jesus Christ. For Strong, the event of the cross is grounded, as was seen above, in the principle of Christ's union with the world from the beginning. In this register, when Strong uses the term "eternity," he seems to be referring to the logical moment between God's determination to create the world and God's determination to provide himself as the atonement for human sin, and thus to the eternal sphere in which God relates to the economy, and not to God's life *in se*.

To support this reading, it might be noted that Strong writes that God "provides that atonement even when he determines to create. . . . In the beginning God gave his Son to die; the provision of redemption antedates the historical existence of sin itself,"[115] and—as noted above—Strong claims that this sacrifice was from eternity. Strong wants to underline that from the beginning, from the eternal moment in which God determines to create human beings and atone for their sins, God suffers the pain of those sins. In his *Systematic Theology*, after employing the term "eternity" to describe the span of this suffering of God, Strong uses the phrase "from the beginning" to clarify his use of the term. In the following paragraph Strong explains that "*from the beginning* he [God] has suffered in all human sin" and again in the next page claims that God "has been our substitute *from the beginning*."[116]

In Strong's writing, then, the term "from the beginning" seems to specify his use of the term "eternity," at least in the context of the atonement. The terms are being used at this point interchangeably, in order to underscore that, as the result of Christ's determination for union with

---

113. Strong, *Ethical Monism*, 95.
114. Strong, *Systematic Theology*, 2:715.
115. Strong, *Ethical Monism*, 95.
116. Strong, *Systematic Theology*, 2:715, emphasis added; 2:716, emphasis added.

the world "from the beginning," his suffering of the pain of the sins of humanity precedes the actual event of creation and the consequent emergence of sin in history.

When Strong's remarks concerning the eternal suffering of God are examined across his entire theological program, however, it becomes clear that this suffering in view of the economy cannot be considered to be attributable to the self-sufficient and self-existing life of God. The distinction between the absolute/immanent attributes and relative/transitive attributes in Strong's doctrine of God serves "to make plain the divine self-sufficiency" and to stress therefore that creation "is not a necessity."[117] For Strong, divine suffering serves as a substitutionary suffering for the transgressions of human beings. Therefore, if God can be God without the world and human beings, God does not have to suffer in this way, which means that divine passibility belongs to the transitive and relative dimensions of God's will and of God's experience with non-divine beings, and not to God in his inner divine life.

Strong himself specifies that "Jesus Christ in his sorrow and sympathy, his tears and agony, is the revealer of God's feelings *toward the race*,"[118] whereas "the divine nature in itself is incapable of . . . suffering . . . [and is] impassible."[119] Besides, if self-sacrifice were to be of the eternal nature of God, God would have to create the world necessarily in order to fulfill his nature; however, for Strong, God's redemptive operation is explicitly his free act: "The relations which God sustains to the world (*predicata*), moreover, such as creation, preservation, government, are not to be denominated attributes; for these are accidental, not necessary or inseparable from the idea of God. God would be God, if he had never created."[120] If the event of the cross is an eternal event of God in the sense of relating to God *in se*, Strong's whole theological system breaks down. Regardless of the rather ambiguous use of the term "eternity," then, Strong's program presents divine suffering as a temporal experience that is related to the world, with God in himself resolutely impassible.

Martensen considers divine suffering in the context of the atonement. As noted above, the manifestation of God's perfections in the world is marked, for Martensen, by antithesis in the face of human sin.

---

117. Strong, *Systematic Theology*, 1:249.
118. Strong, *Systematic Theology*, 1:266, emphasis added.
119. Strong, *Systematic Theology*, 2:697.
120. Strong, *Systematic Theology*, 1:246.

The historical economy of redemption is thus God's attempt to turn the antithesis to the unity. The wrath and suffering of God are the restrained and unfulfilled form of relationship of God's holy love towards the world in sin.[121] In this way, God's wrath and suffering are construed as "a limitation of the divine blessedness."[122] The contradiction between unity and sin can be removed only through the destruction of sin.[123] However, creation cannot overcome the infinite antithesis; only God himself, through the incarnated reconciler, can overcome it.[124]

Martensen's concept of atonement seeks to resist the key arguments of two other positions—at least as Martensen reads them: (1) God's essence of love does not change to wrath and (2) God's essence is too great to be affected by sin and atonement.[125] In his view of the atonement, Martensen claims against both these ideas that, "We, on the contrary, believe that sin is against God, that it does concern him, that it disturbs his divine relations towards us, and therefore we cannot rest satisfied with that seeming reconciliation which is effected on earth but not in heaven."[126] That is, as God is moved by sin and expresses his restrained love through his wrath, propitiation is necessary for God: this is provided on the cross.

Martensen's view of the atonement demonstrates that God is moved by sin and expresses suffering in return and that as God will overcome antithesis caused by sin, his own suffering, the limitation of God's blessedness, will be "swallowed up in the inner life of perfection which God lives, in total independence of his creation, and in triumphant prospect of the fulfilment of his great designs."[127] The suffering of God is thus considered to be his temporal experience.

Along with Strong and Martensen, Clarke's affirmation of divine suffering takes a similar, though not identical, route, and locates sin at the center of God's suffering in the framework of the atonement. In Clarke's system, holiness is the will of God and the purpose of his activity, and love is what accomplishes holiness. God establishes holiness as the life standard for creation: God is perfectly holy, commands an equal

---

121. Martensen, *Christian Dogmatics*, 303.
122. Martensen, *Christian Dogmatics*, 101.
123. Martensen, *Christian Dogmatics*, 303.
124. Martensen, *Christian Dogmatics*, 216.
125. Martensen, *Christian Dogmatics*, 305.
126. Martensen, *Christian Dogmatics*, 305.
127. Martensen, *Christian Dogmatics*, 101.

standard for his human creatures made in his image, and executes holiness in the world.[128] God is essentially the enemy of sin, and if sin exists, God will eternally strive to eradicate sin in the world and is willing to enter the suffering of the world to defeat the eternal enemy.[129] In this way, Clarke states, "God is the great sin-bearer: and this truth he expressed in Christ."[130] Through incarnation God expresses his hatred of sin as a Savior and as a sin-bearer and reveals the main objective of the mission, i.e., winning sinners and satisfying God's offended holiness.

Clarke's understanding of God's attitude towards sin and the atonement points to two types of divine suffering. First, God suffers because he hates sin but loves sinners. Sin burdens the heart of God, who is strongly averse to sin as Clarke describes: "His holiness is offended, and his love is grieved."[131] Second, God suffers in his endeavor to save sinners throughout his redemptive operation. While punishment of sin is one familiar model of this suffering, a less familiar model involves God's work to save sinners from evil and sin even at the cost of the grief and suffering that is entailed. Clarke stresses that an analogue of this type of divine suffering can be understood "by making the endeavour to save some soul from evil, —to reform a drunkard or a gambler, or to cure a man of deep dishonesty."[132] To engage in this righteous endeavor, he explains, one "must put up with evil . . . suffer the disgust, the grief, the weariness . . . [and] be willing to be despised and rejected, ignored and insulted."[133] For Clarke, God endures precisely these experiences to save sinners from their transgressions.[134]

The mediating theologians stage the theological discussion of divine suffering on the platform of God's interaction with sinners, connecting divine suffering with God's response to sin and attributing temporal nature to his suffering. Their propositions claim that God's holiness is

---

128. Clarke, *Outline of Christian Theology*, 91.
129. Clarke, *Outline of Christian Theology*, 92.
130. Clarke, *Outline of Christian Theology*, 341.
131. Clarke, *Outline of Christian Theology*, 342.
132. Clarke, *Outline of Christian Theology*, 342–43.
133. Clarke, *Outline of Christian Theology*, 343.
134. Clarke, *Outline of Christian Theology*, 343. He adds that "upon God comes all that burden of endurance and endeavour that sin casts upon a Saviour. Upon him it comes from all the sin of the world, and all the time. All that the pure One must feel in contact with evil he is made to endure, and upon him is laid all the burden of endeavour against it that a Saviour-God can bear." Clarke, *Outline of Christian Theology*, 343.

grieved by sin. Strong posits that as much as sin has caused humanity's suffering, sin has caused even more suffering for God, supporting the passive dimension of divine suffering. For Martensen, because God is moved by the sin of the world, his love is expressed by anger and grief. In each case, as divine passibility is closely related to and responds to human sins, God's suffering is affirmed and attributed to the economic dimension of God's experience. Clarke's argument for the passibility of God is connected to the sin-bearing nature of God and his righteous endeavor to save sinners.

God's Suffering and Immutability

How Strong, Martensen, and Clarke connect their understanding of divine passibility to the attribute of God's immutability is the next area of exploration. As mentioned in chapter 2, impassibilists base their argument for divine impassibility on the strong immutability of God. Though they differ in their view of divine impassibility, these three theologians do not depart from the classical view of divine immutability, in which God's eternal will, nature, and attributes do not change. However, for them, God's expression of his attributes can take place in different forms, such that divine suffering can represent God's unchanging attributes. They revise the strong immutability of God and appear to support more of the weak version of God's immutability.

Yet unlike those passibilists who argue that divine passibility occurs in the form of change, mediating theologians do not consider divine passibility as change. Mediating theologians treat divine suffering as one of the acts of God with the world and as one of the manifestations of the immutable will, truth, and love of God, and seem to acknowledge the passive aspect of God's passibility.

Strong's definition of divine immutability that "the nature, attributes, and will of God are exempt from all change"[135] and that God is immutable *in se* and *ad extra* is in harmony with that of the impassibilists, and Strong supports the definition with reference to biblical passages referring to the unchanging God (Ps 102:27; Mal 3:6; Jas 1:17). These texts are the backbone of the impassibilist case against the passibilist use of biblical passages that describe God as changing his emotions and mind (Gen 6:6; Num 29:19; 1 Sam 15:11, 29). However, instead of dismissing these passages as

---

135. Strong, *Systematic Theology*, 1:257.

mere metaphors, as impassibilists have done in the past, Strong suggests three complementary ways of viewing biblical references that appear to assign changes to God's nature and argues that these changes are in truth the various expressions of the immutable and eternal truth, love, and purpose of God.

First, the changes should be viewed "[a]s illustrations of the varied methods in which God manifests his immutable truth and wisdom in creation."[136] God is free to choose various methods that may both appear to and involve changes, and is flexible enough to allow himself to be moved by the world to manifest his truth and wisdom. To make this point, Strong references John Caird's argument: "In God infinite consistency is united with infinite flexibility. There is no iron-bound impassibility, but rather an infinite originality in him."[137] The changes that are attested in Scripture are thus the result of God's original and creative activity that he freely chose in order to reveal his truth and wisdom in his infinite freedom and flexibility.

Second, Strong suggests that the biblical references to God's changes should be viewed "[a]s anthropomorphic representations of the revelation of God's unchanging attributes in the changing circumstances and varying moral conditions of creatures."[138] God's unchanging perfection moves him to treat human beings differently. For instance, God's immutable holiness and justice require him respectively to punish the wicked and to reward the righteous. Also, God's immutable love adapts "itself to every varying mood and condition of his children, so as to guide their steps, sympathize with their sorrows, answer their prayers."[139] However, for Strong, these responses and adaptations are not changes in God but in the varying conditions of human beings. Accordingly, they represent the flexibility of God's immutability, so that "God's immutability is not that of the stone, that has no internal experience, but rather that of the column of mercury, that rises and falls with every change in the temperature of the surrounding atmosphere."[140] God adapts to the varying conditions of human beings and responds to them diversely through various manifestations such as joy, anger, and suffering.

136. Strong, *Systematic Theology*, 1:258.
137. Strong, *Systematic Theology*, 1:258. For Caird's view on infinite flexibility, see Caird, *Fundamental Ideas of Christianity*, 2:139.
138. Strong, *Systematic Theology*, 1:258.
139. Strong, *Systematic Theology*, 1:258.
140. Strong, *Systematic Theology*, 1:258.

Third, the changes to God referenced in Scripture are to be viewed "[a]s describing executions, in time, of purposes eternally existing in the mind of God."[141] God has decided in his eternity to respond to certain human conditions and choices in the form of changes. These changes that are recorded in Scripture and that include suffering are the outcome of the perfect execution of God's eternal and immutable purpose in actual history. Strong warns that divine immutability "must not be confounded with immobility" and explains: "This [immobility] would deny the imperative volition of God by which he enters into history. The Scriptures assure us that creation, miracles, incarnation, regeneration, are immediate acts of God. Immutability is consistent with constant activity and perfect freedom."[142] God in his immutable, eternal purposes wills these changes. In this sense, while God remains immutable *in se*, he is free in his infinite flexibility to express his immutable truths, attributes and purposes using different methods and manifestations that involve changes in his relationship with the world.

In describing God as the eternal and self-existent Being who is unchangeable, Martensen underscores the unchangeability of God's life both *ad intra* and *ad extra*. In consideration of God's life *ad intra*, he asserts that it is immutable and yet full of life and dynamism: "The life he lives is unchangeably the same, and yet he never ceases to live his life as something new, because he has in himself an inexhaustible fountain of renovation and of youth."[143] Martensen adds correspondingly that "[God's] unchangeableness is not a dead unchangeableness."[144]

Respective of God's life *ad extra*, Martensen argues that God's reciprocal relationship with his creation does not contradict God's unchangeableness, observing that "God's unchangeability cannot be an empty, meaningless notion; it must be comfortable with the fact of a living activity in him by which he holds free intercourse [or reciprocal relationship] with his creatures."[145] God's unchangeableness does not exclude God's capability to engage in reciprocal relations with the world. This living activity *ad extra* does not represent genuine change, growth, or production in God's immutable nature; rather it illustrates God's willingness to

---

141. Strong, *Systematic Theology*, 1:258.
142. Strong, *Systematic Theology*, 1:258.
143. Martensen, *Christian Dogmatics*, 93.
144. Martensen, *Christian Dogmatics*, 93.
145. Martensen, *Christian Dogmatics*, 304.

harvest "infinite fruitfulness out of himself."[146] God's immutable nature does not exclude his capability to interact with his creatures and to be moved by them. In this way, Martensen's theology of God's immutability considers God's activities toward the world as the manifestations of the unchangeable divine attributes and as the outcome of God's being moved by the world.

Clarke's version of God's immutability is in agreement both with the classical doctrine of immutability and with Strong's (mediating) representation of God's infinite flexibility. He asserts that "God is unchangeable in himself, and in the essential modes of his activity. He is always a personal spirit [being eternal, self-sufficient, and self-existent] with the same elements of nature; he is always the same in character [such as love and holiness]; and he always acts in essentially the same modes [such as omnipresence and omnipotent]."[147] Clarke refines the classical doctrine of divine immutability by introducing his idea of "inexhaustible versatility,"[148] asserting that "immutability must not be conceived as immobility, fixedness, rigidity"[149] and that immutability "is not inability to act variously in various conditions."[150] Instead, God is able to act and react in various ways in accordance with his unchanging will and for the purpose of redeeming the lost. He believes that to accomplish this immutable purpose, God "must act in a thousand ways, varying his action with the occasion for action, while he himself changes never."[151]

Moving beyond the position of the traditional impassibilists, then, Clarke considers the diverse acts of God on various occasions to display God's communication of his unchanging self and will. In this way, God's inexhaustible versatility emerges not because of the mutability of God but because of the way in which the divine, immutable, and determined will to save the world that changes and progresses constantly in act. Clarke is confident in testifying that "[t]he inexhaustible versatility of the divine mind is the true expression of its changelessness."[152] Thus, God's suffering

---

146. Martensen, *Christian Dogmatics*, 93.
147. Clarke, *Outline of Christian Theology*, 88.
148. Clarke, *Outline of Christian Theology*, 89.
149. Clarke, *Outline of Christian Theology*, 88–89.
150. Clarke, *Outline of Christian Theology*, 89.
151. Clarke, *Outline of Christian Theology*, 89.
152. Clarke, *Outline of Christian Theology*, 89.

is considered to be one of the various acts that God willingly takes to accomplish his purpose in his inexhaustible versatility.

Strong and Clarke take one step further in their doctrines of divine immutability, with a view to overcoming any tension or contradiction between divine blessedness and divine suffering. Both theologians expound God's grief as the expression of the love of God towards the world and as a sign of God's infinite flexibility or versatility. However, this explanation only underlines one aspect of God's responding to the situation of the world. At the same time, both theologians also insist that God experiences suffering through joy. Strong remarks, "Love rejoices even in pain, when this brings good to those beloved."[153] God enters the world not to inflict suffering on himself but to accomplish his unchanging will and to convey his impeccable goodness and blessedness to the creatures with a plan to share his eternal blessedness and pleasure. In this way, God rejoices to partake in the suffering of the world.

Clarke similarly resists any tension arising between divine grief and divine blessedness, associating both as part of the redemptive will and act of God. Divine suffering is not a violation of the perfect blessedness of God but includes joy and welcome. Holiness abhors sin but delights even in the course of suffering for the sake of liberating sinners from the shackles of sins. Clarke asserts that "the endurance of redemptive suffering is the highest bliss. To a holy being there is no worthier or more welcome joy than the enduring of whatever may be necessary for the deliverance of souls from sin."[154] Only God knows the full extent of the joy of redemption. The Son of God, foreknowing the intensity of humiliation and suffering and the irreplaceable joy of reconciliation, without grudge, opted to bear sin and suffer on the cross. Clarke adds that "so does the Father, filled with the same *joy*, bear the burden of the sins of the world, and count it bliss to feel the pain that must be borne if his creatures are to be saved."[155] The saving nature of the divine suffering that is rooted in the self-giving and self-sacrificial love of the triune God is thus rendered entirely coherent with the notion of divine blessedness.

The impassibilists and mediating theologians agree that God's eternal and infinite attributes are immutable and yet disagree whether the notion of God's suffering can be consistently maintained with God's

---

153. Strong, *Systematic Theology*, 1:266.

154. Clarke, *Outline of Christian Theology*, 343, emphasis original. Clarke does not explain further the nature of the suffering of the Father.

155. Clarke, *Outline of Christian Theology*, 344, emphasis original.

infinite perfection and blessedness. Strong, Martensen, and Clarke all propose that God can reveal himself and interact with creation in infinite possibilities without change. Strong employs the terminology "infinite flexibility" and considers God's suffering as one of the various manifestations of the way in which God expresses his immutable truth, attributes, and purpose.

Martensen bluntly rejects the strong version of divine immutability, calling it "a dead unchangeableness" and urging that God's immutability must be consistent with God's interaction with his people. For Clarke, God's various responses to different human conditions demonstrate God's inexhaustible versatility and God's immutable will to save his human creatures. As such, the two view God's grief in the context of the infinite flexibilities and versatilities of the living God. These are not a violation of the doctrine of the divine immutability: their approaches underline the triune God's unchanging commitment to pursue, save, and redeem sinners by all means necessary, even adapting himself to the conditions of the world and being flexible in all situations. In this way, they offer support to a modified form of the immutability of God in which God's inner being is immutable while in his relationship with the world God is mutable. Those flexible activities of God serve as expositions of the immutable and infinite perfections of God.

The Self-Limitation of God

Related to the concept of the possibility of God is the idea that God somehow limits himself in becoming involved with the creation and in becoming incarnate in Jesus Christ. Strong, Martensen, and Clarke all employ the notion of self-limitation both to affirm the absolute perfection and personhood of God against pantheism, and stress that God's self-limitation is not a sign of weakness but a demonstration of his omnipotence.

Strong ascribes God's self-limitation to the divine nature *in se*. He opposes the traditional view that God does not limit himself, whether through self-emptying, giving up the divine form, resigning the independent exercise of divine attributes, or self-humbling.[156] In his assessment, the view that "an absolute Being can exist in no relation and that an infinite Being can suffer no co-existence of the finite"[157] is by itself unable

156. Strong, *Ethical Monism*, 87.
157. Strong, *Ethical Monism*, 88, emphasis original.

to sustain the weight of the biblical revelations of the living and personal God.

Strong dissents from employing the ideas of absoluteness and infinity in a way that deprives God of any sense of definiteness and personality, and grapples instead with reviving the biblical portraits of the personal God who is both self-conscious and self-determined: "Mere boundlessness is not perfection; to be perfect, a thing must be definite, not indefinite. For example: God would not be perfect if he were not a *personal* Being. But personality, with its self-consciousness and self-determination, implies definiteness. . . . His very perfection limits him to consciousness and freedom."[158] Strong thus affirms that God's nature includes limitation by way of contrasting definiteness and indefiniteness. He similarly writes: "Righteousness is necessary to perfection. But righteousness involves limitation. God cannot be both truth and untruth; but exclusion of untruth is limitation. God cannot be both purity and impurity; but exclusion of impurity is limitation."[159] For Strong, then, to recognize that there is a definite extent or scope to the being of God is already to affirm the self-limitation of God.

This acknowledgment of divine self-limitation allows Strong to explain God's temporal activity in history. Strong asserts that God's self-limitation is not associated with any weakness of power but with God's omnipotence and serves as "one of the proofs of his greatness."[160] Strong continues, "Omnipotence in God does not exclude, but implies, the power of self-limitation. Since all such self-limitation is free, proceeding from neither external nor internal compulsion, it is the act and manifestation of God's power."[161] In this way, Strong sees self-limitation in a series of acts and revelations of God: in creation, in the decree, and in preservation.

In creation, God lets the universe stand alongside of him. In the decree, in past eternity, abstract omniscience was narrowed down to a definite scheme. In preservation, God withholds his anger and wrath.[162] However, Strong finds the strongest evidence of God's self-limitation in the loving self-sacrifice of the incarnation of the Son of God, the greatest

---

158. Strong, *Ethical Monism*, 88, emphasis original.
159. Strong, *Ethical Monism*, 89.
160. Strong, *Ethical Monism*, 92.
161. Strong, *Systematic Theology*, 1:288.
162. Strong, *Ethical Monism*, 90–91.

form of self-limitation.[163] Strong's thought on God's self-limitation follows this logical sequence: "Perfection involves limitation; revelation involves self-limitation . . . redemption involves an infinite self-limitation. . . . If the love is infinite and the need is infinite, then the sacrificial self-limitation will be infinite also."[164] For Strong, then, the incarnation represents the greatest extent to which God limited himself and the strongest evidence of his self-limitation.

In a similar fashion, Martensen conceives the idea of self-limitation as pertaining to God's unique nature such that it cannot be separated from the divine perfection.[165] He posits that "as the absolute, unconditioned, unlimited being, God must be one and all; as *a person*, he can only be conceived as limited, bounded by a world which is not part of himself."[166] This concept of the self-limitation of God is directly opposed to the pantheist's assertion of a contradiction between the ideas of absolute and personal. Martensen reconciles the absolute and personal aspects of God.

On the one hand, Martensen rejects the unqualified pantheist ascription of ontological limitation to an omnipotent Being.[167] For him, God's inner life lacks no limit, possessing absolute powers and realizing each element of perfection within himself and through the universe. On the other hand, he recognizes that creation itself is an act of self-limitation on God's part. Martensen posits that "God limits his own power by calling into existence, out of the depths of his own eternal life, a world of created beings to whom he gives, in a derivative manner, to have life in themselves."[168] Thus, the self-limiting of God does not alter the degree of the perfections of God, for God is always eternal and omnipotent; at the same time, God's self-limitation is the way God reveals and shares his great power with the creation.

Just as Strong and Martensen argue that self-limitation pertains to God's personal nature, so too Clarke associates self-limitation with divine personality. Clarke construes personal spirit or personality as the essence of God and explains that the traits of the perfect personality include

---

163. Strong, *Ethical Monism*, 94.
164. Strong, *Ethical Monism*, 94.
165. Martensen, *Christian Dogmatics*, 81.
166. Martensen, *Christian Dogmatics*, 80, emphasis original.
167. Martensen, *Christian Dogmatics*, 80–81.
168. Martensen, *Christian Dogmatics*, 81.

sacrifice, self-abnegation, and self-limitation.[169] He therefore maintains that the divine self-limitation is rooted in the infinite perfection of God: "The Infinite has infinite resources, even for self-limitation, and for self-expression within limited ranges of life. . . . For the sake of his own great motive of holy love, the Greatest may limit himself as he will, and manifest himself to his kindred creatures in their own forms of being."[170] Continuing the analogy between the Creator and creatures, Clarke argues that "God made thought, love and volition to be essentially the same in man that they are in him. The life of God is a life of intelligent volition, and so, upon his lower plane, is the life of man."[171] God as the perfect model of personality is able to express those qualities perfectly as he freely and willingly limits himself in his interaction with creation. God's incarnation in the flesh and his entering the world do not represent his intrusion on a foreign territory. Being aware of the critics who resist any notion associated with self-limitation, Clarke considers the incarnation and God's relationship with the world as examples of self-limitation and rejects the traditional notion that the incarnation involves a contradiction.[172]

The mediating theologians, in opposition to pantheism, have each endeavored to develop the meaning of divine personality by considering self-limitation to pertain to God's essence. It could be asked, however, whether this move renders God eternally bound to limit himself by creating the universe and sacrificing himself. Strong and Clarke safeguard their positions from this outcome by referencing God's freedom to exercise his power.

In his discussion of the omnipotence of God, Strong makes a similar claim regarding God's control of his perfections. He writes that God "has power over his power; in other words, his power is under control of his wise and holy will. God can do all he wills, but he will not do all he can. Else his power is mere force acting necessarily, and God is the slave of his own omnipotence."[173] He correspondingly observes that God's "self-limitation is free, proceeding from neither external nor internal compulsion."[174] Likewise, Clarke perceives God's self-sacrifice, self-

169. Clarke, *Outline of Christian Theology*, 296.
170. Clarke, *Outline of Christian Theology*, 297.
171. Clarke, *Outline of Christian Theology*, 292.
172. Clarke, *Outline of Christian Theology*, 297.
173. Strong, *Systematic Theology*, 1:287.
174. Strong, *Systematic Theology*, 1:288.

limitation, and self-negation to be divine possibilities that pertain to his nature. However, God remains in full control of his nature and attributes: "God is so great that he is not a slave to his own greatness."[175] In this way, Strong and Clarke would affirm that God limits himself to engage in personal relationship with the world on the basis of freedom and not necessity. For Martensen, however, God must limit himself to reveal and share his great power with his creatures, for God creates and loves them necessarily.

Constructive Lessons from Strong, Martensen, and Clarke

There are several lessons from these nineteenth-century mediating theologians that will be relevant for our constructive proposal. Three might be named as a summary of their respective arguments.

First, the mediating theologians consider that it is important both to hold the tenets of the classical position and to support divine passibility. Unlike passibilists such as Moltmann, their mediating position does not violate God's infinite attributes and eternal joy. Instead, God's perfections *in se* and particularly his aseity are the basis of his suffering *ad extra*. In what follows, Strong's distinction between God's absolute and relative attributes and Martensen's distinction between God's life *in se* and *ad extra* will be used to develop the constructive dimension of this publication, in order to propose that divine (im)passibility relates to the two modes of the divine life—the immanent Trinity and the economic Trinity.

Second, Strong and Martensen seek to make a distinction between God's love for himself and God's love for the world. They were compelled to make the distinction because of the two radically different moral conditions of the objects of God's love *in se* and *ad extra*. Martensen in particular portrays God's passibility as the expression of his restrained and hindered love for the world. This work will follow a similar path, proposing that divine blessedness is the manifestation of God's love for himself and that divine suffering is the manifestation of God's love for the world, a distinction necessitated by the difference between the Creator and his creatures.

Third, it is noteworthy to observe the way in which the mediating theologians always discuss God's passibility in reference to human sin. They seek to emphasize that as much as sin moves God to feel anger, sin

---

175. Clarke, *Outline of Christian Theology*, 297.

also moves God to feel grief and suffering, as Scripture records. Clarke proposes a particularly creative way to think about God's suffering with reference to divine suffering not only as a response to human sins but also as an inherent part of God's work to save sinners. This present work builds on this mediating position, construing God's suffering in his opposition to sin as a temporal experience for God in his redemptive economy.

4

Mediating Theologians within Evangelical Theology

In recent years, a number of evangelical theologians have advanced a mediating position on the doctrine of the (im)passibility of God.[1] These scholars have sought to affirm both that the triune God is eternally joyous and infinitely perfect within himself and that he suffers in his relationship with his human creatures. Their number includes theologians such as John Frame, Michael Horton, and Clark Pinnock.[2] In arriving at such a mediating position, these scholars have reevaluated the traditional interpretation of biblical passages referring to God's emotions and

---

1. Bloesch, *Essentials of Evangelical Theology*, 2–3. Both now and historically, there has been something of a lack of doctrinal unity among evangelical theologians. However in time general consensus has been reached regarding a series of doctrines that are central to evangelical theology: the importance of evangelism; the doctrine of the Trinity; the inerrancy of the Bible; the deity, virgin birth, miracles, and resurrection of Christ; justification by faith; and final judgment. For these core evangelical doctrines, see Dorrien, *Remaking of Evangelical Theology*, 23; Grenz and Olson, *Twentieth-Century Theology*, 288. Of course, not every evangelical theologian agrees entirely with this list of central beliefs. For example, Bloesch proposes a more moderate terminology for the authority of Scripture than its inerrancy. Bloesch, *Essentials of Evangelical Theology*, 51–79. Such latitude is only to be expected in a movement that spans Arminian, Reformed, Anabaptist, Pentecostal, and other traditions. Regardless of its broad spectrum, however, evangelical theology is fully committed to regarding Scripture as the fulcrum and final authority of evangelical faith.

2. Frame, *Doctrine of God*; Horton, *Christian Faith*. For other evangelicals who hold this mediating position, see Bloesch, *God the Almighty*; Carson, *Difficult Doctrine of Love*; Erickson, *God the Father Almighty*.

suffering and have reassessed the relationship between the transcendence and immanence of God in attending to God's (im)passibility.

In order to explore this mediating position within evangelical theology, the work of Clark Pinnock and John Frame will be investigated for two reasons. First, their theological works present two different models of the Christian God. To explain the dynamics of God's transcendence and immanence, Pinnock employs the concepts of relationality and self-limitation and refutes God's eternal decree and unrestricted transcendence. Frame, meanwhile, reinterprets God's transcendence as his lordship and thus disagrees with Pinnock's version of the limited God.

Second, their theological expositions provide detailed accounts of the suffering of God with attention to both its active and its passive dimensions. For Pinnock, the relationality, limited future knowledge, and thus limited sovereignty of God become the cause of the passive dimension of God's emotions and suffering. Meanwhile, for Frame, God's lordship means that God eternally foreordains his emotions and suffering actively and experiences them passively and that they include both active and passive dimensions. Still, their doctrine of God consequently affirms the passibility of God, but without eternalizing suffering as God's nature in the way that the work of certain passibilist theologians such as Moltmann; it also goes beyond the work of certain impassibilist theologians such as Weinandy, which affirms only the active dimension of God's emotions, to affirm its passive dimension.

The discussion of Pinnock and Frame's theological projects will thus shed further light on the range of mediating positions on the doctrine of the (im)passibility of God and therefore help bolster the premise of this work that the immanent Trinity is impassible but is also passible when acting for the benefit of world in the economy.

Theological Background of Pinnock and Frame

The following analysis provides a concise outline of the theological background of Pinnock and Frame. This background will serve to highlight the motivation and the trajectory of their theological works and will explore the main points of commonality and divergence.

Clark H. Pinnock

A Canadian and evangelical theologian, Clark H. Pinnock (1937–2010) was one of the pioneers of the open theology movement of recent times. He began his faith journey in a liberal congregation and was raised by his paternal grandparents, who were British Methodist missionaries. He later went on to receive a PhD in New Testament from the University of Manchester.[3] The influence of Francis Phillip and the writings of B. B. Warfield led him to resist the anti-inerrantist movements of liberalism and neo-orthodoxy and launched his academic and pastoral career as a defender of the inerrancy of Scripture in the secularizing climate of the West.[4]

Pinnock's influential project on open theism, *The Openness of God*, was published in 1994, after his theological trajectory shifted to the open theism model during the 1970s, but his conviction regarding the authority of Scripture remained strong. With the help of his fellow open theist, John Sanders, Pinnock developed four tenets of open theology:

> First, God loves us and desires for us to enter into reciprocal relations with him.... Second, God has sovereignly decided to make some of his actions contingent on our requests and actions.... Third, God chooses to exercise a general rather than a meticulous providence.... Fourth, God granted us the libertarian freedom necessary for personal relationships of love to develop.[5]

Pinnock's theological enterprise is motivated by his conviction that Scripture is the foundation of Christian theology and that evangelical communities and their doctrines have been shackled by "Reformed scholasticism, Hellenistic perversions, and other cultural accommodations."[6] In response, open theism is conceived by Pinnock as a third model of theology between classical theism and process theology, as "a superior paradigm in light of the relevant biblical, theological, philosophical and practical material."[7] While Pinnock admits that all types of theologies are influenced by philosophies and firmly demands that "conventional

---

3. Callen, *Clark H. Pinnock*, 16–18.
4. Callen, "Clark H. Pinnock," 2–4.
5. Pinnock, *Most Moved Mover*, 4–5.
6. Callen, "Clark H. Pinnock," 9.
7. Pinnock et al., *Openness of God*, 9.

theists should be candid about their dependence on the great Hellenes," he urges his fellow open theists "not to be overly dependent on process philosophy."[8]

In terms of the doctrine of God, Pinnock considers that the teachings of classical theism and of Reformed theology—such as timeless eternity, impassibility, strong immutability, and simplicity—portray God as unaffected, immobile, and all-controlling, and are thus inaccurate descriptions of the relational and biblical God who is temporal, changing, and dynamic in relationship with his people. In sum, Pinnock complains that Hellenic philosophy "infected the Christian doctrine of God."[9] Pinnock and other open theists correspondingly want open theism to function as an "antibiotic to aid the healing process, bringing about a healthier doctrine of God."[10] He therefore seeks to revise the classical doctrine of God by purging from it the fingerprints of Hellenic philosophy.

Pinnock's open theism has drawn both positive and negative comments, and its position under the evangelical umbrella has been sternly questioned. Barry Callen praises Pinnock as being faithful to the biblical foundation and contemporary setting and for being "one of the most prominent, productive, and provocative Christian theologians."[11] Roger Olson infers that Pinnock's theology was "thoroughly and authentically evangelical."[12] Similarly, Stanley Grenz perceives Pinnock to be a theological pioneer and second-generation evangelical who inherited the spirit of the neo-evangelical theology of Carl Henry.[13]

However, other evangelicals have reached a different assessment of open theism. Some theologians such as Gerald Bray question whether the claim that Hellenic philosophies actually "infected" the Christian doctrine of God can be sustained.[14] It has also been suggested that Pinnock's harsh criticism of classical theism may be unfair given that his own theological treatment is developed with the aid of secular philosophies. R. Wright, for example, one of Pinnock's former students, perceives that Pinnock's work shares more affinity with philosophically infused process

---

8. Pinnock, *Most Moved Mover*, 150.
9. Pinnock et al., *Openness of God*, 8.
10. Pinnock et al., *Openness of God*, 9.
11. Callen, "Clark H. Pinnock," 1.
12. Olson, "Post Conservative Evangelical Theology," 20.
13. Grenz, *Renewing the Center*, 125–26.
14. Bray, "Has the Christian Doctrine of God Been Corrupted?," 112.

theism,[15] and Geisler notes that Pinnock's attack on using philosophy in theological work is unfair and self-contradictory given that open theism's "reinterpretations of the biblical texts are influenced by contemporary process philosophy."[16]

Even John Sanders, another prominent open theist, admits the influence of philosophies in freewill theory, which is a crucial aspect of open theism.[17] In their inability to conceive how God's infinite attributes could be limited in the divine economy, other evangelicals have expressed their concerns regarding Pinnock's conception of God's self-limitation.[18] Bruce Ware, for example, notes that "the God of the Bible is not the limited, passive, hand-wringing God open theism portrays,"[19] while R. C. Sproul argues, "This fascination with the openness of God is an assault, not merely on Calvinism, or even on classical theism, but on Christianity itself."[20]

John M. Frame

John M. Frame, an American evangelical theologian influenced by Reformed theology, was born in 1939, and his publications focus on two primary areas: the authority and inerrancy of the Bible and the lordship of the God of Scripture. His undergraduate experience at Princeton University and participation in the Princeton Evangelical Fellowship instigated dissatisfaction with Princeton's liberalism for, in Frame's words, it "was casual religion: no authoritative Bible, no passion for souls, no desire for holiness, no vitality."[21] This theological trajectory towards liberalism led Frame to be, in his words, "biblically oriented (almost

---

15. Wright, *No Place for Sovereignty*, 227.
16. Geisler, *Creating God in the Image of Man?*, 96.
17. Sanders, "Historical Considerations," 71–81. Frame traces the root of the freewill theory in Philo and the early church fathers such as Justin Martyr, Irenaeus, Tertullian, Origen, and even in Greek philosopher Epicurus (341–270 BC). Frame, *No Other God*, 28.
18. For these evangelical theologians, see Barrett, "Does Inclusivist Theology Undermine Evangelism?"; Beilby and Eddy, *Divine Foreknowledge*; Carson, *Gagging of God*.
19. Ware, *God's Lesser Glory*, 216.
20. Sproul, *Willing to Believe*, 143.
21. Frame, "Backgrounds to My Thought," 11.

biblicistic, but I think in a good way), antiliberal, ecumenical, and incipiently perspectivalist."[22]

Frame's experience at Westminster Theological Seminary under Cornelius Van Til's apologetics and theology, G. Dennis O'Brien's thoughts on perspectives, Edmund Clowney's triadic perspective, Meredith Kline's work on biblical covenants, and John Murray's theological method shaped Frame's theological thinking and tri-perspectivalism.[23] Instituting God's lordship as the central perspective of the scriptural descriptions of God, Frame's theological work *Doctrine of God* was the outcome of Frame's lecture material collected over the course of forty-one years of teaching.[24] Frame wanted theological works on the lordship of God, based on Scripture alone, to serve as "antidotes to speculative, scholastic, and liberal approaches such as process theology and open theism."[25]

Frame's theological project is to revitalize Christian doctrines through attending to the everlasting truths of the Scriptures, in association with the appropriate use of philosophy and tradition. Frame rebuts the accusation that biblical Christian teaching was replaced by non-Christian thoughts as the direct outcome of Hellenistic philosophies. He observes instead that philosophical discussion, and extrabiblical vocabulary such as being, substance, and attribute, strengthened the development of the Christian doctrine of God.[26]

Nevertheless, Frame raises two concerns regarding the uncritical adoption of philosophy and tradition within the Reformed tradition. First, Frame complains that the Protestant scholastic doctrine of God was not always firmly established on Scripture.[27] The Reformers, such as John Calvin and Martin Luther, were in his view more concerned with reforming the doctrine of salvation than the doctrine of God, for soteriology was a more urgent theological issue of the day. For Frame, Protestant scholastics uncritically favored adopting medieval views and thus Greek philosophy in their work on the doctrine of God, which correspondingly became more rationalist and philosophical.

22. Frame, "Backgrounds to My Thought," 13.
23. Frame's tri-perspectivalism will be defined in the next section.
24. This chapter uses this book as the primary source of Frame's theological work.
25. Frame, "My Books," 5.
26. Frame, *Doctrine of God*, 3.
27. Frame, *Doctrine of God*, 9.

Second, Frame worries about an indiscriminating commitment among the Reformed to the historical confessions and traditions without any suspicion of error. Frame observes that by the end of the twentieth century, evangelical theology was being constructed by evangelical theologians and scholars "who do their work in dialogue with ancient and recent history,"[28] referring to David Wells, Donald Bloesch, and Michael Horton. Frame expresses his disappointment with the historically oriented theologians for being "uncritical of traditions" and constructing their argument "based on their preferences rather than biblical principle."[29] The Reformed tradition, according to Frame's view, is an object that is itself to be reformed if it strays from the message of Scripture. Frame avers that the Reformed confessions "should not be treated as infallible or as ultimately normative" and that the traditional Christian creeds should not "be elevated to a position of authority equivalent to Scripture."[30]

Frame's approach has also received a mixed reception. Tim Trumper views Frame's approach as a constructive Calvinism that accentuates the priority of Scripture over the Reformed confessions.[31] Others, such as Richard Gambler, are somewhat critical of Frame's great caution concerning the Reformed tradition.[32] Mark Garcia understands Frame's concern but suggests that he is tilting too far against the usage of tradition,[33] while Derek Thomas alleges that Frame departs from Calvin's theology.[34] Still, Frame is not anti-confession or anti-tradition, but simply claims that confessions and traditions must be tested and modified, if necessary, by the Scriptures.[35]

Pinnock and Frame both seek to use Scripture as the normative source for exploring the truths of God over the teachings of philosophy and tradition. On the one hand, Pinnock proposes that open theism is a biblical, balanced, and theological approach that grasps the scriptural revelations of the triune, loving, and relational God. He revises the metaphysics of classical theism with the relationality of open theism. On the

---

28. Frame, "Machen's Warrior Children," 138.
29. Frame, "Machen's Warrior Children," 139.
30. Frame, "Introduction to the Reformed Faith."
31. Trumper, "John Frame's Methodology," 147.
32. Gamble, "Biblical Theology and Systematic Theology," 228–32.
33. Garcia, "Word Made Applicable, 237.
34. Thomas, "Frame on the Attributes of God," 362–67.
35. Frame, *Doctrine of God*, 10.

other hand, Frame finds no issue with using philosophical terms and ideas to develop Christian teaching on God but is committed to modifying any philosophical notions in Christian theology if they contradict the truths of Scripture. He insists that God's lordship is the central idea of the Christian God, not the self-limiting God of open theism. These dynamics drive the theological works of Pinnock and Frame: they shape their views on divine impassibility and passibility and result in their mediating view that God is eternally blessed yet suffers in his interaction with the world that he loves.

Thematic Discussion of Impassibility and Passibility

Having briefly considered the theological backgrounds of Pinnock and Frame, we will now consider their arguments, beginning with their approach to the doctrine of God, then exploring in turn their understanding of the themes of God's emotions, his suffering, love, and sovereignty, his suffering and immutability, and finally his suffering and self-limitation. At points within this discussion the voices of other theologians who support either Pinnock's affirmation of open theism or Frame's approach of lordship theology will be included.

Starting Points in Considering the Doctrine of God

Both Pinnock and Frame start their work on the doctrine of God from God's perfections and ultimately affirm similar views of the doctrine of the Trinity and of God's attributes, such as love, omnipotence, sovereignty, foreknowledge, immutability, aseity, blessedness, and eternity, however they have different theological emphases. The following paragraphs will explain how these theological emphases dictate the interpretations of God's other attributes and render two different understandings of the Christian God.

Pinnock's focal theme as an open theist is the relationality at the heart of the communion of the immanent Trinity. His definition of "person" captures the relational nature of the triune persons. Pinnock argues that the key to the meaning of this term is "intersubjectivity along with mutuality and reciprocity.... [E]ach person is conscious of itself as divine and distinct from the other persons in reciprocal relationships."[36] Under this

---

36. Pinnock, *Flame of Love*, 36.

definition of person, the essence of the communion of the three divine persons is relationality: "Relationality belongs to God's very essence because at the heart of reality is shared life, God's own life, characterized by spontaneity and giving."[37] Pinnock complains that even though classical theism highlights God as person, classical theism is more concerned with "the impression of absolutism."[38] By contrast, he states that God must be liberated from the confinement of metaphysical and substantial categories, and should be considered as a dynamic and relational Being.[39] Pinnock's proposal that "[w]e ought to view God in personal not absolutist terms" because "[t]he primary category in Christian theism is person not substance"[40] shows his commitment to overcoming the metaphysical barrier that often overshadows the relational aspect of God's nature. In this way, he speaks of the relationality of the triune persons as "an open and dynamic structure."[41]

What follows naturally from this doctrine of the immanent Trinity is Pinnock's endorsement of the doctrines of divine aseity and of creation *ex nihilo*. The triune God is self-existent and self-sufficient and exists in his triune fellowship, which is full of abundance, joy, and love.[42] Pinnock describes God's inner life in this way: "God is pure ecstasy—each person exists in loving relationship with the other persons."[43] His doctrine of creation, which is grounded in God's aseity, states that God chose to create in order to share freely his joy and love with the world.

Correspondingly, he posits, "Creation results from the openness of God to make others who could enter into loving relationships with him."[44] Pinnock also claims that "God enjoys the goodness of the world and, by grace, creates (unnecessarily) in order to share his own bliss with others."[45] At this point, his painstaking work to distinguish open theism from process theism is clear. God is not dependent upon the existence of the world, and he creates freely without any necessity to complete his nature and to be loved. Pinnock can therefore conclude that "[c]reation

37. Pinnock, *Most Moved Mover*, 84.
38. Pinnock, *Most Moved Mover*, 80.
39. Pinnock, *Most Moved Mover*, 84.
40. Pinnock, *Most Moved Mover*, 79.
41. Pinnock, *Most Moved Mover*, 84.
42. Pinnock, *Most Moved Mover*, 125–45.
43. Pinnock, *Flame of Love*, 55.
44. Pinnock, *Most Moved Mover*, 28–29.
45. Pinnock, *Most Moved Mover*, 125.

is a gift of grace"[46] and that God "does not need the world in order to be God."[47]

In turning to consider God's immanence, Pinnock invokes the concept of divine self-limitation, the voluntary limitation of those divine attributes associated with divine transcendence. Pinnock finds that within the contemporary evangelical setting, where both transcendence and immanence are theologically confirmed, God's transcendence is emphasized over his immanence.[48] He therefore asserts that the task of his work at this point is "to correct this imbalance in the handling of the transcendence and immanence of God."[49]

At the center of Pinnock's task to amend the balance between God's transcendence and God's immanence is the divine act of self-limitation, by which God freely limits the scope of his foreknowledge and governance and participates in personal and temporal relationship with the world in order to carry out the trinitarian vision. Pinnock warns that "placing too much distance between God and creation takes away from God's glory . . . if it obscures the freely chosen relationships that God seeks to have with creatures."[50] In this way, Pinnock recasts the transcendence of classical theology without tilting towards the immanence of process theology.[51]

Shifting to the work of Frame, his doctrine of God is dictated by the focus upon God's lordship. His lordship includes the attributes of conventional theism such as exhaustive foreknowledge, meticulous sovereignty, aseity, existence, eternity, omnipotence, and immutability, and the attributes that are related to emotions such as jealousy, wrath, joy, and blessedness.[52] Frame observes that God's lordship—as Yahweh—is the central message of the Old and New Testaments, "[s]ince God chose the name Lord . . . for himself, since it is found thousands of times in Scripture, and since it is at the heart of the fundamental confession of faith of God's people."[53]

---

46. Pinnock, *Most Moved Mover*, 29.
47. Pinnock, *Most Moved Mover*, 145.
48. Pinnock, "Systematic Theology," 107.
49. Pinnock, "Systematic Theology," 107.
50. Pinnock, *Most Moved Mover*, xii.
51. Pinnock, "Systematic Theology," 107.
52. Frame, *Doctrine of God*, 399.
53. Frame, *Doctrine of God*, 12.

Frame identifies divine lordship as the unchanging nature of God and conceives the other divine attributes in conjunction with the lordship of Yahweh: "With regard to the divine nature, we shall see that all of God's attributes are forms and manifestations of his lordship."[54] Frame's acceptance of lordship as the main theme of his doctrine of God does not mean that he dismisses the traditional concept of transcendence. He simply considers that the term "transcendence" by itself is insufficient to grasp fully the biblical description of God as both transcendent and immanent. Therefore, Frame interprets "transcendence in terms of God's kingship or lordship: God is not infinitely removed from us in Scripture; rather, he rules us."[55]

With God's lordship as the paramount theme of God's attributes, Frame proceeds to recommend a complicated classification of God's attributes. Before proceeding to outline this, it is necessary first to introduce his tri-perspectivalism, which is his theological methodology.[56] Frame's tri-perspectivalism explains that human beings can know God only through limited and multiple perspectives and that knowledge of God is derived from numerous triad patterns in Scripture.[57] These patterns can be observed in the triune revelation of three-ness (the Father, Son, and Holy Spirit), in the divine lordship (authority, power, and presence), in revelation (general, special, and existential revelations), in the offices of Christ (prophet, priest, and king), and so forth.

In his description of the divine attributes that define God's lordship, Frame first posits a triadic pattern of three divine attributes—God's control, authority, and presence—and then moves to explain each of these attributes further by means of a triadic pattern of divine attributes—God's

---

54. Frame, *Doctrine of God*, 237.

55. Frame, "Backgrounds to My Thought," 15.

56. Frame's methodology is not without critique within Reformed circles. Trumper, for instance, admits the positive contributions of Frame's tri-perspectivalism but questions whether perspectivalism must entail these triads, for "Scripture does not always speak in terms of triads." Trumper, "John Frame's Methodology," 163. Likewise, Mark Karlberg is not satisfied with Frame's theological method and complains that "Frame prefers to reduce theological debate to mere differences in emphasis (i.e., perspectival differences)" and that "Frame appears more interested in establishing the legitimacy of his own methodology (with which we take vigorous exception) than he is in doing justice to traditional Reformed dogmatics." Karlberg, "On the Theological Correlation," 104. For Frame's response to Karlberg, see Frame, "Reply to Mark W. Karlberg," 297–308.

57. Frame, "Primer on Perspectivalism."

goodness, knowledge, and power.[58] First, then, there are the attributes that are related to divine control, which "draw much of their meaning from God's actions in history."[59] These are identified as wrath and jealousy (relating to God's goodness); speech and incomprehensibility (relating to God's knowledge); and eternity and existence (relating to God's power). Second, there are the attributes that highlight the divine authority and thus "denote constancies in God's nature, a structure that defines the limits of his possible actions" and "his standards of right and wrong."[60] These are identified as justice and righteousness (God's goodness); truth (his knowledge); and aseity and simplicity (his power). Finally there are the attributes that pertain to the divine presence, which indicate that they "present in God" and "indwell him."[61] These attributes are identified as blessedness, joy, and holiness (God's goodness); knowledge, wisdom, and mind (his knowledge); and glory, spirituality, and omnipresence (his power).

Frame's idea of divine lordship indicates that God is the Lord of his own knowledge and emotional life. For Frame, this view of God relates to the doctrine of aseity, which, he writes, "is equally important in the epistemological and ethical areas. . . . He not only exists without receiving existence from something else, but also gains his knowledge only from himself (his nature and his plan) and serves as his own criterion of truth."[62] Frame affirms that God is the Lord over his own eternal blessedness and gains his happiness only from himself.

Being self-existent, self-contained, and self-sufficient, God is eternally at peace within himself because "God . . . is completely in harmony with himself. His three persons glorify and serve one another willingly and cheerfully. He is whole, well, and prosperous—blessed and happy."[63] Frame continues, "God is supremely blessed, because he is the full embodiment, indeed the archetype, of the virtues described in the beatitudes and elsewhere in Scripture. Those virtues bring about the best life

---

58. Frame, *Doctrine of God*, 398–99.
59. Frame, *Doctrine of God*, 398.
60. Frame, *Doctrine of God*, 398–99.
61. Frame, *Doctrine of God*, 399.
62. Frame, *Doctrine of God*, 602.
63. Frame, *Doctrine of God*, 444.

possible, including supreme satisfaction, and that satisfaction belongs to God."[64] God who is the Lord of his emotional life is eternally joyous.

The core disagreement between Pinnock and Frame concerns how to manage the balance between God's transcendence and immanence. Both theologians admit that God's transcendence is prior to his immanence, without neglecting or minimizing the significance of the immanence of God, and that God's inner life is complete blessedness and glory. At this point, however, their thoughts diverge. On the one hand, Pinnock believes that classical theism's commitment to God's transcendence violates the realm of his immanence[65] and moves to modify the traditional conceptions of God's transcendence. On the other hand, for Frame, only sustained attention to God's lordship, which is a reinterpreted definition of transcendence, is the way to reconcile God's transcendence and immanence: as he argues, "The 'give-and-take' between God and the creation requires, not a reduced, but an enhanced, view of God's sovereignty."[66] These theological positions in turn shape the way in which they describe how God experiences various emotions and suffering, to which theme we now turn.

God's Emotions

Various contemporary evangelical theologians openly affirm God's emotions as recorded in Scripture, instead of interpreting them as metaphors and anthropopathism. For instance, Gordon Lewis and Bruce Demarest claim that God is an ethical and personal being with intelligence, will, and emotions, and experiences both displeasure and pleasure.[67] As will be seen, Pinnock and Frame affirm God's emotions as well; however, they do so in different ways, and one way of capturing this distinction is to draw on the language of active and passive emotions.

For Pinnock, the relational and dynamic communion of the three divine persons not only describes the existence of the immanent Trinity but also serves as a prototype for understanding the economic Trinity. Pinnock notes, "Being socially triune, God has made a world with freedom, in which loving relationships can flourish. It is an ecosystem

64. Frame, *Doctrine of God*,
65. Pinnock, *Most Moved Mover*, 107.
66. Frame, *No Other God*, 559.
67. Lewis and Demarest, *Integrative Theology*, 1:236.

MEDIATING THEOLOGIANS WITHIN EVANGELICAL THEOLOGY

capable of echoing back the triune life of God."[68] That is, the triune God created human beings with the ability to engage reciprocally with him in such a way that God is moved by human beings.

Grounded in the inner fellowship of the triune God, God's relationship with the world has the same open and dynamic structure. God's reciprocity with the world means that God does not want control over it: as Pinnock writes, "It seems God did not create the world in order to exercise total control over it. Rather, he wants to enjoy the loving relationship—mutual, reciprocal and give-and-take—that is possible if it is not controlled."[69] Sanders makes the same point: "Relationality is an *essential* aspect of God. . . . The members of the Trinity mutually share and relate to one another."[70] He adds, "A God who is antecedently relational and self-sufficient is free to create significant others and enter into genuine reciprocal relations with them."[71] God thus has a reciprocal relationship with the world.

The result is that God experiences various emotions passively. Unlike impassibilists, who assert that God decrees his emotional responses without being moved and conditioned in a temporal sense by the affairs of human creatures, Pinnock, along with many passibilists such as Oord, argues that divine emotions are the direct outcome of God's responding to human beings.[72] He writes, "God does not simply rule over creation, he is moved and affected by what happens in history. Events arouse joy or sorrow, pleasure or wrath in him. Our deeds move, grieve, gladden, or please him. His nature is not characterized merely by intelligence but is also characterized by pathos."[73] In a similar way, Peckham argues that "God is voluntarily passible in relation to the world, meaning he freely chose to create this world and freely opened himself up to being affected by it. . . . Because God has voluntarily opened himself up to love relationship with creatures, God may be emotionally affected by, and responsive to, the actions of creatures."[74] God is moved by the world and thus, we can say, experiences passive emotions. Thus, Pinnock repudiates the

---

68. Pinnock, "Systematic Theology," 110.
69. Pinnock, *Most Moved Mover*, 25.
70. Sanders, *God Who Risks*, 177, emphasis original.
71. Sanders, *God Who Risks*, 178.
72. Oord, "Strong Passibility," 129–51.
73. Pinnock, *Most Moved Mover*, 55.
74. Peckham, "Qualified Passibility," 98.

doctrine of divine impassibility, charging the traditional dogma as offering a nonbiblical and philosophical picture of God, and arguing that scriptural revelation must direct the content of the Christian doctrine of the passibility of God.[75]

Frame affirms both God's impassibility and his capability of emotions as recorded in Scriptures. He articulates his view of God's impassibility in this way: "[T]he doctrine of impassibility should not be used to deny that God has emotions, or to deny that God the Son suffered real injury and death on the cross. But God in his transcendent nature cannot be harmed in any way, nor can he suffer loss to his being.... In this sense, God is impassible."[76] Frame grapples with sustaining both respective of God's impassibility and the biblical descriptions of divine emotions, instead of denying the latter. In this way, he is disappointed with the stance of traditional and Reformed theologians who dismiss the biblical references to God's emotions as anthropomorphism and as metaphors that delineate God's mysteriousness.[77] Frame's disappointment is captured well in this statement: "On this view, for example, when Scripture says that God knows his people, he really does know them, but when it says that God is angry, he is not 'really' angry."[78] Frame thus resists the traditional understanding of divine emotions on the basis that Scripture truly witnesses to God's emotions. For Frame, as God has intellect and will, so too he has emotions. Indeed, he claims, "Scripture does not distinguish 'the emotions' as a part of the mind that is radically different from the intellect and the will."[79] Therefore, God's emotions cannot be carved out of his impassible nature simply because of the negative association of emotions.

Frame recognizes the full reality of divine emotions in three ways. First, he affirms God's capacities for emotion as God's attributes, making two categories of divine emotions: those that are present in and indwell God and those that are related to God's actions in history. Frame assigns joy, blessedness, beauty, perfection, and holiness to the former category, and goodness, love, grace, mercy, patience, compassion, jealousy, and

---

75. Pinnock, *Most Moved Mover*, 55–59.
76. Frame, *Doctrine of God*, 614.
77. Frame, *Doctrine of God*, 609.
78. Frame, *Doctrine of God*, 609
79. Frame, *Doctrine of God*, 609.

wrath to the latter category.[80] In this sense, there are certain emotions such as blessedness that God experiences only *in se* and others such as jealousy that he experiences only in his relationship with the world.

Second, Frame posits that the divine emotions that belong to the divine economy are interwoven into and thus predetermined in the content of the eternal decree. Frame observes:

> Doctrines like God's eternal decree, his immutability, and his aseity sometimes lead us to think that he cannot truly respond to what happens in the world. Responding seems to assume passivity and change in God. Now emotions are usually responses to events. They are, indeed, sometimes called "passions," a term that suggests passivity. This consideration is one reason why theologians have resisted ascribing emotions to God.[81]

However, instead of refusing the ascription of emotions to God, Frame asserts that in ordaining the sequence of historical events, God also ordains his sovereign and unconditioned emotional responses to them, by way of God's exhaustive foreknowledge of every future situation.[82]

In the terms of this publication, then, Frame affirms the active dimension of God's emotions. His emotional responses are not in the first instance the outcome of being temporally moved or changed by human beings. Frame is aware that God's anger and jealousy could be viewed as changes to God's nature, for the triune God was eternally joyous before the world existed. However, Frame avoids this conclusion by tying these emotions to God's eternal decree and explains that although "God's eternal decree does not change, it does ordain change."[83] Therefore, Frame affirms the active dimension of God's emotional responses as the result of his eternal decree.

Third, Frame posits that God not only decrees in eternity his emotional responses in time, but he also experiences these same emotions at the predetermined time and in the predetermined place. God is both transcendent and immanent, and for Frame, God's immanence means that he is in time and changes as history changes.[84] He notes, "History

---

80. Frame, *Doctrine of God*, 398–99. Other evangelicals, such as Grudem, categorize God's emotions, such as jealousy, wrath, and blessedness, to be communicable attributes of God. Grudem, *Systematic Theology*, 205–18.

81. Frame, *Doctrine of God*, 610.

82. Frame, *Doctrine of God*, 610.

83. Frame, *Doctrine of God*, 610.

84. The details of the discussion in reference to God's mutability and time will be

involves constant change, and so, as an agent in history, God himself changes.... God is not merely *like* an agent in time; he really is *in* time, changing as others change."[85] In this way, Frame affirms that God's presence in the world allows him to respond mutably and temporally to the circumstances of the world, for "[i]t is not wrong to describe them [emotions] as responses to these events."[86] God is indeed moved by the world in history and experiences emotions that are associated with response and change, emotions that we have throughout referred to as passive emotions. Correspondingly, the passive dimension of emotions is an authentic experience for God, who is fully present in all times and spaces and responds to the events and conditions of human beings. As noted above, these emotions occur as the result of God's eternally decreeing his emotional response and change. And therefore Frame observes that "God responds (both transcendently and immanently) only to what he has himself ordained."[87] In this way, Frame supports the view that God's emotions include both transcendent (active) and immanent (passive) aspects.

In sum, Pinnock's approach to God's emotions is based on God's will to engage in a truly reciprocal relationship with the world. In his work, the passive dimension of God's emotions is stressed without any place for an active dimension, for God does not foreordain his emotional responses to human beings. Frame, meanwhile, posits that God who is impassible decrees his emotional responses from the beginning of creation and foreordains his experience of emotions in response to the conditions of human beings. At the same time, God's emotional responses are experienced by God in time and space; therefore, the divine emotions include both the active and passive dimensions. The ramifications of these positions are explored further in what follows.

God's Suffering, Love, and Sovereignty

As evangelical theologians began to consider more seriously what certain impassibilist scholars previously considered as the anthropopathic and metaphorical testimonies of Scripture, the transition to affirming

---

provided later in this chapter.
85. Frame, *Doctrine of God*, 571, emphasis original.
86. Frame, *Doctrine of God*, 610.
87. Frame, *Doctrine of God*, 610.

the reality of God's suffering in his relationship with the world occurred naturally. However, a number of more conservative Reformed evangelical theologians, such as Geisler, continued to view suffering as a negative quality that is not to be ascribed to God's immutable, timeless, and perfect nature: "God cannot undergo passion or suffering; nothing in the created universe can make God feel pain or inflict misery on him."[88] Passibilists, by contrast, argue that if God is love then he cannot *not* suffer because suffering and love are inseparable. In their respective works, both Pinnock and Frame engage with this theme of the suffering of God: Pinnock explicitly addresses divine love as a pivotal dimension of God's experience of suffering, while Frame occasionally connects God's love to his suffering but primarily frames the divine suffering with reference to his affirmation of God's sovereignty. This section explores in detail the distinct views of divine passibility that arise in their work on the basis of these differing emphases.

The relationality of trinitarian love serves as the foundation of Pinnock's doctrine of divine passibility. In Pinnock's open theism, love is the nature of God. He complains that love is considered as a secondary attribute of God in conventional theism because of the influence of Greek thought that prioritizes metaphysical conceptions such as immutability, timeless eternity, and simplicity.[89] The triune God desires having this loving and reciprocal relationship with his creation and receiving their devoted and free love. Pinnock alleges that "God sovereignly chooses to love us and is conditioned by our willingness or unwillingness to receive or refuse love."[90] As relationality is the essence of the love of the triune God, for Pinnock "[i]t is natural for God to make a world that would reflect relationality back to him. . . . [It is] natural for God as social Trinity to create beings capable of hearing and responding to his word and capable of relating to each other also."[91] As God's love is reciprocal in nature and expression *in se* and *ad extra*, God undergoes a passive form of suffering in his relation with the world. In agreement with passibilists, he remarks, "The fact that God is love rules out the doctrine of impassibility."[92]

88. Geisler, *Systematic Theology*, 112–24. Other evangelical impassibilists hold that God cannot experience any suffering *in se* and *ad extra*. See Bray, *Doctrine of God*; Dolezal, "Still Impassible"; Duby, *Divine Simplicity*.

89. Pinnock, *Most Moved Mover*, 81–82.

90. Pinnock, *Most Moved Mover*, 81.

91. Pinnock, *Flame of Love*, 44.

92. Pinnock, *Most Moved Mover*, 88.

Pinnock explains four aspects of divine suffering. First, he argues that "*God suffers because of his people.*"[93] God suffers when his covenantal relationship with human beings is broken. Second, Pinnock asserts that "*God suffers with his people.*"[94] When his people cry out to him and express their afflictions, he suffers with them, just as he was afflicted when the Israelites cried out to him in the midst of their exiles. Third, Pinnock contends that "*God suffers for his people.*"[95] God is moved by human sins and rejections and is burdened by them. This leads to him responding to human sins and suffering: "God immerses himself in the depths of their sufferings and thereby overcomes the powers of death. God gives himself and extends his life for the sake of his people."[96] He chooses to redeem his people from their sins and suffering through his own suffering and death. Lastly, all three triune persons suffer during the event of the cross. Pinnock, acknowledging the distinct personhood of each person of the Trinity, sees the event of the cross as "a trinitarian event in which the three Persons experience the mutuality and reciprocity characteristic of the triune God."[97] In this way, the Father and the Holy Spirit are moved by the suffering of the Son who suffers in his both divine and human natures and experience their own distinct afflictions. Pinnock notes, "Father, Son and Spirit . . . suffer. . . . The Father suffers the death of his Son and the Spirit feels both the Father's pain and the Son's self-surrender."[98] As the title of his book indicates, Pinnock's view of God is that he is the "Most Moved Mover," who is always moved by human beings and experiences grief and pain in response to their conditions.

For all the suffering that Pinnock attributes to God in the divine economy, he does not attribute any suffering to God's inner reality and nature. In his 1996 publication, *Flame of Love*, Pinnock clearly distinguishes between the immanent Trinity and the economic Trinity: "We assume that the economic Trinity is the immanent Trinity. The immanent Trinity (God in himself) is revealed by the economic Trinity (God in history)."[99] However, Pinnock also maintains a corresponding distinction

---

93. Pinnock, *Most Moved Mover*, 56, emphasis original.
94. Pinnock, *Most Moved Mover*, 56, emphasis original.
95. Pinnock, *Most Moved Mover*, 56, emphasis original.
96. Pinnock, *Most Moved Mover*, 56, emphasis original.
97. Pinnock, *Flame of Love*, 93.
98. Pinnock, *Most Moved Mover*, 58.
99. Pinnock, *Flame of Love*, 32.

between the mystery of the eternal life of the Trinity and the salvation history of the Trinity, remarking that "the economic Trinity does not exhaust the immanent Trinity, since the divine mystery overflows revelation and is unattainable by the creature."[100] The result is that "the economy of salvation does allow a *glimpse* into [but not a complete vision of] the divine life."[101] Pinnock posits that suffering is not of the nature of God, and if it were otherwise, he would not be able to affirm that God is pure ecstasy.[102] Correspondingly, Pinnock's publication *The Most Moved Mover* (2001), which is a more comprehensive form of his work, shows no sign of attributing the suffering of the cross to the eternal nature of God and instead consistently supports the self-sufficiency of God who is not "metaphysically limited."[103]

A special characteristic of Pinnock's account of love must receive comment in order to appreciate the full scope of his doctrine of divine passibility. To love always involves the risk of that love not being reciprocated. Pinnock depicts the risk factor in God's reciprocal relationship with the world as follows: "Love is precarious and makes even God vulnerable because it may not be reciprocated.... In a word, lovers are vulnerable because love is precarious."[104] He draws here on the analogy of the parent-child relationship: "On another level, giving birth to children and raising them is also a risky business because parents can influence, but not control, their children."[105] In open theism, the libertarian model of freedom is the main ingredient for such a personal relationship.[106] Without such freedom on the part of human beings, any divine fellowship of love with creation is a pre-programmed and non-genuine relationship because the true freedom of human beings is not conditioned on anything or anyone, even God. Open theists agree with Pinnock's description of the risk factor that attends God's love.

Gregory Boyd comments that taking risks is a better form of love than attempting to control another person, and he applies this logic to

---

100. Pinnock, *Flame of Love*, 32.
101. Pinnock, *Flame of Love*, 36, emphasis added.
102. Pinnock, *Flame of Love*, 55.
103. Pinnock, *Most Moved Mover*, 149.
104. Pinnock, *Most Moved Mover*, 81.
105. Pinnock, *Most Moved Mover*, 81.
106. Pinnock, *Most Moved Mover*, 127.

explain how God loves his creation.[107] Sanders remarks that "[b]y creating us with libertarian freedom God takes risks for some things because God is not tightly controlling everything that happens."[108] However, other evangelical theologians resist any notion associated with God's taking risks, considering God instead to be always in control of all events and human affairs. Ware correspondingly posits that "none of God's creation, heavenly or earthly, can challenge, disrupt, thwart, or frustrate his comprehensive will."[109] Frame also rejects the argument that God is precarious and risk-taking, for in his view the main theme of Scripture is not the open model of a risk-taking God, but the full sovereignty associated with God's lordship.[110]

Unlike Pinnock, Frame's own understanding of divine love is derived from his view of the way in which God's lordship is expressed in sovereign love. Even though God's lordship is the central theme of his doctrine of God, Frame does not dismiss God's love as a secondary or inferior attribute but identifies three distinct aspects of sovereign love: God's self-love, God's universal love, and God's saving love (redemptive and covenantal love).[111] Frame underscores the fellowship of the three divine persons of the immanent Trinity as the starting point of God's economic relationship with the world. The act of creation thus represents a transition from God's love for himself (necessary love) to his universal and finally his saving love (free love).

For Frame, it is God's saving love that is the heart of the biblical message: "the form of divine love most central to Scripture's message is the love of God in saving sinners."[112] God unconditionally and freely initiates his redemptive covenant with human beings tainted by their sins. Unlike Pinnock, who considered reciprocal love to be the essence of God's love *ad extra*, Frame identifies God's love for sinners as sovereign love. Frame remarks, "It is God's love that initiates his covenant with Israel, and, indeed, all his covenants with men. His love chooses us for salvation before the foundation of the world. So his love is *controlling*, sovereign."[113]

---

107. Boyd, *God of the Possible*, 57–58.
108. Sanders, *God Who Risks*, 14.
109. Ware, *God's Lesser Glory*, 150.
110. Frame, *No Other God*, 45.
111. Frame, *Doctrine of God*, 416–23.
112. Frame, *Doctrine of God*, 420.
113. Frame, *Doctrine of God*, 423, emphasis original.

There are a small number of places where Frame connects God's love to his suffering explicitly,[114] but unlike in Pinnock's view of God's love, it is God's sovereignty that provides the overarching framework for Frame's consideration of the divine suffering, with the love of God therefore attendant only implicitly. It is illuminating at this point to consider the various dimensions of divine suffering that Frame identifies as falling under the divine sovereignty.

First, divine suffering has an active dimension. Frame's affirmation of the passibility of God is related to his understanding of God's eternal decree, as was the case with the divine emotions. God's lordship over the world eternally determines how in future situations he will respond to the ever-changing and fluctuating circumstances of human beings. Frame remarks, "In his atemporal and nonspatial transcendent existence, God ordains grievous events and evaluates them appropriately. He grieves in that sense, but does not suffer injury or loss."[115] That is, God suffers without being moved by the world as the result of an ordained act determined from before the foundation of the creation—indeed, in the atemporal life of God. In this active dimension, God suffers without being moved by events in history or being overwhelmed by his suffering.

Second, God also experiences passive forms of suffering. He eternally decrees to suffer in time in response to human sin and suffering and therefore also experiences suffering passively. If the active dimension of suffering explained above is unconditioned and unmoved, this passive dimension of suffering is a conditioned and moved suffering, the outcome of God being moved by his human creatures. Frame stresses that God in his immanence is in time: "He can mourn one moment and rejoice the next. He can hear and respond to prayer in time. Since God dwells in time, therefore, there is give-and-take between him and human beings."[116]

It is important to acknowledge that Frame does not ascribe passion to God's nature itself; indeed, he argues explicitly that God "has chosen

---

114. Such a connection can be found in Frame's discussion of Moltmann's view of divine passibility. Frame seems to support the idea that God's love indicates the capacity to enter reciprocal relations with the world: "As to Moltmann's second point, I would agree that love involves reciprocity." Frame, *Doctrine of God*, 615. In the wider context of this passage, Frame affirms that the redemptive suffering of the Son on the cross is grounded in God's self-sacrificing love. Frame, *Doctrine of God*, 613–16. Further discussion of this matter proceeds below.

115. Frame, *Doctrine of God*, 614.

116. Frame, *Doctrine of God*, 558–59.

to create a world that will often grieve him.... [H]e is active, rather than passive."[117] However, Frame is simply indicating here his commitment to the view that God is impassible first and that God's passibility in the economy only results from his eternal decree. Thus, while Frame considers his conception of God's suffering to be "active, rather than passive" in this particular sense, the fact that he affirms that divine suffering takes place within time and in response to human suffering means that in the terms of this work, he affirms the passive dimension of the suffering of God.

Third, Frame explains divine passibility with reference to the immanence of God (God's temporal and spatial omnipresence). For Frame, the transcendent God is historically present in all places and times and undergoes grief and sorrow with all his creation. He posits that God "grieves with his creatures, and he undergoes temporary defeats on his way to the complete victory he has foreordained."[118] God's suffering thus relates to his immanence, which in turn is grounded in his transcendence and in his eternal decree and lordship.

Fourth, God suffers with his people who are in distress in his theophanic presence. God co-suffered with his people who were in exile on account of the rejection of their covenant with God.[119] Even though God appoints their exile and burdens, he does not leave his people in the dark valley but is present with them throughout the journey. However, it is critical to understand that Frame's assessment of this covenantal suffering differs from the general vicarious divine suffering of process theology that describes God as a fellow sufferer who suffers with his people without being able to deliver them from their miseries through his mighty power.[120] Rather, Frame insists that God "promises complete victory and vindication both for himself and for his faithful ones."[121] Regardless of God's voluntary participation in covenantal suffering, the lordship of Yahweh in Frame's work never diminishes.

Finally, in common with Pinnock, Frame affirms that the Son and Father suffer on the cross, without suggesting that the pain is ascribed to the eternal life of the triune God. Frame contends, first, that the Son

---

117. Frame, *Doctrine of God*, 610.
118. Frame, *Doctrine of God*, 614.
119. Frame, *Doctrine of God*, 614.
120. Whitehead, *Process and Reality*, 351.
121. Frame, *Doctrine of God*, 614.

suffered as a person and that this suffering was God's experience.[122] Second, unlike Weinandy, who rejects the suffering of the Father, Frame insists that the suffering of the Son must have had a significant impact on the Father, because the Father and the Son are always united, mutually indwelling each other. Distinguishing the suffering of the Son from that of the Father, Frame writes that "the Father empathized, agonized, and grieved over the death of his Son, but he did not experience death in the same way that the Son did."[123] Third, and unlike Moltmann, Frame is not willing to view the suffering of the Son as an eternal part of God. Instead of interpreting God's love as weakness and vulnerability and thus seeing the Father and the Son as bound together in eternal suffering, Frame sees the divine love as sovereign and powerful love; therefore, suffering cannot be in the category of God's absolute perfections.

In sum, Frame argues that "this principle [the event of the cross] should not be magnified into a metaphysical assertion about God's vulnerability [suffering], for, as we have seen, God's eternal nature is invulnerable, and that invulnerability is also precious to the believer."[124] Indeed, if the suffering of Christ were to be considered an eternal attribute of God, it would imply "losing some attribute, being defeated in his war with Satan, or otherwise failing to accomplish his eternal plan."[125] Therefore, Frame rejects the view that the cross is an eternal event for the triune God.

It should be noted that Frame's doctrine of God has met scholarly resistance. Thomas considers Frame's view of God's suffering to be a departure from the Reformed tradition, observing that the Westminster Confession and the sixteenth- and seventeenth-century theologians never attributed any form of passion or suffering to God.[126] What concerns Thomas particularly is the attribution to God of the negative notions related to emotions and suffering. Thomas claims that "the implications of a doctrine of divine passibility when applied to God (in his divine essence or nature) are catastrophic. We are left with a God who is crippled with pain and whose ability to engage in more than just empathy is severely

---

122. In his discussion of Moltmann's theology of divine passibility, Frame writes, "Certainly Jesus suffered injury and loss on the cross. And I agree with Moltmann that Christ's sufferings are the sufferings of God." Frame, *Doctrine of God*, 613.

123. Frame, *Doctrine of God*, 613–14.

124. Frame, *Doctrine of God*, 615.

125. Frame, *Doctrine of God*, 614.

126. Thomas, "Attributes of God," 363–65.

curtailed as a consequence."[127] Understanding the gravity of ascribing any human form of emotions and suffering to God's nature, however, Frame both restricts divine suffering to what God freely decrees to experience in his relationship with the world and insists that God is impassible in his nature. God's infinite perfections are the foundation of his temporal experience of suffering; therefore, God is always in control and is never overwhelmed or restrained by his suffering. In this way, Frame distinguishes his position carefully from other, more radical passibilists.

To summarize this section, as their respective expositions on divine aseity and triune fellowship indicate, Pinnock and Frame both prioritize God's eternal self-sufficiency and blessedness. In their turn to the divine economy, however, their different theological emphases cause their theologies to diverge. Pinnock portrays divine suffering as the outcome of God's truly reciprocal relationship of love with the world. For Frame, God's lordship dictates his relationship with the world, such that divine passibility is both his active (unmoved) and passive (moved) suffering, as God foreordains himself to suffer with the world actively and to experience the world's suffering passively. Still, Frame prioritizes God's active suffering over his passive suffering and stresses that the passive suffering is only part of God's eternal and immutable decree. The next section will describe how Pinnock and Frame portray divine passibility in relation to mutability and time.

God's Suffering and Immutability

Starting in the mid- to late twentieth century, evangelical theology, which had inherited the traditional understanding of divine immutability, began to devise alternative doctrines of the immutability of God in light of the biblical witness and specifically those references that seemed to denote changes in God, particularly in his emotions.[128] Ware proposes a developed account of the immutability and mutability of the God of the Bible, reformulating the traditional doctrine of God's immutability to make room for a relational and emotional mutability.[129] Oden, mean-

---

127. Thomas, "Attributes of God," 367.

128. For relevant evangelical works that followed this path, see Henry, *God, Revelation and Authority*, 295–306; Davis, *Logic and the Nature of God*, 41–51; Ware, "Evangelical Reformulation," 431.

129. Ware, "Evangelical Reformulation," 438–46.

while, uses the term "divine constancy" to identify God's unchangeable essence and will as well as his personal and mutable reciprocity with the world.[130]

Within this creative theological space, and in line with the earlier works of Strong, Martensen, and Clarke, both Pinnock and Frame affirm God's immutability *in se* and his mutability *ad extra*. Where they depart from the work of these earlier thinkers is in their view of God's emotions and suffering as representing changes and temporal experiences. This section delineates in more detail how Pinnock and Frame view divine passibility in relation to God's immutability and mutability and to God's relation to eternity and time.

Pinnock proposes the expression "changeable faithfulness" to account for what he considers to be the unchanging and changing natures of the God of Scripture. Pinnock is not satisfied with traditional thinking about divine immutability, for he believes that Scripture reveals that God changes in his dealings with human beings.[131] He points here to the revelation of Jesus: "God is not an Unmoved Mover but the God of Jesus Christ, who goes out of himself and acts in history, who becomes involved in the affairs of his people and enters into conversation with them."[132] At the same time, Pinnock is unwilling to give up entirely on divine immutability:

> One way to express this is to say that God is necessary and changeless in some respects but free and changing in others, or that God is necessary and changeless in nature but that in his nature is that of a temporal and personal agent.... [W]ho God is does not change but *what* God *experiences* changes. God's nature does not change but his activities and relationships are dynamic. God's character is stable but God is not static when it comes to associating with creation.[133]

Pinnock seems to affirm the major tenets of the classical understanding of God's attributes such as God's omnipotence, immutability, eternity, omnipresence, sovereignty, and omniscience *in se*.[134] God in his nature and inner activity is not subject to change ontologically, as if God's

---

130. Oden, *Living God*, 1:111.
131. Pinnock, *Most Moved Mover*, 85.
132. Pinnock, *Flame of Love*, 44.
133. Pinnock, *Most Moved Mover*, 85, emphasis original.
134. Pinnock, *Most Moved Mover*, 79–104.

relational, personal, loving, and trinitarian nature could change. However, in being open to the changing developments and events in world history and in allowing truly reciprocal relationships between himself and human beings, God changes in experiencing various emotions and even in the extent of his knowledge and sovereignty.[135] Connecting the discussion of God's immutability to his love, Boyd agrees that "[i]f we believe God is unchanging in his perfect love, we must believe he *perfectly changes* in response to the changing situations of the people he loves."[136]

Pinnock insists that the God of Scripture is the God of time who is a temporally everlasting being, present in the world and experiencing the process of time and change.[137] Asserting the impossibility of connecting timeless eternity to time, he posits that God's eternity must include the possibility and capacity to enter into time in order to begin and to sustain his personal fellowship with humanity. Instead of affirming the timeless eternity of God, then, he affirms that God is everlastingly eternal and is capable of having a temporal relationship with the world: "God is a temporal agent. He is above time in the sense that he is above finite experience and measurement of time but he is not beyond 'before and after' or beyond sequence of events."[138] God unfolds his plans in history and responds to the affairs of the world in the temporal domain, not by working from outside it.[139] Pinnock explains: "If God is personal he is temporal, and if he is temporal then he is inside and not outside of time. Time is not a 'thing' that God may or may not have created. Time is the concomitant of God and personal life. It exists because of God's nature."[140] William Hasker supports this view of God and time: "God is everlasting—without beginning or end but nevertheless undergoing a sequence of experiences, even apart from God's relation to creation."[141]

135. Pinnock, *Most Moved Mover*, 88.

136. Boyd, *Is God to Blame?*, 59, emphasis original.

137. As noted in chapter 2, many scholars support the temporally everlasting view of God's eternity instead of the traditional conception of the timeless eternity view. For these advocates, see Boyd, *Is God to Blame?*, 50–60; Kenny, *God of the Philosophers*; Pike, *God and Timelessness*; Rowe, *Philosophy of Religion*.

138. Pinnock, *Most Moved Mover*, 96.

139. Wolterstorff, who argues against timeless eternity, writes, "If God were eternal, he could not be aware, concerning any temporal event, whether it was occurring, nor aware that it will be occurring, nor could he remember that it had occurred, nor could he plan to bring it about." Wolterstorff, "God Everlasting," 200.

140. Pinnock, *Most Moved Mover*, 98.

141. Hasker, "Adequate God," 218. Other evangelicals resist this conception of time

Recognizing the complexity of the doctrine of divine immutability, Frame agrees with Pinnock's position that God's nature is immutable while his relationship with the world changes, but he also explicitly identifies four ways in which God does not change. First, God's eternal and perfect attributes do not change: "God is a Spirit, infinite, eternal, and unchangeable, in his being, wisdom, power, holiness, justice, goodness, and truth."[142] Second, God's eternal will does not change. Frame posits that "God governs all things by the story he has written, his eternal decree that governs the entire course of nature and history. That story has already been written; it cannot and will not be changed."[143] Third, God's covenantal faithfulness does not change. God is the initiator of the covenant he establishes with his people and is faithful to his promises and words. This is his "covenantal immutability."[144] Fourth, the truthfulness of the revelations recorded in Scripture does not change: they serve as revelations of the eternal truths of God.[145]

What differentiates Frame from Pinnock at this point is that Frame seeks to uphold both God's immutable and atemporal existence and his mutable and temporal interaction with the world. First, having established the ways in which God does not change, Frame affirms the testimony of those episodes in Scripture that bear witness to God's relational and temporal mutability. God being present in and engaging with his creation from within time means God partaking in the course of history in a way that requires change: "History involves constant change, and so, as an agent in history, God himself changes.... God is not merely *like* an agent in time; he really is *in* time, changing as others change."[146] As the principal agent in history, God grieves over his people's suffering and rejoices over the worship of his people. Frame notes, "He can hear and respond to prayer in time. Since God dwells in time, therefore, there is give-and-take

---

because time is considered as created by God for human beings, as the main characteristic of creatures, and as a change that a purely atemporal God cannot experience. Lewis and Demarest, *Integrative Theology*, 1:199. Geisler condemns the supposition that God must be temporal because he acts in time: "*It makes no more sense to say God has to be temporal in order to relate to a temporal world than to say he has to be a creature in order to create.*" Geisler, *Creating God in the Image*, 33, emphasis original.

142. Frame, *Doctrine of God*, 568. Frame quotes here the Westminster Shorter Catechism's answer to question four, "What is God?"

143. Frame, *Doctrine of God*, 569.

144. Frame, *Doctrine of God*, 570.

145. Frame, *Doctrine of God*, 570.

146. Frame, *Doctrine of God*, 571, emphasis original.

between him and human beings.¹⁴⁷ Other evangelical theologians, such as John Feinberg, endorse this view of God's immutability in his plan, will, and ontological attributes and his mutability in his relationship with the world through emotions and suffering.¹⁴⁸ Ware comments that God's "relational changeableness includes . . . his experience of variable emotions as he interacts with us at every level and expresses himself in ways that accord both with his unchangeable character and our changeable states."¹⁴⁹

Second, Frame asserts that God's temporal mutability occurs within the broader context of God being the Lord over time and in time. God is the Lord over the limitations of time such as temporal change, ignorance, and frustration.¹⁵⁰ Time means limitation for human beings, but time has no impact upon God. Time does not force God to change, does not limit his foreknowledge to be dependent on the past and present, and does not frustrate him into being impatient. This God who is the Lord over the limitations of time is also in time. Frame argues that "God is the Lord *in* time as well as the Lord *above* time. . . . God is temporal after all. . . . He really exists in time."¹⁵¹ Still, Frame opposes the view that God is merely in time, as if God were trapped in a box that limits him.¹⁵²

Frame prefers instead to affirm God's lordship over time: "God's transcendence is not his being outside or beyond history, but rather his being Lord and King, in control of all things and speaking with authority over all things. So God's special relation to time, whether temporal or atemporal, should not be defined first in terms of temporality, but in terms of lordship."¹⁵³ A similar argument is made by Erickson, in slightly different terms, when he writes that God "is atemporal/aspatial in his fundamental nature, or is ontologically atemporal/aspatial, but actively or influentially present within the space-time universe."¹⁵⁴ The point of transition for God between being only eternal and being eternal and

147. Frame, *Doctrine of God*, 557–58.
148. Feinberg, *No One Like Him*, 273–74.
149. Ware, "Evangelical Reformulation," 446.
150. Frame, *Doctrine of God*, 554–56, emphasis original.
151. Frame, *Doctrine of God*, 559.
152. Frame, *Doctrine of God*, 557.
153. Frame, *Doctrine of God*, 557.

154. Erickson, *God the Father Almighty*, 139. Horton and Erickson posit that for God to be transcendent and immanent means that he is atemporal and temporal. Erickson, *God the Father Almighty*, 139–40; 274; Horton, *Christian Faith*, 255–56.

temporal is the event of creation. It is at the moment of the creation, Ware writes, that "God became both omnipresent and omnitemporal, while remaining, in himself and apart from creation, fully nonspatial and timelessly eternal."[155] In Frame's thought on God's eternity, God's lordship frees him to be atemporally immutable and temporally mutable simultaneously.

Frame insists that God's temporal interaction does not betray the integrity of God's atemporal existence. God's temporal reciprocity, which seems for Frame to be God's disposition towards the affairs of the world, represents the way in which God responds to the unfolding of his eternal decree, for God "acts and then responds to his own act."[156] No time or change is assigned to God's nature, for "God responds (both transcendently and immanently) only to what he has himself ordained."[157]

Some open theists, such as Sanders and Hasker, are skeptical concerning whether an atemporal God can be temporal.[158] Sanders, for example, contends that "God experiences sequence (before and after) in his changing relationships with us. God is not timeless since a timeless being has no history. A timeless deity is more like an abstract concept such as the number 5, it just is and does not change or have reciprocal relations with us."[159] Frame, however, seeks to uphold the dynamics of God's atemporal and temporal existence without compromise and even warns about the danger of stressing only God's transcendent and eternal existence over his immanent and temporal existence.

Frame highlights that both God's transcendence and immanence are real, noting, "Neither form of existence contradicts the other. God's transcendence never compromises his immanence, nor do his control and authority compromise his covenant presence."[160] Connecting God's suffering to the eternal decree is a creative approach that Frame

---

155. Ware, "Modified Calvinist Doctrine," 88–89. Lister makes a similar argument that God is both eternal and temporal simultaneously. Lister, *God Is Impassible*, 226–30.

156. Frame, *Doctrine of God*, 572.

157. Frame, *Doctrine of God*, 610.

158. Hasker, *Providence, Evil*, 97–106; Sanders, *God Who Risks*, 200. As chapter 2 outlined, various scholars such as Pike and Swinburne complain that an atemporal God cannot have personal relationship with his creatures and thus argue that God is everlastingly temporal. Pike, *God and Timelessness*; Swinburne, *Coherence of Theism*.

159. Sanders, *God Who Risks*, 200.

160. Frame, *Doctrine of God*, 571.

developed to uplift the lordship of God over change and time without ascribing passion to God's nature. At the same time, God experiences passively what he has eternally decreed actively, without going through change *in se*.

Despite their disagreement concerning the conception of God's eternity, both Pinnock and Frame agree that the divine joy that is grounded in God's eternal perfection is the foundation of his passibility. At the heart of their agreement is the way in which they both affirm a mediating position, upholding both God's joy within himself and his suffering in relation to the process of history. Pinnock posits that "God's happiness is greater than the sufferings of the world.... God shares in our sorrows and transmutes them into something better. God suffers on account of creation, but his joy cannot be destroyed."[161] He adds, "In the world, there is much suffering and, because God is good, he shares in it and does not ignore it. Yet God can be blissful and suffer at the same time because he can contemplate the values contained in his own being and the values being realized in the world."[162]

Frame concurs that the inner life of the triune God is eternally joyous: "God . . . is completely in harmony with himself. His three persons glorify and serve one another willingly and cheerfully. He is whole, well, and prosperous—blessed and happy."[163] Even though he goes through travails temporally in his redemptive relationship with sinners, God in his immutable and blessedness *in se* "rejoices that his overall plan is wonderful, that it achieves all his purposes."[164] Both thinkers thus highlight and affirm the divine blessedness, as it is sustained in the eternal and immutable fellowship of the triune persons, and thus the divine joy that is more powerful than the pain that follows from the disobedience and travail of his creatures.[165]

In sum, both Pinnock and Frame recognize that God does not change in his inner being, and both affirm God's passibility in the form mutable and temporal experience. Still, they differ in respect of the ways

---

161. Pinnock, *Most Moved Mover*, 92.
162. Pinnock, *Most Moved Mover*, 92.
163. Frame, *Doctrine of God*, 444.
164. Frame, *Doctrine of God*, 444–45.
165. In a similar way, Bloesch holds that "God freely involves himself in the travail of his creation, yet he does not cease to be joyous as he looks forward to the overcoming of this travail. God remains above pain and suffering even while descending into the world of confusion and misery." Bloesch, *God the Almighty*, 94–95.

in which they conceive God's passibility. Pinnock, by contrast, considers that God is capable of participating in temporal and reciprocal relationships and defines divine passibility accordingly as a mutable and temporal response to human beings, rejecting completely the notion of God as a being in timeless eternity. In contrast, Frame, arguing that God is the Lord over change and time, interprets God's mutability as a temporal mutability that God decrees at the beginning of the creation without assigning change and time to God's immutable and eternal nature.

God's Suffering and Self-Limitation[166]

One issue that has aroused great tension in evangelical circles in the debate around divine self-limitation is the question of whether or not self-limitation is a logical possibility of God's omnipotence. Pinnock and proponents of open theism contend that God is able in his omnipotence to limit his own attributes, such as knowledge and control, freely and without any diminishment of his power. If God is thought to be unable to limit himself, it is argued, it would be ascribing a limitation to God's omnipotence. This leads to God's sovereignty, providence, and foreknowledge all being reinterpreted through the concept of self-limitation.

For Frame and the opponents of open theism, however, God's sovereignty and foreknowledge cannot be limited or decreased because these attributes are necessary for God's lordship and represent his utmost perfections. In this way of thinking, any limitation of one of God's attributes would impact the other attributes, and all the attributes are interconnected and indistinguishable from his nature and existence.[167] This debate concerning divine self-limitation is significant for the discussion of the doctrine of divine (im)passibility because the extent of God's foreknowledge and sovereignty determines the shape of God's emotional responses and suffering. This section will outline Pinnock's account of the way in which God limits his sovereignty and foreknowledge and Frame's argument for divine foreordination and exhaustive foreknowledge and

---

166. The mediating theologians noted in the previous chapter apply the concept of self-limitation to God's nature to stress that God is person without using it to limit divine attributes.

167. Horton, *Christian Faith*, 230. Horton opposes this understanding of divine self-limitation, asserting that "God is never free to be not-God. None of his attributes can be suspended, withdrawn, diminished, or altered, since his attributes are identical with his existence."

explore further their implications for their respective accounts of divine passibility.

Pinnock's understanding of God's self-limitation restricts the scope of God's foreknowledge concerning the future events in the world, including the future choices of human beings. God does know all incidents past and present and also knows certain decisions that he himself will make in the future. In the process of realizing reciprocal relationships with his creations and endowing them with libertarian freedom, God takes the risk of not fully accomplishing his own desire and will, for, as Pinnock writes, "no being, not even God, can know in advance precisely what free agents will do, even though he may predict it with great accuracy."[168] On the one hand, Pinnock emphasizes that God is not "metaphysically limited."[169] As omnipotent, God is able to determine every event in history and every human decision and is able to have exhaustive foreknowledge, just as Frame and traditional theologians hold. On the other hand, however, by voluntarily limiting himself, God's knowledge is rendered dependent on historical proceedings. God's knowledge therefore advances and increases as history proceeds and as new information emerges each moment because, in Pinnock's words, "[t]hough God knows all there is to know about the world, there are aspects about the future that even God does not know."[170] God's foreknowledge is limited foreknowledge in its extent.

Other open theists similarly exclude the possibility of exhaustive divine foreknowledge, though not all connect this view with divine self-limitation. Lorenzo McCabe, for example, writes that "God can have no knowledge until from the realm of the possible a free being originates their conception and determines to actualize those conceptions into entities."[171] Referring to the relationship between divine foreknowledge and biblical prophecies, Boyd claims that biblical prophecies relating to human actions are merely high-probability predictions, based on God's past and present knowledge, not based on God's exhaustive foreknowledge.[172] Instead of the traditional view of God's prophecy that is based on God's foreknowledge alone, Richard Rice suggests what he calls "conditional prophecies," which are "prophecies whose fulfillment depended

---

168. Pinnock, *Most Moved Mover*, 100.
169. Pinnock, *Most Moved Mover*, 149.
170. Pinnock, *Most Moved Mover*, 32.
171. McCabe, *Divine Nescience of Future Contingencies*, 24–25.
172. Boyd, *God of the Possible*, 35–39.

on certain human responses," arguing that not all of God's predictions occurred.[173] However, other evangelical theologians pursue a more traditional view of divine foreknowledge. In this vein, Lewis and Demarest oppose this view, arguing that divine foreknowledge is not dependent on the unfolding of history: "God does not learn line upon line, or observation after observation, or conclusion after premise. . . . Since God is not limited by the succession of events in time, his knowledge is not contingent on history."[174] Jack Cottrell similarly notes, "To say that God could not foreknow truly free human decisions is either to exalt man too highly or to reduce God to a creaturely status."[175]

Pinnock's view of God's self-limitation also impacts upon his understanding of God's sovereignty. Pinnock stresses that "God limits his own power in allowing us to be free. The power itself is unlimited but God chooses to actualize a particular world whose development he leaves largely in the hands of creatures. This leaves the future open and largely under our control."[176] In the absence of any eternal decree or foreordination, God is still able to fulfill his words and promises as recorded in Scripture and to accommodate the fluctuations of the world. However, he does so not through dominating power, but through the vulnerable yet superior power that he shares with creation. Pinnock explains: "God is so sovereign that he saves the world by choosing weakness. This self-limitation of God coincides with the act of creation. It is a self-limitation that God himself established for the sake of a measured independence of the world and the possibility of genuine freedom in the world."[177]

However, Pinnock does not thereby dismiss the scriptural witness to God's sovereignty. He endorses instead a general form of sovereignty that makes room for God to support the affairs and unfolding of world history and to accomplish some of his long term and overall goals, including by way of miracles and victories over evil.[178] He posits that "God's sov-

---

173. Rice, "Biblical Support for a New Perspective," 50. Unlike Pinnock and Sanders, who use the term "self-limitation" to describe the open view of God, Rice recommends avoiding use of the term, because it suggests that "the open view of God is somehow deficient in comparison to the traditional alternatives; it lacks something that they affirm." Rice, "Does Open Theism Limit God?," 43.

174. Lewis and Demarest, *Integrative Theology*, 1:199.

175. Cottrell, "Conditional Election," 69.

176. Pinnock, *Most Moved Mover*, 94.

177. Pinnock, *Most Moved Mover*, 93.

178. Pinnock, *Most Moved Mover*, 146.

ereignty is interactive and general, not all-determining and meticulous. God's will is not unchangeably fixed like a blueprint, nor God's power manipulative."[179] Rejecting the idea that God has an eternal blueprint for humanity and focusing on Jesus Christ as revealing the eternal nature of God, Boyd claims that God does not allow or permit evil but actually grapples to overcome it.[180] The ministry of Jesus, in the course of which not everyone accepted his message, suggests to Boyd that "God does not always get what he wants."[181] David Basinger connects this partial understanding of divine sovereignty to God's moral choice: "Freewill theists acknowledge that God does not control much of what occurs. However, unlike process theists, they are adamant in their belief that this is the result of a moral choice, not an external restriction."[182] God is absolutely free in this view to exercise his own power to limit the exercise of his sovereignty over his creation.

Frame does not accept this position on divine self-limitation, for the sovereignty and foreknowledge that are said to be limited are the very elements that define and testify to the identity of God and his lordship over all things. He asks, "Is it possible, then, that God could renounce, or be robbed of, his lordship? Could he be the same God without his control, authority, and presence?"[183] For Frame, such a prospect is unthinkable. For God to limit his sovereignty and foreknowledge would be to deny his own identity as the Lord; therefore, divine self-limitation is an impossible undertaking.[184]

Indeed, Frame's view of divine aseity indicates that God's existence is dependent on nothing but himself, and his omniscience is not conditioned by any historical process of deriving knowledge, for God "gains his knowledge only from himself (his nature and his plan) and serves as his own criterion of truth."[185] Frame does distinguish God's omniscience into two categories: "God's necessary knowledge (his knowledge of his own nature) and his free knowledge (his knowledge of his freely chosen

---

179. Pinnock, *Most Moved Mover*, 94.
180. Boyd, *Is God to Blame?*, 60.
181. Boyd, *Is God to Blame?*, 67.
182. Basinger, *Case for Freewill Theism*, 36.
183. Frame, *Doctrine of God*, 228.
184. Frame, *Doctrine of God*, 518–21.
185. Frame, *Doctrine of God*, 602.

decrees and of the world as determined by those decrees)."[186] But for Frame, God's free knowledge, which in Pinnock's case is dependent upon the world, can only have one source: God himself.

Frame's understanding of omniscience is thus tightly connected with his view of divine foreknowledge. God as the Lord over time, space, and knowledge manages and foreordains every event in history, including every detail of the past, present, and future. Frame writes, "Does God's omniscience include knowledge of the future? Certainly it does, in the view of Scripture. We have seen that God foreordains the whole course of history by his eternal plan. If he plans and foreordains all things, surely he knows them."[187]

Even though Frame may seem to prioritize God's foreordination as the necessary condition for and cause of his exhaustive foreknowledge, the two attributes operate in an entirely reciprocal way:

> There is in God's mind a reciprocity between foreknowledge and foreordination. Neither is simply "prior" to the other. Both are eternal. And, logically, God's knowledge is based on what he foreordains. But his foreordination is not an ignorant foreordination. He does not foreordain at random a set of circumstances and then look upon those circumstances with surprise. His plan is a wise one, formulated according to knowledge.[188]

Frame is convinced that exhaustive foreknowledge is the major factor in Scripture that differentiates the God of Israel from other pagan deities in the context of the prophetic writings: "Knowledge of the future is not only the test of a true prophet. It is also the test of a true God. In the contest between Yahweh and the false gods of the ancient Near East, a major issue is which God knows the future."[189] As such, for Frame, the prophecies attested in Scripture could not be proclaimed or actualized without God's exhaustive foreknowledge.

At this point, a number of questions arise in connection with God's foreknowledge and sovereignty on the one hand, and his suffering on the other hand: Does God suffer because of insufficient foreknowledge? If he ordains his own suffering, is it an authentic form of suffering? And is he in control of his own suffering or overwhelmed by it? Attention will be

186. Frame, *Doctrine of God*, 236.
187. Frame, *Doctrine of God*, 485.
188. Frame, *Doctrine of God*, 150.
189. Frame, *Doctrine of God*, 487.

given below to how Pinnock and Frame would answer these questions and how they portray the characteristic of God's suffering in relation to God's self-limitation and lordship.

First, it should be noted that Pinnock and the proponents of open theism propose that even though God does not foreordain every event in history and does not have exhaustive foreknowledge, he is still able broadly to predict future events by knowing the present and past,[190] because he knows his creation perfectly.[191] Referring to 1 Samuel, which narrates God's repentance for choosing Saul and God's new plan to use David to establish the kingdom of Israel, Pinnock claims that God's repentance, which is *naham* in Hebrew and has the meaning of both regret and intense pain, indicates God's willingness to change the course of his plan, not his weakness and limitations. He writes, "it appears that God is willing to change course, especially where judgment is concerned, because he loves to be merciful and to relent from punishing."[192] In this vein, Sanders makes a similar comment that "given the depth and breadth of God's knowledge of the present situation, God forecasts what is most likely to happen. In this regard God is the consummate social scientist predicting what will happen."[193] Likewise, Boyd, despite denying divine foreordination of all events, concurs that God "is certain about everything that could be and thus is never caught off guard."[194] What is important about Pinnock's position is that God's ability to change plans is not a sign of weakness but a demonstration of God's willingness to adapt to the changes of the world and to work together with the free decisions of human beings.

Whether or not God's changing plan should be interpreted as divine flexibility, God's incomplete foreknowledge in Pinnock's theology is clearly related to Pinnock's position regarding the limitation of divine sovereignty. God, who at one point planned to carry out his covenantal promises through Saul, had to change course because "plan A" failed. Wright criticizes Pinnock at this point, on the basis that this view could be interpreted as God's having no "plan As," for "it also seems to involve God's continually adjusting his plans to whatever I might do in such a

---

190. Pinnock, *Grace of God*, 2–26.
191. Boyd, *God of the Possible*, 35.
192. Pinnock, *Most Moved Mover*, 43.
193. Sanders, *God Who Risks*, 133.
194. Boyd, *God of the Possible*, 150.

way that he could have no 'plan A' at all, only an infinitude of continuously variable 'plan Bs.' And all of his 'plan Bs' are wrong too, except the last, which he has not invented yet."[195] Without his exhaustive foreknowledge, God will always need another plan to accomplish his covenant, and if God only knows the future by way of anticipation and prediction and adjusts his plans in response to failures unforeseen without exhaustive foreknowledge, then God's knowledge and plan do not seem too different from those of human beings. Wright therefore argues against Pinnock's view that "it just does not seem to be enough that God is only finitely smarter than we are.... Does he really only mean that he will be smart enough to invent a new plan when our free will frustrates the old one, as it must, statistically?"[196] Similarly, if God in Pinnock's view suffers when he has to repent of courses of action caused by his own limited knowledge, there is a danger that the distinction between divine suffering and human suffering collapses, despite Pinnock's efforts to distinguish clearly between them.[197]

The result is that Pinnock's view of divine self-limitation deprives God of the ability to control his own suffering. Even if God suffers because he limits himself voluntarily, his suffering exists because of the failed plans, broken anticipations, and repeated repentances caused by the absence of perfect foreknowledge and incomplete sovereignty. Pinnock's view of divine self-limitation appears once again to assign human characteristics to divine possibility.

In the writing of Frame, by contrast, God knows that he will accomplish his unchanging, eternal decree through his sovereign love and omnipotence and therefore that he will eternally triumph over evil, sin, and suffering. Frame notes that "while he [God] grieves about particular evils, he rejoices that his overall plan is wonderful, that it achieves all his purposes."[198] Frame's interpretation of the story of Saul is correspondingly different from that of Pinnock. Frame's analysis of God's repentance is that it is a foreknown and decreed form of suffering. God chooses in eternity to experience the suffering of repentance in time that Scripture describes. Throughout, God is sovereign, which means that God's suffering is controlled pain, and thus very different from the suffering that

---

195. Wright, *No Place for Sovereignty*, 224.
196. Wright, *No Place for Sovereignty*, 225.
197. Pinnock, "Systematic Theology," 119.
198. Frame, *Doctrine of God*, 444–45.

human beings experience. Lister makes a helpful remark concerning God's exhaustive foreknowledge and suffering in this connection: "God's exhaustive foreknowledge entails that God is never surprised into an emotional reaction."[199] Frame does not attribute any inappropriate, human emotions to God and denies that God is overwhelmed by pain as humans can be.[200] God, for Frame, suffers no injury or loss.[201]

Frame's doctrine of divine passibility is grounded in his view of God's lordship, which distinguishes it from Pinnock's view of divine passibility and its basis in the divine self-limitation. For Frame, God is Lord even over his own suffering and has full control over the active and passive dimensions of his suffering. Frame recognizes God's suffering to be determined in his eternal decree; therefore, God's suffering is an active form of suffering. God's suffering is also, and only on this basis, a temporal and passive response to the affairs of human beings as God participates in the unfolding of history. In this way, through his lordship model, Frame resolutely affirms that God's passibility is foreknown and sovereign.

In sum, Pinnock argues that God's limitation of his foreknowledge and sovereignty is motivated by his love to have truly reciprocal relationships with his human creatures. God's limited foreknowledge and sovereignty also seem to shape the characteristic of his emotions and suffering, as unanticipated and uncontrolled. For Pinnock, that is the cost and risk of God's self-limitation and love. Frame, however, understands God as Lord such that God is the source of his own knowledge and sovereignty, which cannot be dependent on anything other than himself; therefore, self-limitation would be a violation of God's lordship. In this way, God's lordship over his knowledge and sovereignty paints the pictures of God's emotional responses and passibility as foreknown and controlled.

Constructive Lessons from Pinnock and Frame

There are several lessons that can be drawn from the work of these more recent mediating theologians in respect of our constructive proposal, to be developed in chapters 5 and 6, that will serve as a summary of the assertion of Pinnock and Frame.

---

199. Lister, *God Is Impassible*, 194.
200. Frame, *Doctrine of God*, 610–11.
201. Frame, *Doctrine of God*, 613.

First, we learn from Frame's approach that emphasizes the sovereignty of God over his relationality. Both Pinnock and Frame seek to preserve the notion of God's relationality with the world; however, Pinnock does so by revising the infinite attributes of God such as God's sovereignty and stressing the self-limitation of God, while Frame builds God's relationality on the foundation of his sovereignty and infinite attributes. Frame's approach preserves both God's sovereignty and relationality, and at this point our constructive proposal will follow Frame's understanding of God's sovereignty and depart from Pinnock's notion of the self-limitation of God.

Second, it should be noted that both mediating theologians feel that it is imperative to hold together the balance between the immanent Trinity and economic Trinity. They posit that the triune God is immutable in his attributes and blessedness *in se* and temporally passible in his experience of various emotions *ad extra* as recorded in Scripture. In doing so, Pinnock rejects the timeless eternity view of God and supports the temporally everlasting view, whereas Frame accepts both the atemporal and the temporal existence of God. In agreement with Frame, we will argue that the God who is the Lord of both eternity and time can be both atemporal and immutable *in se*, and temporal and mutable *ad extra*, without making any compromise on either side.

Third, we can learn from the ways in which Frame sought to hold together both the active and the passive aspects of God's suffering. The strength of affirming God's active suffering is its preservation of God's unlimited perfection and of God's sovereignty over his emotions, whereas the strength of affirming God's passive suffering is its affirmation of the biblical description of God's suffering and of his reciprocal relationship with his creatures. Frame's approach draws on both strengths, and the constructive premise of this work seeks similarly to affirm both that the impassible God decrees his emotional responses actively and that the passible God suffers and experiences them passively in time.

5

The Immanent Trinity Is Impassible

We will now develop the premise of this publication that the triune God is both impassible and passible—the immanent Trinity is impassible but is also passible when acting for the benefit of the world in the economy. Drawing on the strengths and weaknesses of the arguments provided by the impassibilists and passibilists covered in chapter 2, this present work builds on some of the insights offered by the mediating theologians previously reviewed, especially the ways in which these theologians attempt to make a distinction between God's eternal blessedness *in se* and his suffering in relation to the world without compromising the inner perfections of God. The rest of this work explores both the particular characteristics of the reciprocal relations that exist between the divine persons in eternity and the emotions of the triune God *ad intra*, and consider how these relations and emotions relate to an understanding of the relations that exist between the divine persons in time and the emotions and suffering of the triune God *ad extra*.

The Self-Movement of the Immanent Trinity

The doctrine of divine (im)passibility asks whether or not the triune God is moved by the world. Impassibilists answer that God, who is fully actualized within himself, cannot be moved by the world. Passibilists reply that God, who engages in fully reciprocal relationships with the world, is able to be moved by the world. To answer the question whether and how God is moved by the world—the topic of the following chapter—this section explores how the triune God moves himself actively and is moved by himself passively *ad intra* in order to be able to posit this inner trinitarian movement as the foundation of the reciprocal movement and engagement of the persons of the Trinity *ad extra*.

The self-moving God is the only subject of his eternal and dynamic movement. John Webster describes the self-movement of God as "his self-moved self-presentation"[1] and adds, "This movement, without cause or condition, and depending on nothing other than itself, is God's being from himself."[2] Nothing causes God's eternal movement, and no condition moves him to move as he does eternally, for God is the self-moving and self-motivating Being.[3] He is the source of his own activities[4] and the foundation of all movements external and internal to himself, for the determining cause of his life is not outside him but only inside him.[5] No one has any claim on the flow of his movement or can alter the direction of this movement: God directs his own movement.[6] He moves himself eternally and is independent and *a se*, being in and of himself fully realized, satisfied, and sufficient. According to Thomas Torrance, God is "the self-existing, self-living, self-affirming God whose being is his ever-continuing life and whose life is his ever-continuing being."[7] As God moves himself eternally, he is moved by himself. Karl Barth explains that God is moved by himself in his own personal freedom and free power: "God's being is being which knows, wills and decides of itself, and is moved by itself."[8] Samuel Harris argues that God is moved by his love, by "a rational free choice" and by "his own eternal and free determination in the light of absolute reason."[9] As such, God, who moves himself and is moved by himself, is the only subject who determines his own course and mode of activities.

The self-movement of the triune God can also be considered with reference to the personal movements of the Father, Son, and Holy Spirit, who move themselves and are moved by one another. The three subjects of

1. Webster, *God without Measure*, 1:14.
2. Webster, *God without Measure*, 1:20.
3. Barth, *Church Dogmatics*, II/1, 268–69.
4. Strong, *Systematic Theology*, 1:252.
5. Schleiermacher, *Christian Faith*, 219.
6. Clarke, *Outline of Christian Theology*, 67.
7. Torrance, *Christian Doctrine of God*, 235.
8. Barth, *Church Dogmatics*, II/1, 268.
9. Harris, *God the Creator*, 1:205–6.

these movements in the eternal Trinity are equally and completely divine. Oden emphatically claims that "the Father is God (*est Deus*), nothing less, and the Son is God, nothing less, and the Holy Spirit is God, nothing less, and God is essentially one."[10] Each of the divine persons is fully relational and interrelational with the other divine persons. Weinandy stresses the relational interplay of the subsistence of the triune persons, who "are fully in act in that they are constituted and defined only in the act of being inter-related to one another."[11] This interrelationship can be more precisely described by considering the reciprocity of the three divine persons. The Father moves the Son and the Holy Spirit, who are moved by the Father, and the Father is moved by the Son and the Holy Spirit. The Son actively moves the Father and the Holy Spirit, who are moved by the Son, and the Son passively is moved by the Father and the Holy Spirit. And lastly, the Holy Spirit moves the Father and the Son, who are moved by the Holy Spirit, and the Holy Spirit is moved by the Father and the Son.

Simultaneously, all three divine persons, having their own wills and freedom, will to move themselves and will to be moved by the other divine persons in their trinitarian unity. They are fully intentional, moving themselves and each other actively and being moved by themselves and each other passively. Only the three divine persons can move and be moved only by themselves and by the other divine persons. In this context, the reciprocity of the inner life of the trinitarian persons is the interaction of the active and passive movements of the immanent Trinity.

The inner trinitarian persons exist in timeless eternity.[12] Time does not exist within timeless eternity: There is no beginning or end, no duration and no before or after caused by succession of time. As Helm comments, the triune persons are timelessly eternal "in the sense of being time-free."[13] Timeless eternity is an attribute of the triune God and therefore also an attribute of each divine person of the Trinity. All three divine persons are timelessly eternal. In this realm of timeless eternity, the Father, Son, and Holy Spirit subsist together without a moment of absence, moving themselves actively and passively.

10. Oden, *Systematic Theology*, 1:221.

11. Weinandy, *Does God Suffer?*, 127.

12. As chapter 2 noted, there are two major views with respect to God's eternity: God is timelessly eternal or he is temporally everlasting. This present work chooses the former view of God's eternity.

13. Helm, *Eternal God*, 39.

The doctrine of the eternal processions of the Son and Holy Spirit indicates that the Father begets the Son who is begotten by the Father, and the Father with (or through) the Son breathe(s) the Holy Spirit who proceeds from the Father and (or through) the Son. However, this order of the processions of the Son and Holy Spirit does not describe their chronological or temporal origins. The Father's act of generation of the Son does not give birth to the Son, nor does the spirating of the Father and (or through) the Son bring a new existence of the Holy Spirit.

These eternal processions are not past and completed acts, or future and unrealized acts to be accomplished by the triune persons.[14] The three divine persons are not bound by human understanding of cause and effect. Leonardo Boff explains the relationship between cause and effect in the realm of the eternity of the Trinity: "In the Trinity, the 'cause' (the Father) is not anterior to the 'effects' (the Son and Holy Spirit). The 'effects' possess the same eternity and dignity as the 'cause.'"[15] Gregory Nazianzus likewise argues that "a cause is not necessarily prior to its effects—the Sun is not prior to its light."[16] The Father, Son, and Holy Spirit are co-eternal and move themselves actively and passively in their timeless eternity.

Dynamic Reciprocity Model

This work illuminates this self-movement of the triune persons by introducing the dynamic reciprocity model that was outlined previously in chapter 1. The dynamic reciprocity model seeks to offer a new way of thinking about the self-movement and reciprocal relations of the divine three persons of the immanent and economic Trinity. It does so by suggesting that in eternity, passion can be considered as prior to action (and vice versa) and that both eternal action and eternal passion function in similar, if logically opposite, ways.

The tradition of the church already affirms the notion of the self-moving God and acknowledges the distinction between the eternal actions and eternal passions of the three divine persons of the immanent Trinity. The three divine persons move themselves and, in turn, are moved by one another. What the dynamic reciprocity model suggests is that the eternal actions and eternal passions of God are co-constitutive,

---

14. Webster, *God without Measure*, 1:34.
15. Boff, *Trinity and Society*, 142.
16. St. Gregory of Nazianzus, "Third Theological Oration," 71.

such that either one can be considered in light of the other, as prior to the other. This will in turn have constructive implications both for the understanding of the persons of the immanent Trinity as well as for the understanding of the persons of the Trinity in the economy. Two insights of the dynamic reciprocity model can be considered for the present.

The first insight of the dynamic reciprocity model that requires further explanation is the claim that within the timeless eternal life of the triune God, eternal passion can be considered a prior movement to eternal action. In the human dynamic of action and passion, passion is considered "a caused state of being into which one is moved by the activity of some agent,"[17] or "the reception of change in the being acted upon."[18] Thus, passion is always subsequent and secondary to action in the creaturely realm.

However, the claim made by the dynamic reciprocity model is that this dynamic does not apply to the eternal action and eternal passion of the triune God. For every action of one trinitarian person upon another, there is a corresponding passion on the part of the trinitarian person acted upon. The eternal action is not the creating cause of the eternal passion as if the object of the passion were motionless and did not exist before the eternal action took place and caused the passion. In eternity, passion is not a secondary movement only or the mere result of the action.

By contrast, as the three divine persons always coexist in timeless eternity without a moment of absence, so action and passion similarly always operate in eternity without a moment of absence. The eternal three persons are at the same time the subjects and objects of each action and passion. Just as eternal action can be considered—by imperfect analogy with our experience of the creaturely realm—prior and subsequent to passion, so eternal passion can equally be considered as prior and subsequent to action—something not conceivable in the context of the creaturely realm. In one view, then, the Father, Son, and Holy Spirit move themselves and, in turn, are moved by one another. At the same time, in another view, the Father, Son, and Holy Spirit are moved by one another and, in turn, move themselves. In this sense, eternal actions and passions can be both prior and subsequent movements.

The second insight of the dynamic reciprocity model is that eternal action and eternal passion both condition and are conditioned by the

---

17. Dolezal, "Strong Impassibility," 16.
18. Wuellner, "Passion," 88–89.

other. This insight follows directly from the first insight. According to the human understanding of action and passion, action possesses the giving and creating factors, while passion only receives such that "all passions are [considered as] finite, dependent, time bound, and mutable states of being."[19] This subordinating dynamic between the functions attached to action and passion in human terms does not apply to the eternal action and passion of the triune persons, for eternal action and passion are equally divine and perfect without any subordination or limitation.

Because eternal action and passion can both be considered as prior and subsequent to each other, they can both be considered to condition and to be conditioned by each other. To refer to the conventional way of thinking about eternal action and passion, this relates to the way in which the three divine persons move themselves and, in turn, are moved by one another. Eternal action conditions eternal passion, which is thus conditioned by the eternal action. At the same time, however, eternal passion can be considered to condition eternal action, which is thus conditioned by the eternal passion. The three divine persons are moved by the other divine persons and, in turn, move themselves. Therefore, both the eternal action and the eternal passion condition and are conditioned by each other and operate in unity without any subordination.

This construal of the eternal action and eternal passion of the Father, Son, and Holy Spirit as set forth in the dynamic reciprocity model has three particular advantages. First, God can be perceived in a more trinitarian fashion than a concept of God as pure act allows. This traditional conception suggests that divine passion or receiving were somehow alien to him or inappropriate for him. God's full relationality *in se* is helpfully emphasized through the dynamic reciprocity model, where eternal action and passion are both considered as divine movements that have equal value and function. A second advantage is that applying the dynamic reciprocity model can help to illuminate the reciprocal interplay among the trinitarian persons both *in se* and *ad extra* as will be seen in the next chapter.

Employing the dynamic reciprocity model allows for a deeper consideration of how the triune persons exist in their inner fellowship with one another, engage in redemptive operations, and interact with human beings. A third advantage is that the dynamic reciprocity model allows for a new perspective upon God's eternal reality. Eternity is God's

---

19. Dolezal, "Strong Impassibility," 16.

incommunicable attribute, an attribute which belongs to him alone and is beyond the scope of human understanding. This new way of discussing God's eternal action and passion functions as a creative way to reflect on the mystery of the eternal operation of the inner trinitarian persons.

The self-movement of the immanent Trinity is independent of any external cause, condition, or need and is directed to the most beautiful and glorious beings who are and deserve nothing less than perfection, the Father, Son, and Holy Spirit. Within their eternal movements, the three divine persons move themselves and are moved by one another: They exist in the reciprocity of eternal active and eternal passive movements. This eternal reciprocity is possible because the subjects and objects of the active and passive interaction are divine persons, and because only the Father, Son, and Holy Spirit can move themselves and be moved by the divine others. As their eternal actions condition corresponding eternal passions, so too the eternal passions can be considered to condition corresponding eternal actions because these actions and passions are movements of the divine persons that occur in eternity, without succession of time. The inner trinitarian persons exist in this dynamic reciprocity of eternal action and passion.

The Characteristics of the Reciprocity of the Immanent Trinity

Two particular characteristics of the operations of the immanent Trinity are necessity and freedom. Necessity is the reciprocal relations of the inner trinitarian persons involve the necessary reciprocity of love. Freedom is another distinctive characteristic of the reciprocal love of the three divine persons of the immanent Trinity. The dynamic reciprocity model sheds further light on the interplay of the necessary and free dimensions of the inner trinitarian relations.

Necessary Reciprocity of Love

The reciprocal relations of the immanent Trinity in the context of the divine communion of love are *necessary*. The Father, Son, and Holy Spirit of the immanent Trinity exist in an eternal fellowship of love, loving each other and being loved by one another. This reciprocity of love of the divine persons is intrinsic to and even constitutive of the being of each divine person of the immanent Trinity and serves as the essence of the movement of the Father, Son, and Holy Spirit.[20] Frame notes that "it is not necessarily wrong to think of God's triunity as an attribute (and therefore as God's nature). . . . God's triunity is related to . . . acts of love and communication among the three persons."[21] The reciprocity of love of the three divine persons is the nature of the triune God. In this way, the divine persons reciprocate their love with each other necessarily.

In the reciprocity of the inner trinitarian persons, their active love towards themselves and the other divine persons is necessary. Frame holds that "[t]he love between the persons of the Trinity is eternal. And since God does not exist without his three persons, the love among those persons is *necessary* to his nature. So God's love is first of all directed toward himself, but even his self-love is self-giving."[22] The declaration that the triune God loves himself does not refer to a self-indulgent love. Clarke's proposal that God deserves the most perfect form of love explains: "[I]t would seem also that there must eternally be an object fully worthy of his affection. But such an object must be as great as himself, and as good. He must have such an object within himself if he has it all, and it must be an object that he can love without becoming selfishly self-centred."[23] Simultaneously, the love of the inner trinitarian persons is towards the other divine persons. There was never a moment when any person of the Trinity did not love the others. Each divine person who is God loves himself and the other divine persons who are God, and God's active love for himself is a necessary love of three persons who are equally divine.

This active necessity reflects a simultaneous passive necessity. Receiving divine love from the other divine persons is another necessary

---

20. Torrance's remark is helpful to understand how the communion of love of the three persons is necessary to the triune God: "The one triune Being of God is to be thought of, then, as essentially and intrinsically a mutual movement of loving self-communication between the Father, the Son and the Holy Spirit, an intensely personal Communion . . . which the three divine Persons have in common. . . . Since the one Being is three Persons, and God *is* Love, and by its nature love involves reciprocal personal relations, we must go on to consider rather fully the reciprocal perichoretic relations between the Persons of the Father, the Son and the Holy Spirit which are the onto-relations of their mutual love for one another." Torrance, *Christian Doctrine of God*, 133, emphasis original.

21. Frame, *Doctrine of God*, 619.

22. Frame, *Doctrine of God*, 416, emphasis original.

23. Clarke, *Outline of Christian Theology*, 176.

characteristic relating to the reciprocity of the immanent Trinity. Just as the persons of the Father, Son, and Holy Spirit give their love to one another, so too they receive love from one another. As the Father loves the Son and Holy Spirit, they receive the love of the Father; as the Son and Holy Spirit love the Father, he in turn receives their everlasting love for himself. Colin Gunton's definition of love requires precisely this act of receiving, as it states that "the relations of the three are summarized in the concept of love, which involve a dynamic of both giving and receiving."[24] Moltmann finds this act of receiving to be a dimension of the existence of each of the triune persons and relates it in turn to eternal life: "By virtue of the love they have for one another they exist totally in the other. . . . Each person receives the fullness of eternal life from the other."[25] If the focus is only on the giving of love in the life of the immanent Trinity, an incomplete and imperfect depiction of that life is provided, for the giving of love would be an aimless movement without the receiving of that love by the intended recipients. As loving the triune persons is a necessary movement of the divine life, so too receiving the love that is given is part of the inner trinitarian event of love. Therefore, receiving love is as necessary as giving love.

Giving and receiving love are necessary acts of the divine persons. This reciprocity of love represents an eternal and immutable movement of the immanent Trinity, which Catherine LaCugna describes as "an eternal movement of reciprocal giving and receiving, giving again and receiving again."[26] The reciprocity of the triune love is the mode of the existence of the inner life of the triune God, as Highfield explains: "The actions of loving and being loved, of giving, receiving, and returning, constitute the divine life—blessed, full, and overflowing."[27]

As this reciprocity of love is a constitutive movement of the triune persons, they cannot not love themselves and cannot cease their eternal reciprocity of love. However, there is a further important aspect of this reciprocity: the love of the three divine persons is given by perfect divine persons and received by perfect divine persons. As the reciprocity of love is the nature of the triune God, so this particular triune love can be given to and received by the three divine persons only. The triune persons

---

24. Gunton, *Promise of Trinitarian Theology*, 143.
25. Moltmann, *Trinity and the Kingdom*, 173-74.
26. LaCugna, *God for Us*, 272.
27. Highfield, *Great Is the Lord*, 254.

necessarily engage in this reciprocal love according to their nature, in such a way that this necessary triune love binds the three distinct divine persons in their triunity of love and cannot be broken by any internal or external factors.

The necessary reciprocity of the inner trinitarian love just presented can be further elucidated by drawing on the dynamic reciprocity model. The conventional way of discussing the giving and receiving of love between the divine persons is focused on conceptualizing the act of giving love as the only factor in the event of love. However, all three divine persons not only love themselves but, in logical turn, they are also loved by one another. This means, each divine person is the Lover and Loved simultaneously. The Father is the Lover who actively moves himself to love the Son and Holy Spirit, and they in turn are loved by his love. Simultaneously, the Father is the Loved who is passively moved by his Lovers and their love for him. Similar statements then arise in respect of the Son and Holy Spirit: The Son is the Lover of the Father and Holy Spirit and actively moves himself to love the Father and Holy Spirit, who in turn are both moved by the love of the Son. The Son is also the Loved who is loved by the everlasting love of the Father and Holy Spirit for the Son. The Holy Spirit is the Lover who actively loves the Father and Son. The Holy Spirit is also the Loved who is loved in turn by the Father and Son and thus moved by his Lovers. It is important to note that each divine person has always been both Lover and Loved simultaneously so that he does ever not become *only* the Lover or the Loved: there was never a moment when each person was not loved by the other divine persons.

Thus far, attention has focused on the way in which the active love of one divine person conditions the passive love of another divine person. However, the dynamic reciprocity model takes it a further step. This model suggests that, in eternity, not only can the action be considered to move the passion, but the passion can be considered to move the action; not only can the passion be considered to be moved by the action, but the action can be considered to be moved by the passion. So, for example, the Father's active love moves the Son and Holy Spirit to be loved by him, and the Father's passive love to be loved by the Son and Holy Spirit moves them to love the Father. The Son's passive love to be loved by the Father and Holy Spirit moves them to love the Son as the Son actively loves the Father and Holy Spirit. The Father and Son actively love the Holy Spirit because the Holy Spirit's passive love moves the Father and Son to love him. The Lovers move and are moved by the Loved Ones, the Loved

Ones move and are moved by the Lovers. Each divine person loves the divine others and is loved by them simultaneously. Therefore, each divine person is both a Lover and Loved in these reciprocal relationships.

The first distinctive characteristic of the immanent Trinity has now been described as necessity. The divine persons give their love to each other and receive love from one another eternally and ceaselessly, for such a reciprocity is the essence of each divine person and of the fellowship of the trinitarian persons. What is new to the articulation of this characteristic here is the idea that there is a dynamic interplay at stake between the eternal active and eternal passive movements. The active love can be considered to occur prior and subsequent to the passive love, and vice versa; both the active love and passive love can be considered to condition mutually and be conditioned by each other in harmonious unity. The dynamic reciprocal model can thus serve as a heuristic tool to explore further the eternal fellowship of the triune persons and to demonstrate that both their actions and their passions have equal value and function.

Free and Necessary Reciprocity of Love

The subjects and objects of the necessary reciprocity of love in the immanent Trinity are the Father, Son, and Holy Spirit. The divine persons are free and will to love themselves and the other divine persons actively and to be loved by the others passively. This eternal reciprocity cannot be the self-moving, self-motivating, and self-directing movement of the triune God without this exercise of divine freedom. The freedom of the triune God is grounded in his infinite perfection, self-movement, and self-determination without being limited, conditioned, or constrained by anything or anyone.

The triune God moves himself and is moved by himself completely in his sovereign freedom. Concerning the freedom of God, Highfield explains that "God is free not because he could have been (and can be) other than himself.... God is free because he is himself completely in his action, which is his eternal life. God is free precisely in his 'inability' to contradict himself."[28] As the triune God is the fellowship of love and is completely free in his action and passion, the trinitarian reciprocity is not only necessary but also free movements of the three divine persons, who

---

28. Highfield, *Great Is the Lord*, 174.

are free to act according to their unchanging nature without contradicting themselves. To examine how the immanent Trinity is the reciprocal communion of love not only *necessarily* but also *freely*, particular attention will be given in this section to the work of Frame.[29] Thereafter, the necessary and free reciprocity of the Trinity will be considered through the lens of the dynamic reciprocity model in order to reflect more deeply on the *opera Trinitatis ad intra*.

Frame's program underlines both necessity and freedom as two distinctive characteristics of the intra-trinitarian movement. Necessity, for Frame, is the primary characteristic of the operation of the immanent Trinity. Frame asserts that the three divine persons will to reciprocate their love with one another. At this point, to avoid equating the will that God exercises *ad intra* and the will that God exercises *ad extra*, Frame makes a distinction between "God's necessary will (the will by which the Father begets the Son and the Spirit proceeds from the Father and the Son eternally, the will by which God loves, knows, and communicates within the Trinity) and his free will (the will which decrees and governs the world)."[30] In this way, the triune God loves himself necessarily.

Still, Frame does not interpret the reciprocity of triune love as having the character of necessity only, for the reciprocity of triune love is the nature and inner life of the divine persons who each have their own wills and freedom.[31] He maintains that the triune reciprocity is a free act of the internal divine persons, for the triune God has freedom to act according to his perfect nature[32] and for "all of God's actions [whether *ad intra* or *ad extra*] are equally free."[33] Simultaneously, God's necessary will is not a complete contradiction of his freedom, because the necessary will of God, that by which he wills himself and his own goodness, is free in the sense of spontaneity. As Richard Muller notes, "God's necessary willing is subject to no external compulsion and is, therefore, characterized by

---

29. For others who recognize the free characteristic of the reciprocity of the loving fellowship of the divine persons, see Strong, *Systematic Theology*, 1:326; McCall, *Which Trinity?*, 236; Coppedge, *God Who Is Triune*, 177.

30. Frame, *Doctrine of God*, 236.

31. Frame, *Doctrine of God*, 236.

32. Frame, *Doctrine of God*, 233.

33. Frame, *Doctrine of God*, 233.

freedom of spontaneity."³⁴ Thus, the reciprocity of the triune love is a free and necessary act of the inner trinitarian persons.³⁵

All the eternal actions and passions of the divine persons are carried out with both necessity and freedom. The reciprocity of love of the triune persons is of the nature of each divine person of the Trinity so that they give and receive their divine love necessarily. Frame writes that "since God does not exist without his three persons, the love among those persons is *necessary* to his nature."³⁶ Simultaneously, the Father, Son, and Holy Spirit willingly and freely love one another because they subsist in the unity of their reciprocal love. They fully know their perfect and glorious conditions and engage in the fellowship of love willingly and freely.

However, this does not mean that the free characteristic of the Trinity's movement somehow overrides the necessary aspect of the movement, as if the divine persons could will to break their communion of love. As the triunity of love is their nature, they cannot will to deny themselves and cannot will something contrary to their being. Whatever God wills himself freely *in se* according to his nature, he does so necessarily, for he is already himself and can only will to be himself. Highfield's comment is helpful to understand this dynamic between the free and the necessary characteristics of the reciprocal relations of love of the inner triune persons: "In Trinitarian love we see unity of being and action and of necessity and freedom.... His natural and necessary love is free because God is completely himself in his action of love."³⁷ God's love for

---

34. Muller, *Divine Essence and Attributes*, 559–60. Turretin's understanding of the necessary will also include the connotation of freedom: "For so the things which God wills most necessarily, he wills also freely." Turretin, *Institutes of Elenctic Theology*, 1:219.

35. Barth understands the significance of grasping the necessary and free aspects of the inner operations of the triune God, although he does not speak explicitly of the distinct freedom of each of the trinitarian persons. He remarks that God's "inner union is marked off from the circular course of a natural process as his own free act, an act of majesty ... [I]t is not subject to any necessity." Barth, *Church Dogmatics*, II/1, 345. He adds, "[God] is the One who loves in freedom, the One who is free in his love, and therefore not his own prisoner." Barth, *Church Dogmatics*, IV/1, 186–87. At the same time, Barth wants to affirm the necessary characteristic of the inner relations of the immanent Trinity. Thus, he stresses that the inner fellowship of the triune persons is "the indestructible fellowship between the two [the Father and Son] which is not grounded in choice but in their two-sided existence." Barth, *Church Dogmatics*, I/1, 432.

36. Frame, *Doctrine of God*, 236, emphasis original.

37. Highfield, *Great Is the Lord*, 168.

himself is necessary and free and is "without any possibility of not loving him."[38] Therefore, as the reciprocity of love—both active love and passive love—is the nature of the eternal Trinity and as the three divine persons are free to love themselves and to be loved by one another, the reciprocity of the inner life of the trinitarian persons is not only necessary but also free.

The necessary and free reciprocity of the love of the immanent Trinity explored in this section can be further illuminated by a way of the dynamic reciprocity model. As noted in chapter 1, the active will is defined as the prior will to act, and the passive will is defined as the subsequent will to be acted upon by virtue of the prior will. In the conventional way of considering the divine reciprocity, the active will to love is the only factor in the event of the passive will of receiving love. The Father is the Lover who wills to love the Son and Holy Spirit, and they in turn will to be loved by him. The active will of love of the Son moves the passive will of love of the Father and Holy Spirit, who in turn will to be loved by the Son. The Holy Spirit wills to love the Father and Holy Spirit, who in turn will to be loved by the Son. Only the active will to love causes the passive will to receive love, whereas the passive will does not directly move the active will; and only the passive will to receive love is moved by the active will to love, whereas the active will is not moved by the passive will.

In the dynamic reciprocity model, however, the active wills to love can condition and be conditioned by the passive wills to be loved, which can then in turn be conditioned by and condition the active wills. The Son and Holy Spirit will to be loved by the Father, and in turn the Father wills to love them such that their passive wills move the Father's active will to love them. The active wills of the Son and Holy Spirit move the Father's passive will to be loved by them, and the passive will of the Father moves the Son and Holy Spirit's active will to love the Father. The Holy Spirit's passive will to be loved by the Father and Son move their active wills to love the Holy Spirit, whose active will to love the Father and Son also move their passive wills to be loved him. As each divine person can will actively and passively, the divine wills are dynamically reciprocal.

The ability to consider this reciprocity of the active and the passive wills is a significant point of this present work. The conventional model explains that the divine persons will to love each other and will to be loved by one another. The dynamic reciprocity model goes further: both

---

38. Highfield, *Great Is the Lord*, 173.

the active will to love and the passive will to be loved by the eternal three persons can condition each other. The passive wills of love of the divine persons can be moved by and move the active wills of love of the other divine persons. Likewise, the active wills of love of the divine persons can move and be moved by the passive wills of love of the other triune persons. In this dynamic reciprocity model, then, the active wills and passive wills of the three divine persons mutually condition one another dynamically.

This section has explored two distinct characteristics of the immanent Trinity—necessity and freedom—through reflecting on the reciprocity of love of the inner triune persons. By stressing that the reciprocity of the love of the three divine persons is the nature of each divine person of the Trinity, the reciprocity of love was construed as a necessary operation of the triune persons who cannot deny themselves. However, the inner triune persons also exist in the mode of their reciprocity of love freely, for they are not prisoners of their nature. The dynamic reciprocity model was employed to help to explore further the interplay of the active and passive wills of love of the triune persons that mutually move and are moved by one another.

The Impassibility of the Immanent Trinity

Having explored the movements and relations of the trinitarian persons *ad intra*, our attention now turns to developing the concept that the immanent Trinity is impassible in two ways: it is not moved by the world, and the emotional life of the divine persons of the immanent Trinity is characterized by eternal blessedness.

The Immanent Trinity Is Not Moved by the World

The doctrine of divine impassibility rejects the notion that God is moved by the world. The notion of divine passibility has been associated with time, change, and passion, and has often been considered as an imperfection that would be wrong to attribute to God. With reference to the infinite ontological distinction between the Creator and creatures, impassibilists argue that God's immutability cannot be associated with mutability, that God's timeless eternity cannot be intermixed with time, and that God's pure act cannot be penetrated by passion. These arguments correctly portray the impassibility of the triune God in so far as reference is made to the life of the triune God *ad intra*. That is, the immanent Trinity is not moved by the world.

The inner trinitarian persons are not moved by anything except by the other divine persons. As indicated earlier, the eternal movement of the inner trinitarian persons is the reciprocity of the eternal Father, Son, and Holy Spirit and is thereby exclusively and essentially divine movement. As the three divine persons move themselves and are moved by the other divine persons, they can be moved by divine persons only. While human beings have received the capacity to move themselves and to be moved by one another, they do not have any ontological ability to move the triune persons *ad intra* either directly or by their choices and conditions. Geisler's understanding of God grasps this point: "God can and does act. However, others do not move him, for He is the Unmoved Mover of all else."[39] Divine status is the only qualification to move the triune persons; only divine persons can move themselves actively and passively. Because human beings are not divine ontologically and cannot and do not become divine, the immanent Trinity is not moved by the world and is, in this sense, impassible.

The Eternal Blessedness of the Immanent Trinity

The emotional life of the divine persons of the immanent Trinity is characterized by eternal blessedness. All three divine persons are infinite and absolute and reciprocate their love, joy, and glory with one another. Eternal joy and glory are the expression of the perfection of the fellowship of love of the inner trinitarian persons; the emotional life of the triune God *in se* is fundamentally distinct from his emotional life *ad extra*.

The emotions of the inner trinitarian persons are grounded in their infinite perfection. Richard of Saint Victor articulates how the fullness of happiness of the triune God is connected to his absolute perfections: "Fullness of highest happiness requires fullness of highest joy. Fullness of highest joy requires fullness of highest charity-love. Fullness of highest charity-love demands fullness of absolute perfection."[40] This eternal

---

39. Geisler, *Systematic Theology*, 462.

40. Richard of Saint Victor, *On the Trinity*, 3.21, 134. Edwards concurs with Richard's understanding that God's eternal happiness is closely related to the perfections of the triune God: "When we speak of God's happiness, the account that we are wont to give of it is that God is infinitely happy in the enjoyment of himself, in perfectly

happiness is so deeply founded in the nature of the divine persons of the immanent Trinity that they are completely sufficient and satisfied within themselves and cannot be detached from their happiness. Jonathan Edwards writes that God's "happiness is *in himself*; as his being is necessary and underived, so is his happiness and glory."[41] The triune God, who alone is magnificent and infinite in his perfections, is the source of his own emotional life and can experience the fullest degree of true peace and joy because, as Herman Bavinck correctly estimates, "the degree of blessedness corresponds to the measure of perfection that pertains to a being."[42] To stress this intimate relationship between God's perfection and blessedness, Wayne Grudem even considers blessedness as the corollary or the summary attribute that describes the perfection of the divine attributes: "*God delights fully in himself and in all that reflects his character.*"[43] Thus, if God's blessedness is incomplete or in need of fully becoming, he would be an incomplete and imperfect God and in need of becoming: as Randles writes, "A God of imperfect blessedness were an imperfect God."[44] Correspondingly, the opposite is also the case: God is perfect and God's blessedness is complete. Only the divine persons are responsible for this blessedness. As Bavinck correctly states of God, "He cannot be blessed except in and through himself."[45] Because of the immutable and eternal landscape of the inner emotional life of the Trinity, this eternal and pure blessedness cannot be compromised by and is completely independent from external conditions.

The three divine persons of the immanent Trinity, who have their own feelings and the capacity to affect one another both actively and passively, reciprocate dynamically their eternal blessedness with one another both necessarily and freely. As blessedness is rooted in the perfect nature of the divine three persons, they are eternally joyous necessarily. The three divine persons are moved by the joy of the other divine persons and experience joy in response eternally. The Father shares his blessedness with the Son and Holy Spirit, and in turn the Son and Holy Spirit are affected by the Father's blessedness. The Son is conditioned by the

---

beholding and infinitely loving, and rejoicing in, his own essence and perfections." Edwards, *Works of Jonathan Edwards*, 21:118.

41. Edwards, *Works of Jonathan Edwards*, 25:662–63, emphasis original.
42. Bavinck, *Doctrine of God*, 248.
43. Grudem, *Systematic Theology*, 218, emphasis original.
44. Randles, *Blessed God*, 43.
45. Bavinck, *Doctrine of God*, 227.

joy of the Father and Holy Spirit, and they share their joy with the Son. Likewise, the Son actively shares his joy with the Father and Holy Spirit, and they are conditioned by the joy the Son. The Father and Son actively share their happiness with the Holy Spirit because the passive affection of the Holy Spirit moves the Father and Son to share their happiness with him. Simultaneously, the Son and Holy Spirit are affected by the Father passively, and in turn the Father shares his joy with them. Furthermore, the divine persons reciprocate their happiness with each other and are affected by the happiness of the other divine persons in accordance with their divine wills and freedom. In this way, as the three divine persons share their blessedness, they are moved by the perfect joy of the divine others both necessarily and freely.

Eternal joy and glory are the expressions of the reciprocity of love of the three divine persons. The reciprocal love leads to eternal joy, as it is the joy of the inner trinitarian persons to reciprocate their love with the other divine persons who are infinitely perfect and therefore most worthy to deserve their holy and glorious love. Vanhoozer describes the inner fellowship of the love of the Trinity as "the eternal delight of the dialogical dance of call, response, acknowledgment, and affirmation,"[46] and Leonardo Boff considers it "the ecstasy of love."[47] In the divine life, the degree of the perfection determines the degree of the happiness of the fellowship of love. The intra-trinitarian love is the eternal fountain of the impassible joy and the embodiment of the perfect fellowship of the three divine persons. No deviation or fluctuation of the eternal joy occurs within the fellowship, for—in Lister's terms—there is "only the perfectly pitched ontology of love, glory, holiness, and intra-Trinitarian delight."[48] There can be no other emotional expression of this fellowship of the love of the inner divine persons than joy. David Hart offers the following insight against the view that the joy and peace of the inner trinitarian persons can be intermixed with suffering: "[God's] love is an infinite peace and so needs no violence to shape it, no death over which to triumph."[49] As such, God's supreme happiness and the triune communion of love cannot be separated from each other.[50]

46. Vanhoozer, *Remythologizing Theology*, 258–59.
47. Boff, *Trinity and Society*, 218.
48. Lister, *God Is Impassible*, 176.
49. Hart, *Beauty of the Infinite*, 167.
50. Richard of Saint Victor, *On the Trinity*, 3:3, 118.

In a similar manner, the reciprocal love of the Trinity leads to eternal glory. Only the one who is infinitely absolute and praiseworthy can glorify himself to the fullest degree and deserves to be glorified. In God, this takes place as he exercises the divine attributes. Vladimir Lossky explains this relationship between God and glory in detail: "God has from all eternity enjoyed the sublimity of his glory.... His glory is the revelation, the manifestation, the reflection, the garment of his inner perfection.... In this glory, uniquely proper to himself, God dwells in perfect felicity above all glory, without having need of any witness, without admitting of any division."[51] All three divine persons glorify themselves and are glorified by one another. Highfield insists that all the activities of the triune God are glorious: "God manifests his glory in all his actions. His love is great, magnificent, and excellent; hence his loving actions are glorious. His mercy, righteousness, grace, and patience are equally great, excellent, and glorious. His acts of power, knowledge, and presence manifest his greatness and thus are glorious."[52] Nothing short of the triune glory can be part of this communion of the divine persons of the immanent Trinity. In their reciprocity of love, the Father, Son, and Holy Spirit express nothing but joy and glory to each other, being moved by the beauty and greatness of the other divine persons.

The inner trinitarian persons exist in eternal blessedness and reciprocate their love, blessedness, and glory with one another mutually and immutably without any room or need to be affected, influenced, or enhanced, by any external condition or movement. The degree and condition of the emotional life of the immanent Trinity is determined by the perfection of the attributes, happiness, and reciprocity of the triune persons. Anything less than his holiness and glory cannot be part of the eternal blessedness. This is why the triune God is fully satisfied and sufficient within himself, existing in perfect blessedness without any need or deficit.

Two Contrasting Points

The picture of the emotional life of the inner trinitarian persons that this present work has presented thus far in this chapter contrasts with the way in which Moltmann tends to depict the eternal life of the immanent

51. Lossky, *Mystical Theology*, 75.
52. Highfield, *Great Is the Lord*, 391–92.

Trinity. At least two contrasting points between this work and Moltmann's position might be observed briefly. First, while this chapter has posited that the immanent Trinity is eternally joyous, Moltmann argues that the triune God is in the process of overcoming his eternal suffering through his external operations in creation.[53] Second, while this chapter has posited that the inner trinitarian life is not influenced by any external event, Moltmann asserts that because the triune event of the cross determines the life of the triune God both *in se* and *ad extra*, sustaining the distinction between the immanent and economic Trinity is not for him a necessary theological task. These points of contrast will now be examined in turn.

The first contrasting point is that Moltmann asserts that an eternally suffering God achieves his final and complete blessedness through a process of works *ad extra*. As noted in chapter 2, Moltmann believes that within the emotional life of the immanent Trinity both joy and pain coexist simultaneously from eternity. Moltmann also asserts that the emotions of the inner divine persons can be affected by external events. He notes, "The pain of the cross determines the inner life of the triune God from eternity to eternity. If that is true, then the joy of responsive love in glorification through the Spirit determines the inner life of the triune God from eternity and eternity too."[54] Of course, God does not remain in his pain eternally, for the eternal joy of the immanent Trinity is accomplished through the works of the economic Trinity, through "the history of the Spirit [that] moulds the inner life of the triune God through the joy of liberated creation when it is united with God."[55] The eternal suffering love that shapes the life of the triune God from eternity to eternity reaches "its fulfilment in the love that is bliss,"[56] which is accomplished when human beings are liberated from their affliction. In other words, Moltmann explains that "the deliverance or redemption of the world is bound up with the self-deliverance of God from his sufferings."[57] He adds, "The economic Trinity completes and perfects itself to the immanent Trinity when the history and experience of salvation are completed

---

53. Moltmann, *Crucified God*, 228–34.
54. Moltmann, *Trinity and the Kingdom*, 161.
55. Moltmann, *Trinity and the Kingdom*, 161.
56. Moltmann, *Trinity and the Kingdom*, 60.
57. Moltmann, *Trinity and the Kingdom*, 60.

and perfected."[58] The fulfillment of God's joy and the liberation of human beings from suffering are interdependent events; the latter is the only way in which God can deliver himself from his incompleteness and enjoy the joy of the eternal sabbath.

The effect of Moltmann's approach is that it undermines the richness and self-sufficiency of the life of the inner triune persons. If the eternal serenity of the immanent Trinity were dependent on the completion of the Trinity's redemptive operation in the world, God's invitation into a fellowship of love and blessedness could be construed as an invitation into the deficiency characteristic of the inner life of God. In Moltmann's program, God's deficiency or incompleteness is overcome only when his eternal suffering love moves out of the immanent Trinity's fellowship of love and heals the brokenness of human suffering through the Trinity's own suffering. To borrow the words of Storr, such a version of God "is in danger of defeat unless man comes to his assistance."[59] Don Schweitzer is thus correct to observe that Moltmann's concept of God's invitation and love is "to fulfil what is lacking within the divine life" and that there is "a deficiency in the divine being that makes creation and redemption necessary for God to experience fulfilment and peace."[60] In addition, it can be argued that to eternalize suffering in the way that Moltmann does is to divinize suffering and horror.[61] In contrast to Moltmann's claim that the economic Trinity completes the immanent Trinity, this publication argues that the inner life of the immanent Trinity is already a communion of eternal joy and peace without a hint of suffering and sorrow, and is therefore not in any way dependent on the temporal experiences of subordinate and sinful creatures. As Strong affirms, "the existence of the universe is not necessary to his serenity and joy."[62]

Against Moltmann's view that God is dependent on the world, Vanhoozer asserts that such a God "ceases to be worthy of worship."[63] The inner divine life does not need a process of becoming for realization or completion, for as Lossky states, "There is no interior process in the Godhead; no 'dialectic' of the three persons; no becoming; no 'tragedy

---

58. Moltmann, *Trinity and the Kingdom*, 161.

59. Storr, *Problem of the Cross*, 125.

60. Schweitzer, "Aspects of God's Relationship," 8.

61. Horton, *Christian Faith*, 247.

62. Strong, *Systematic Theology*, 1:265.

63. Vanhoozer, *Remythologizing Theology*, 458; Long, "Aquinas on God's Sovereignty," 184.

in the Absolute."'[64] By contrast, the triune God is completely sufficient *in se* and the ultimate ground of all creaturely actualizations.[65] If the Trinity's communion of love is not in itself sufficient, then it is not clear how interaction with non-divine beings, who are sinful and finite and lack the divine attributes, can truly complete or perfect the existing communion of the Trinity. Therefore, the emotional life of the immanent Trinity is already complete without room for any process of development.

Moltmann, along with the late nineteenth and early twentieth centuries' passibilists, might reply that the notion of the eternal suffering of the Son is a biblical doctrine, citing Revelation 13:8: "all whose names have not been written in the Lamb's book of life, the Lamb who was slain from the creation of the world."[66] However, the interpretation of this text is still debated in contemporary theology, and two common options might be noted here briefly. The first option is to interpret the text as the revelation of God's eternal plan to provide redemptive atonement in Jesus Christ before the foundation of the world. Against passibilists, Mozley argues that the phrase, "the Lamb that was slain from the creation of the world," should be viewed "as implying something which has been part of God's eternal purpose" but not "as an eternal truth."[67] What has occurred temporally cannot be transferred to eternity.[68] The second option is to use the prepositional phrase, "from the creation of the world," to modify "the written names in the book of life," which would mean that the names were written from the creation of the world, not that the Lamb was slain from the creation of the world. Charles claims that the phrase "is by almost all scholars [of the late nineteenth and early twentieth centuries] connected with γέγραπται [written] as in xvii.8."[69] In Revelation 17:8, the phrase "from the creation of the world," modifies "the written names in the book of life." These two options are more theologically balanced in

---

64. Lossky, *Theology of the Eastern Church*, 45.

65. Barth, *Church Dogmatics*, IV/2, 113.

66. Moltmann, *Kingdom and the Trinity*, 159; Morgan, *Bible and the Cross*, 58; Ohlrich, *Suffering God*, 50.

67. Mozley, *Doctrine of the Atonement*, 90.

68. Mozley, *Impassibility of God*, 183.

69. Charles, "Critical and Exegetical Commentary on the Revelation of St. John," 1:354. Mozley similarly comments that this option was the common way of interpreting the text in his days, though does not provide any references. Mozley, *Doctrine of the Atonement*, 91.

the context of the whole salvific story of the triune God than Moltmann's literal interpretation of the text.[70]

The second contrasting point between the argument of this present work and Moltmann concerns the way in which his work collapses the distinction between the immanent and economic Trinity. Moltmann observes that this distinction limits him from understanding the meaning of the cross for God himself. Moltmann writes that "to grasp the death of the Son in its significance for God himself, I found myself bound to surrender the traditional distinction between the immanent and the economic Trinity, according to which the cross comes to stand only in the economy of salvation, but not within the immanent Trinity."[71]

By contrast, according to Moltmann, the event of the cross serves as the determining factor for both the economic and the immanent Trinity so that the life of the triune God *in se* and *ad extra* is indistinguishable. In this line of thinking, it is only natural for Moltmann to state, "The pain of the cross determines the inner life of the triune God from eternity to eternity. If that is true, then the joy of responsive love in glorification through the Spirit determines the inner life of the triune God from eternity to and eternity too."[72] Moltmann believes that the economic Trinity reveals the immanent Trinity and "has a retroactive effect on it."[73] The suffering on the cross of the triune God in particular and the work of the economic Trinity in general therefore cannot *not* affect the immanent Trinity. As noted above, God's relationship with the world completes the reality of the life of the immanent Trinity.[74] In this way, Moltmann accepts to the fullest possible degree Rahner's axiom that "the economic Trinity is the immanent Trinity, and vice versa."[75]

However, in the view of this work, the effect of collapsing the distinction between the immanent and economic Trinity jeopardizes the self-identity of the triune God.[76] If the economic Trinity is indistinguish-

---

70. Aune and Blount are two other scholars who choose this interpretive option. Aune, *Revelation 6–16*, 746; Blount, *Revelation*, 252.

71. Moltmann, *Trinity and the Kingdom*, 160.

72. Moltmann, *Trinity and the Kingdom*, 161.

73. Moltmann, *Trinity and the Kingdom*, 160.

74. Moltmann, *Trinity and the Kingdom*, 161.

75. Moltmann, *Trinity and the Kingdom*, 160; for Rahner's axiom, see Rahner, *Trinity*, 22.

76. For other theologians who maintain the immanent and economic distinction, see Sanders, "Entangled in the Trinity"; Baik, *Holy Trinity*, 188–89; Gunton, preface

able from the immanent Trinity, the identity of the triune God would be determined by the sinful and imperfect conditions of fallen human beings.[77] Highfield suggests that along these lines "God's life and the world process become intertwined in a way that resembles pantheism."[78] By contrast, however, as God is self-moving, self-motivating, and self-sufficient, his immanent identity is a self-defined identity that is not dependent on the economic Trinity. In this sense, Hart notes, "If the identity of the immanent Trinity with the economic is taken to mean that history is the theatre within which God . . . finds or determines himself as God, there can be no way of convincingly avoiding the conclusion . . . that God depends upon creation to be God . . . so that God is robbed of his true transcendence."[79]

In other words, when the identity of the immanent Trinity is shaped by the world, the mystery of the inner life of the divine persons becomes a merely historical reality.[80] Yet, the position of this work is that the inner life of the divine persons contains the unfathomable mystery aspect that is beyond the reach of finite beings. Veli-Matti Kärkkäinen correctly warns of the danger that "we claim to know more about the inner life of God than we indeed do. . . . There is still the unknown, as the apophatic

---

to *Promise of Trinitarian Theology*, xvii–xix. Not all theologians believe that maintaining the immanent and economic distinction is a necessary theological task. For those theologians, see Wiles, "Some Reflections on the Origins of the Doctrine of the Trinity," 92; Richardson, *Doctrine of the Trinity*, 148; LaCugna, *God for Us*, 228.

77. Hart, "No Shadow of Turning," 191. Torrance stresses the same point, writing: "[W]e cannot think of the ontological Trinity as if it were constituted by or dependent on the economic Trinity, but must rather think of the economic Trinity as the freely predetermined manifestation in the history of salvation of the eternal Trinity which God himself was before the foundation of the world, and eternally is." Torrance, *Christian Doctrine of God*, 108–9.

78. Highfield, *Great Is the Lord*, 124.

79. Hart, *Beauty of the Infinite*, 157.

80. Transforming this mystery of God *in se* into the history of the revelation of the cross is the very purpose of Moltmann's project. Moltmann argues, "Anyone who really talks of the Trinity talks of the cross of Jesus and does not speculate in heavenly riddles" and adds, "We cannot say of God who he is of himself and in himself; we can only say who he is for us in the history of Christ which reaches us in our history. Nor can we achieve it in the forms of modern thought which are so related to experience and practice . . . [W]e would have to give up the distinction made in the early church and in tradition between the 'God in himself' and the 'God for us,' or between 'God in his majesty' and 'God veiled in the flesh of Christ.'" Moltmann, *Crucified God*, 207; 238–39.

tradition, both Eastern and Western, has always emphasized."[81] To collapse the distinction between God *in se* and God *pro nobis* may be to reduce the incomprehensible majesty and beauty of the triune God to the level of human limitation and to an object of understanding, not an object of faith.[82] Therefore, sustaining the distinction between the immanent and economic Trinity is a necessary theological task because without the immanent Trinity, only understanding remains without room for mystery and miracle.

The economic Trinity should certainly be interpreted as the epistemological ground of the knowledge of the life of the immanent Trinity, but not in such a way as to provide comprehensive knowledge of the three divine persons in their eternity. Grenz notes, "If the twentieth-century conversation reached any point of consensus regarding this issue, it is that any truly helpful explication of the doctrine of the Trinity must give epistemological priority to the presence of the trinitarian members in the divine economy but reserve ontological primacy for the dynamic of their relationality within the triune life."[83] Not every element of God's external operation, such as God's involvement in the suffering of Jesus Christ, can be legitimately read back into the life of the immanent Trinity.[84] Paul Molnar agrees: "what God is in time does not define who God is in eternity, even by way of anticipation."[85] In this trajectory of thought, Webster helpfully illuminates the dynamics between God *in se* and God *pro nobis*:

> [The coherence between God in himself and his outer works]
> can best be accomplished by first contemplating the infinite

---

81. Kärkkäinen, *Trinity Global Perspective*, 392.

82. In addition, Castelo believes that the immanent Trinity provides "the conceptual space for doctrinal articulations and theological safeguards that are not as clearly presented in specific passages of Scripture, including the case for the crucifixion." Castelo, *Apathetic God*, 95.

83. Grenz, *Rediscovering the Triune God*, 222. Boff emphasizes the mystery of God's life *in se* and states that this mystery "will be partially revealed to us in the bliss of eternal life" and that "not the whole of the immanent Trinity is the economic Trinity." Boff, *Trinity and Society*, 215.

84. Torrance, *Christian Doctrine of God*, 199. Torrance rejects reading every aspect of the economy back into the immanent Trinity in order to avoid subordinating the Son to the Father: "the subjection of Christ to the Father in his incarnate economy as the suffering and obedient Servant cannot be read back into the eternal hypostatic relations and distinctions subsisting in the Holy Trinity." Torrance, *Christian Doctrine of God*, 180.

85. Molnar, *Faith, Freedom and the Spirit*, 182.

depth of God in himself, out of which his temporal acts arise. The divine agent of revelatory acts is not fully understood if the phenomenality of those acts is treated as something primordial, a wholly sufficient presentation of the agent. God's outer works bear a surplus within themselves; they refer back to the divine agent who exceeds them.[86]

The distinction between the immanent and economic Trinity must be made because the distinction between God and human beings exists eternally: The Father, Son, and Holy Spirit, who subsist eternally in the fellowship of love, blessedness, and glory, are not eternally the Creator, Redeemer, and Sanctifier. Therefore, the economic Trinity should be considered, primarily, as the epistemological ground of knowledge of the mystery of the immanent Trinity.

In sum, the triune God *ad intra*, who moves himself and is moved by himself, is impossible in the sense that he is not moved by anything but himself and exists in eternal blessedness within himself. As the degree of the infinite perfection of God determines the degree of his happiness in his eternal life and as God is infinitely perfect, the divine life *in se* involves the greatest possible delight, an overflowing fountain of happiness without fluctuation or deviation. The three divine persons express their communion of love with eternal joy and exist in the reciprocity of blessedness necessarily and freely. Therefore, within the life of the inner trinitarian persons, suffering cannot be part of the emotional state of the inner trinitarian persons. If suffering were part of the immanent Trinity, it could jeopardize the consistent identity of the triune God, minimize the sufficiency and completeness of the inner life of the Trinity and dissolve the immanent Trinity into the economic Trinity.

---

86. Webster, *God without Measure*, 1:8.

6

The Economic Trinity Is Passible

The three divine persons of the economic Trinity move themselves both so as to move towards the world and so as to be moved by the world voluntarily. Thus, they chose to be able to suffer with human creatures actively and experience that suffering with them passively. A detailed discussion of the economic Trinity requires a description both of the identities and natures of the three divine persons and of the way in which the three eternal persons of the immanent Trinity move to engage in personal relationships with created and sinful beings.

This chapter will draw on three insights from the previous chapter to describe the possibility of the economic Trinity. First, it draws on the insight regarding the self-movement of the inner trinitarian persons in order to explore how the triune God, who is impassible within himself, moves himself to move the world and to be moved by it, and how he thereby undergoes suffering freely. Second, it draws on the insight regarding the characteristics of the immanent Trinity in order to contrast these with the characteristics of the economic Trinity. In the last chapter, it was shown that *necessity* and *freedom* are the distinctive characteristics of the operations of the immanent Trinity; this chapter considers how these characteristics differ in the operations of the economic Trinity. Third, this chapter draws on the insight of the dynamic reciprocity model as it was applied to the immanent Trinity in order to explore the movements of the three persons of the economic Trinity, and to shed new light on the ways in which they engage with the economy in general and the event of the cross specifically.

The Self-Movement of the Economic Trinity

The doctrine of divine (im)passibility asks whether God is moved by the world, and if so, how he is moved by the world. In responding to these questions, the previous chapter explored how the triune God moves himself actively and passively *ad intra* and argued that because the inner trinitarian persons are moved only by the other divine persons, they are not moved by the world. Drawing on this understanding of the self-movement of the triune God and supplementing this with insights from the dynamic reciprocity model, we will now explore how the three divine persons move themselves to engage with the world in their roles as Creator, Redeemer, and Sanctifier, and how they move themselves to move the world actively, and to be moved by it passively so as to engage in their operations *ad extra*.

The three persons of the economic Trinity, according to their wills and freedom, choose to engage in salvation history together as the Creator, Redeemer, and Sanctifier. Their economic actions and passions occur in the historical realm. This means that—unlike in the case of their actions and passions in eternity that were considered in chapter 5—there is a logical and chronological priority of action over passion. Nonetheless, each of the three divine persons of the economic Trinity resolves both to move himself and to be moved by the other divine persons freely. Hasker observes that each divine person can propose and will specific actions in the economy: "First, it must be possible that one of the trinitarian persons in effect 'proposes' some action for consideration. That is to say, one person can initiate such a 'proposal' by himself; this does not need to be done by the entire Trinity acting together."[1] Erickson affirms the distinct will of each of the three persons and suggests that "the person of the Trinity who became incarnate and thus also took upon himself the responsibility of dying an atoning death did so voluntarily, in conjunction with the decision of the other two persons. . . . It was the will in which the Son had participated, in the original decision."[2] All three divine persons in agreement engage in the roles of the Creator, Redeemer, and Sanctifier.

Building on these claims, and drawing on the dynamic reciprocity model, it can be suggested that the three divine persons will to move themselves and will to be moved by the other divine persons. The Father

---

1. Hasker, *Tri-Personal God*, 208. He adds that the proposals of the divine persons could be rejected by the other divine persons. Hasker, *Tri-Personal God*, 208.

2. Erickson, *God in Three Persons*, 309–10.

wills to be the Creator of the universe and is moved by the Son and Holy Spirit, who also both will the Father to be the Creator. The Son wills to be the Redeemer of created beings and is moved by the Father and Holy Spirit, who also both will the Son to redeem his creatures through his self-sacrifice. The Holy Spirit wills to be God's agent of reconciliation in the broken world and is moved by the wills of the Father and Son, who also both will the Holy Spirit to take the economic role of the Sanctifier.[3] All three persons are fully intentional and committed to their own roles as they are mutually moved by one another in perfect conjunction.[4]

The three divine persons of the economic Trinity, who are free to move themselves *ad intra* and *ad extra*, thus move themselves and each other to move towards the world and to be moved by it. As previously explained, the trinitarian persons *ad intra* are not moved by the world because they can be moved only by the divine others and because creaturely beings ontologically have no intrinsic power to move the triune God. Crucially, however, this view does not prevent the self-moving God to move himself as he wills, directs, and determines: the impassibility of God does not mean that he cannot be moved by himself. Barth helpfully suggests that God, who "cannot be moved from outside by an extraneous power," is capable of moving himself and is "moved and touched by Himself . . . in the full scope of God's own personal freedom."[5] Nothing except the three divine persons can move themselves to engage in external activities with human beings—but they move themselves to move towards the world and allow themselves to be moved by the world. Horton suggests that God is not moved by the world and yet affirms that "God is affected by us but is not determined in his being, will, nor actions by us. God freely allows us to affect him."[6]

---

3. Erickson, *God in Three Persons*, 310. Erickson affirms a distinct role of the Holy Spirit, namely "calling to remembrance the words of Jesus, directing persons' thinking toward him, and glorifying him," and concurs that the Holy Spirit fully participates in the decision-making process without simply submitting to the Father and Son. It is important to note that Erickson's proposal that all three divine persons are fully involved in the process of choosing their economic functions is motivated by his stress on the three distinct wills of the triune persons and by his attempt to avoid any notion of the subordination of the Son and Spirit. Erickson, *God in Three Persons*, 309–10.

4. In this way, even though the divine three persons propose their own desires, they are in agreement with one another, contrary to Hasker's claim.

5. Barth, *Church Dogmatics*, II/1, 370.

6. Horton, *Christian Faith*, 249.

Thus, while the triune God is fully relational and complete within himself, the fullness of God does not limit God's freedom and capability to move towards his human creatures (in temporal action) and to be moved by them (in temporal passion). God himself is the ground of his own self-movement and is capable of reciprocity *ad intra* and *ad extra*. This understanding of the self-moving God still recognizes the ontological distinction between the Creator and creation and stresses the sovereign freedom of God, yet it also acknowledges the way in which God can move himself to move the world and to be moved by it without compromising his infinite and eternal perfections.

The triune God is the Subject of all of his actions and passions, whether eternal or temporal, thus if God is perfect, all of his actions and passions are equally perfect. As suggested in chapter 5, it is critical to avoid making the mistake of interpreting divine passions through negative conceptions of human passions. For human beings, as actions condition and precede passions, "all passions are [considered as] finite, dependent, time bound, and mutable states of being."[7] But, this negative view of passion does not apply to God's passion. Likewise, the human presumption that actions are superior to passions is not true of divine actions and passions, because God chooses both to act upon and be acted upon by human conditions and choices, so that divine action has no special effect, status, or privilege over divine passion.

This section has explored how the triune God engages in his redemptive operations—how he moves the world actively and is moved by the world passively. It first used the dynamic reciprocity model to discuss how the three divine persons choose to be the Creator, Redeemer, and Sanctifier, showing that all three divine persons are involved with the process of choosing their economic roles. Then it explored how the self-moving God moves himself to move towards the world and to be moved by it. Both God's actions and passions were considered as the outcome of God's sovereign freedom, thereby indicating that God's passion is not a necessary movement or simply a fulfillment of God's relational nature (against the passibilists), and that action and passion are divine movements without construing passion as a negative conception and viewing action as intrinsically superior (against the impassibilists). The triune God determines his own movement *ad extra* and is the Lord of his own temporal action and passion in his sovereign freedom over the world.

---

7. Dolezal, "Strong Impassibility," 16.

The Characteristics of the Operations of the Economic Trinity

Karl Rahner's axiom that the immanent Trinity is the economic Trinity, and vice versa,[8] seems an accurate description in so far as the three persons of the immanent Trinity are the same three persons who are engaged in personal relationships with the world. That said, different characteristics among the movement of the persons as considered *ad intra* and the movement of the divine persons in the economy, relating to the ontological differences between divine beings and non-divine beings.

A number of writers have sought to express this difference. Frame, for example, writes, "There is a difference between what God is necessarily [the immanent Trinity] and what he freely chooses to do in his plan for creation [the economic Trinity]."[9] Meanwhile, Lister suggests that "though God's actions in the economy are all expressions and manifestations of his essential being and character, God's action in eternity is not identical in every respect to his action in the economy, because in eternity past, God was not engaged with a finite and fallen creation."[10]

In the preceding chapter, it was argued that the movements of the three divine persons of the immanent Trinity have two primary characteristics: necessity and freedom. In this chapter, it is suggested that the primary characteristics of the operations of the economic Trinity are God's freedom and his creative, redemptive, and sanctifying love for the world. The next section explores the two distinctions between the characteristics of the immanent and economic Trinity in their operations, and posits that divine passibility is God's freely chosen expression of his love for the world.

Free Operations of the Economic Trinity

The first distinct characteristic between the operations of the immanent and economic Trinity is that the movements of the economic Trinity are free movements. The condition that describes the necessary mode of the reciprocity of the inner life of the Trinity—that each divine person must be part of the fellowship of love and the indwelling relationship with the

---

8. Rahner, *Trinity*, 22
9. Frame, *Doctrine of God*, 707.
10. Lister, *God Is Impassible*, 247; Ware raises the same concern. Ware, "How Shall We Think About the Trinity?," 258–59.

other divine persons—is not the same in the case of the economic Trinity. As will be seen, the difference results from the fact that the world has never been a part of the reciprocity of love of the immanent Trinity, and thus necessity does not arise in the same way in the case of the movements of the Trinity in the economy. Correspondingly, the modes of the life of the immanent Trinity (necessity and freedom) reduce to just one—freedom—in respect of the way in which the triune God interacts with the world. The characteristic of the economic Trinity is thus freedom without necessity because God, who is a free and necessary Being, freely creates and interacts with human beings, who are ontologically contingent and dependent on him. Each of these claims will now be explored in greater detail.

The first characteristic of the economic Trinity is that all of God's movements *ad extra* are free movements. The condition that shapes the necessity of the reciprocity of the inner life of the triune God is irrelevant to the mode of his interaction with non-divine beings. The former condition is that the fellowship of love of the Father, Son, and Holy Spirit is simply the nature of each divine person. This essential triune love defines the necessary condition of the immanent Trinity. However, this is not the case for human beings. They were created to participate in the triune fellowship of love, not with the nature of the triune love. Also, the three divine persons indwell one another ontologically. Torrance notes, "[The divine persons] coinhere in one Another by virtue of their one Being for one Another and by virtue of the dynamic Communion which they constitute in their belonging to one Another."[11] The Creator and the creation do not dwell in one another in this way, however, even though proponents of panentheism may speak otherwise.[12] The Scriptures state that God made human beings in his own image and that Jesus prayed that believers may be one with him as the Father, Son, and Holy Spirit are one in the unity of communion (John 17:21). The fellowship of believers with the triune God is thus the result of salvation history, not a necessary ontological state. Unlike the mode of the inter-trinitarian relationships, therefore, the mode of God's external relationships is not one of necessity.

Besides, as noted previously, the immanent Trinity is the self-movement of the inner divine persons, who are the only subjects and objects of their movements. In the communion of love of God the Father, God

11. Torrance, *Christian Doctrine of God*, 133.

12. For panentheists, see Jantzen, *God's World, God's Body*; McFague, *Body of God*; Moltmann, *God in Creation*.

the Son, and God the Holy Spirit, there is immutable and ceaseless movement.[13] Only the triune persons can move themselves in these eternal and unchanging movements, and each of these persons is fully divine. In God's relationship with non-divine beings, however, the dynamics are utterly different. The world has never been part of the triune movement and is not qualified of itself to participate in the inner trinitarian life. Thus, the world cannot move God and cannot be moved by him necessarily, unless God freely wills to move the world and to be moved by the world in a certain way, for God himself is alone the ground of his inner and external movements.[14]

Another reason why the mode of the movements of the economic Trinity is freedom is that the necessary characteristic of the will and movement of the persons of the immanent Trinity does not remain the same in the economic operations of the Trinity. What the triune God wills and moves towards himself has the characteristics of necessity and freedom, but what he wills and moves towards the world has the characteristic of freedom only. This is because of the nature of the objects of God's willing and acting in the economy.

The ontological distinction between the divine as necessary and independent, and the non-divine as contingent and dependent led the Reformers and their followers, such as Francis Turretin,[15] Edward Leigh,[16] and John Frame,[17] to posit that God wills all actions related to himself necessarily and freely, but wills all action related to the world only freely.[18] The transition from necessity and freedom to freedom alone takes place because the triune God, as the one necessary and free Being, freely made human beings. Even without the creation, God, being independent from the world and self-existent, would still be God.[19] Thus all the external operations of the Trinity that are connected with creation and redemption have the characteristic of freedom.

---

13. Meerson, *Trinity of Love*, 177.
14. Schleiermacher, *Christian Faith*, 219.
15. Turretin, *Institutes of Elenctic Theology*, 1:219.
16. Leigh, *Treatise of Divinity*, 2:67.
17. Frame, *Doctrine of God*, 236.
18. Muller, *Divine Essence and Attributes*, 453; Other theologians offer similar observations in reference to God's necessary and free willing such as Webster, *God without Measure*, 34–35; Berkhof, *Systematic Theology*, 78.
19. Barth, *Church Dogmatics*, I/1, 434–44.

In the absence of the necessity that governs the reciprocity of the immanent Trinity, the movements of the economic Trinity are free and unconditioned movements. The triune God moves himself and is moved by himself only; however, created beings cannot move God unless God first moves himself and allows himself to be moved by them. All God's movements *ad extra* are therefore determined and executed by the triune God in sovereign freedom.

God's Creative, Redemptive, and Sanctifying Love for the World

The second distinct characteristic of the operation of the economic Trinity is that just as God loves himself with his love for himself, he loves the world with his creative, redemptive, and sanctifying love. The sphere of divine love now includes not only purely divine relationships with the other divine persons, who are the perfect subjects and objects of their eternal fellowship of love, but also relationships with objects of the divine love that are not only created but also fallen. Here, the distinction between God's love for himself and his love for the world is important—not to separate them into two different kinds of love, but to demonstrate that God's love can be communicated in different types and expressions according to the different conditions of the objects of his divine and holy love.[20]

As previously discussed, eternal blessedness is the necessary and free expression of the fellowship of love of the inner-trinitarian persons; however, this dynamic changes in God's relationship with human beings and in his expression of his love for them. In what follows, this distinction is explored more fully, before three modes of the divine love towards the world are considered. This section concludes that divine suffering is the free expression of God's love for the world.

The inner trinitarian love is the most beautiful and perfect form of love, because of the conditions of the subjects and objects of their fellowship of love. As the last chapter explained, the life of the immanent Trinity is the interaction of the love of the three divine persons, who as perfect subjects can fully love the objects of their actions and as perfect objects, can fully receive the divine love bestowed upon them. The perfect form of the reciprocal love requires the most worthy and supreme subjects and

---

20. Clarke, *Christian Doctrine of God*, 98.

objects, nothing less.²¹ Julius Müller, defending the doctrine of divine aseity, asserts that "God has in himself the eternal and wholly adequate object of his love, independently of his relation to the world."²² Hasker holds, "Perfect love requires for its fulfilment a perfect object, which can only be another divine person."²³ Others such as Strong and Barth similarly posit that the intra-trinitarian love necessitates none other than that God be the object of the everlasting and absolute divine love.²⁴

The dynamic of God's relationship with the new objects of his love changes in his redemptive economy. Leigh and Turretin define God's willingness to love himself as the chief and first good and his willingness to love creation as the secondary and subordinate good. Because God first loves himself and then loves the world, men and women "become subordinate objects of that love."²⁵ Strong makes a similar distinction between God's love for himself as immanent love and his love for the world as relative love.²⁶ Nevertheless, the love of the triune God for the world is not a deficient form of love, for all God's actions—internal and external—are perfect as they manifest the same holy love of the same triune God.

The additional complicating factor in turning to an external object of the divine love is that the recipients of divine love in the divine economy are not simply created and finite, but also sinful and unrighteous. Strong describes the relative love of God as mercy in its relationship to the disobedient, highlighting mercy as the "eternal principle of God's nature which leads him to seek the temporal good and eternal salvation of those who have opposed themselves to his will, even at the cost of infinite self-sacrifice."²⁷ The conditions of recipients of God's love are not without significance, for his love is not a love without any foundation or standard.

With this context in mind, three dimensions of God's love towards the world can be observed.²⁸ First, God's love for the world is his free

21. Richard of Saint Victor, *On the Trinity*, 3.7, 121.
22. Müller, *Christian Doctrine of Sin*, 2:136.
23. Hasker, *Tri-Personal God*, 220–21
24. Strong agrees, "The only sufficient object of his love is the image of his own perfections [holiness], for that alone is equal to himself." Strong, *Systematic Theology*, 1:266; Barth posits that "God is sufficient in Himself as object and therefore as object of His love." Barth, *Church Dogmatics*, II/1, 280.
25. Strong, *Systematic Theology*, 1:290.
26. Strong, *Systematic Theology*, 1:249.
27. Strong, *Systematic Theology*, 1:289.
28. Other theologians distinguish the various dimensions of God's love differently.

love to non-divine beings. As noted above, the first characteristic of the economic Trinity is freedom; all divine movement towards the world is carried out freely, and Scripture calls this "grace" (Eph 2:8). Frame attests, "The very idea of grace is that God is not required to give it. If God is required, even by his own nature, to give grace to us, then we have a certain claim on him. But grace excludes such claims."[29] God is not obligated to love non-divine beings and freely chooses to love the world.

The second dimension of God's love toward the world is his creative love, which is encompassing of all that he has made. God, who is love, loves all human persons. Every human being is the image of God and is created from God's goodness. Jack Cottrell provides a helpful description of this creative aspect of God's love for the world: "His self-giving affection for his image-bearing creatures and his unselfish concern for their well-being leads him to act on their behalf for their happiness and welfare."[30] Webster interprets God's love for the world in terms of providence: "Providence is that work of divine love for temporal creatures whereby God ordains and executes their fulfilment in fellowship with himself. God loves creatures and so himself orders their course to perfection."[31] God loves all human beings as his own creatures.

The third dimension of God's love towards the world is God's redemptive and sanctifying love for fallen and sinful creatures. The created objects of God's love have become the objects of divine wrath and condemnation by violating his holiness and righteousness. Paul observes that human beings made in God's image and likeness became his enemies instead (Rom 5:9-10).[32] Nevertheless, God has extended his redemptive love towards those who need redemption from sin, suffering, and death, and reconciliation with their Creator. God's sanctifying love for the world is sufficient for weak and sinful human beings, restores their

---

For example, Carson and Frame outline five dimensions of God's love, depending on the different conditions of the objects of divine love: inner-trinitarian love, general love for all creation, redemptive love for sinners, special love for the elect and covenant community, and conditioned love for the response (obedience or disobedience) of his people. Carson, *Difficult Doctrine of Love*, 16-17; Frame, *Doctrine of God*, 416-30.

29. Frame, *Doctrine of God*, 235.
30. Cottrell, *About God the Redeemer*, 336.
31. Webster, *God without Measure*, 1:127.
32. Paul writes, "Since we have now been justified by his blood, how much more shall we be saved from God's wrath through him! For if, while we were God's enemies, we were reconciled to him through the death of his Son, how much more, having been reconciled, shall we be saved through his life!" (Rom 5:9-10).

broken images of God to divine holiness, and reconciles them to the full and abundant life of the triune God in a way that cannot be said of the inner-trinitarian love of God.

In the work of the economy, therefore, God is able to choose the mode of his love based on the conditions and needs of the objects of his holy love. It is the position of this work that God chooses to demonstrate his love for his sinful creatures through his own suffering and especially through the event of the cross. God expresses his holy love through inflicting suffering on himself: "God demonstrates his own love for us in this: While we were still sinners, Christ died for us" (Rom 5:8). Human beings cannot understand the depth of God's love for them; therefore, as John remarks, the suffering and death of the Son is the way to know God's love: "This is how we know what love is: Jesus Christ laid down his life for us" (1 John 3:16).[33] Similarly, Martensen asserts that God's grief or distress is the manifestation of his love for the world.[34] God is not obligated to choose suffering to demonstrate his creative, redemptive, and sanctifying love but insists on doing so because he knows that such an expression is the only means for stubborn and wicked beings to understand even a glimpse of his love.

If the triune God were not to choose the mode of his love based on the conditions and needs of the objects of his holy love, two possibilities could follow. First, if God were to choose to love the world with the exact form of his love for himself, sharing his glory and majesty without hesitation, then he would be unable to express his anger and wrath against sinners. D. A. Carson is correct when he states that "an exclusive focus in this direction [the inner-trinitarian model as God's love for the world] takes too little account of how God manifests himself toward his rebellious image-bearers in wrath, in love, in the cross."[35]

Second, and as a corollary, if God were to choose to love himself with his love for the world, he could only become the object of his own wrath and then forgiveness, with the implication that each person of the immanent Trinity would be the object of redeeming and sanctifying love. As Carson insists, however, "There is no sense in which the love of the

---

33. Other scriptural testimonies concerning God's expression of his love through his suffering include Gal 2:20, Eph 5:2, and 1 John 4:9–10.

34. Martensen, *Christian Dogmatics*, 303.

35. Carson, *Difficult Doctrine of Love*, 21.

Father redeems the Son, or the love of the Son is expressed in a relationship of forgiveness granted and received."[36]

In contrast to both these scenarios, therefore, the divine persons are not blinded from seeing the beauty of each other and the wicked condition of human beings, and are transcendently free to manifest their creative, redemptive, and sanctifying love to these different objects of love in different modes, expressing love to the divine persons through radiant glory and blessedness, and love to sinful creatures in the context of fierce wrath against sin and voluntary undertaking of suffering.

All economic movements are initiated and executed by the triune God freely and that God chooses to love the world with his creative, redemptive, and sanctifying love. This served to provide a space within which the free expressions of God's love for the world could be seen in their true distinction from the free and necessary expressions of God's love for himself. In this way, this section explained that God chooses divine passibility as a means to express freely his creative, redemptive, and sanctifying love for human beings who sin against God.

The Passibility of the Economic Trinity

Having sketched above the contours of a possible doctrine of divine (im)passibility, attention will now be given to examining this doctrine more deeply through engaging a series of theological themes. The themes to be explored in turn are God's suffering and human sin, his active and passive emotions, his suffering and immutability, and his suffering on the cross.

God's Suffering and Human Sin

As God has chosen suffering as the free expression of his love for the world, he responds through his own suffering to his human creatures who are implicated in sin and suffering.[37] Scripture forcefully and frequently testifies to ways in which divine suffering is caused by human

---

36. Carson, *Difficult Doctrine of Love*, 21.

37. This work affirms that God suffers in his response to human suffering but stresses the suffering of God that is closely related to human sin, because this aspect of the discussion of the passibility of God is often dismissed in the contemporary conversation of the doctrine of divine (im)passibility.

sin.³⁸ However, as noted in chapter 2, unlike other passibilists who affirm the suffering of God related to human sin, for Moltmann, a theological treatment of God's relationship with human transgression is rather neglected and even becomes unnecessary in considering the suffering of God, while impassibilists such as Weinandy consider that all suffering is related to sin and evil and thus reject attributing suffering to a holy God. Thus, both passibilist and impassibilist strategies lead to a neglect of the biblical testimonies of God's suffering. By contrast, mediating theologies pursue a different trajectory of thought. This section considers the relationship between God's suffering and human sin in the context of God's redemptive history in order to develop a position that limits divine suffering to the domain of redemptive history. The views of Moltmann and Weinandy will serve as conversation points in order to explore how this mediating treatment of the suffering of God and its connection with human sin provide further insights into the doctrine of divine (im)passibility.

God experiences suffering in response to human sin in the following ways. First, God is grieved by sin because he hates sin and because sin disturbs the relationship between God and his creatures. God therefore suffers "by way of endurance, as a hater of sin and a lover of men."³⁹ Because God hates sin and evil but loves his creatures, human transgressions are a burden upon his heart, disturbing God's relationship with human beings and molding them to the image of evil. The account of the flood in Genesis 6:6–7 indicates that human hearts were filled with every evil and iniquity. This passage reveals that Yahweh is deeply affected by and grieves over the evil thoughts and wickedness of human beings.⁴⁰

Second, God experiences suffering in his redemptive work to save and atone for sinners on the cross. Clarke unpacks the details of the suffering that the Son endured on Golgotha as follows:

> In seeking to save us Christ offered and submitted himself to endure the closest contact with the moral evil that he abhorred; to feel all the grossness, selfishness, blindness, ingratitude, violence, of the sinful hearts of men . . . to be despised, rejected and murdered by those over whom he yearned in undying affection;

---

38. Gen 6:6, 7; Exod 32:10–14; 1 Sam 15:11; Ps 78:40; Isa 43:23; Jonah 3:10.
39. Clarke, *Outline of Christian Theology*, 342.
40. Arnold, "Genesis," 91.

to suffer the shame of a criminal's position and the agony of a disgraceful death.[41]

As God's righteousness requires the punishment of sinners for their wickedness, it also compels him to suffer and die to save sinners. The Son's salvific suffering is provided through his free act of taking suffering upon himself to redeem fallen human beings.

Third, in addition to the specific and time-bound suffering of the Son on the cross, God suffers in the course of his work to save sinners throughout his redemptive economy. God does not merely sympathize with sinful and suffering creatures, but wills and chooses to work for their salvation, work that brings with it suffering, weariness, rejection, and insult.[42] Clarke remarks, "A sinful world throws upon God the burden of a Savior's work."[43] God thus suffers across time in his work to save transgressors.

In opposition to the argument that God suffers before the foundation of the world, the position being advanced here is that divine passibility relates to redemptive history only. God wills to deliver human beings from their sins and the effects of their sins, such as suffering and death. The origin of the suffering and death of humanity is human sin; before the presence of sin, suffering and death did not exist. Only when the holiness of God was offended did human suffering appear in the world, and at this point the suffering of God in time began, for from then on, he had to bear the sin and pain of his human creatures.

To resolve the problem of all sin and suffering of human beings, God himself provides the way to deliver them from their transgressions and suffering, as Torrance writes: "God provides a way for the saving and healing of the world and the vanquishing of all its evil, and he does so by paying for it at infinite cost to himself in the sacrifice of Christ as the Lamb of God."[44] In this sense, Strong correctly observes, "Sin has cost God more than it has cost man."[45] In God's love for the world, through the suffering and death of the Son, sin and death have been swallowed up once and for all, through the resurrecting and mighty power of God (e.g.,

---

41. Clarke, *Outline of Christian Theology*, 346.
42. Clarke, *Outline of Christian Theology*, 343.
43. Clarke, *Outline of Christian Theology*, 342.
44. Torrance, *Christian Doctrine of God*, 248.
45. Strong, *Ethical Monism*, 95.

1 Cor 15:54–56).[46] At the end of time, when the kingdom of God is fully established, human sin and suffering will no longer exist (Rev 21:4).[47] Correspondingly, the loving God will not have to bear the sorrow of his people any longer. God's passibility can therefore only be a temporal experience that he chooses to undergo in the presence of and in response to the sin and suffering of his beloved creatures.

Having discussed the theme of divine suffering with reference to human sin in the context of a mediating position on divine (im)passibility, the following examines how this theme is considered in Weinandy's and Moltmann's views on the passibility of God. Weinandy interprets all types of suffering as evil and sinful and stresses the negative origin of suffering, while Moltmann discusses divine suffering without the emphasis of sins of men and women. Each of these arguments will be explored in turn.

Weinandy has offered two reasons for opposing the ascription to God of any form of suffering. The first reason is connected to sustaining an absolute distinction between the ontological locations of God and suffering.[48] For Weinandy, God exists in the uncreated order, whereas sin, suffering, and evil exist only in the created order. While God is able to influence the created order, sin, suffering, and evil cannot impact the uncreated order. If God were to suffer, it would mean that God somehow existed in and became part of the created order, and the distinction between the Creator and creation would collapse.

Correspondingly, God cannot be "infected by the evil that takes place within the created order" and is therefore "immune to suffering."[49] The second reason is that, for Weinandy, all suffering is evil, which is in turn deprivation of goodness. Weinandy observes that it is sin that "has brought the evil of suffering into the world."[50] He correspondingly

---

46. Paul quotes Isaiah 25:8 and Hosea 13:14 when he writes that the suffering and death of the Son overcame sin and death once and for all: "'Death has been swallowed up in victory.' 'Where, O death, is your victory? Where, O death, is your sting?' The sting of death is sin, and the power of sin is the law. But thanks be to God! He gives us the victory through our Lord Jesus Christ" (1 Cor 15:54–56).

47. The book of Revelation makes this point clear: "He [God] will wipe every tear from their eyes. There will be no more death or mourning or crying or pain, for the old order of things has passed away" (Rev 21:4). Other biblical references speak of the eternal joy and gladness of the last days (Ps 30:5; Isa 25:8; Heb 12:2; 1 Pet 1:18).

48. Weinandy, *Does God Suffer?*, 153–54.

49. Weinandy, *Does God Suffer?*, 154.

50. Weinandy, *Does God Suffer?*, 149.

describes suffering as "not a good in itself, but rather an evil . . . for suffering is always caused by the absence of some good."[51] If God were to experience suffering, it would imply that God was being deprived of his own goodness; therefore God, whose goodness is fully actualized and complete, cannot undergo any form of suffering.

Weinandy acknowledges that human love is often tested by the degree of suffering that a subject is willing to undergo for his or her love for another. Nonetheless, he denies any intrinsic relationship between love and suffering, because he views love and suffering as having different origins, highlighting the divine origin of love and the purely *negative* origin of suffering.[52] Other impassibilists, in a similar manner, interpret suffering only as a negative and imperfect experience; the obvious consequence is that it cannot be ascribed to God.[53]

Nevertheless, the origin of God's suffering must be distinguished from the origin of human suffering. Weinandy is correct to acknowledge that the origin of human suffering is sin, evil, and "a free misuse of what is good,"[54] and that God's goodness *in se* cannot be affected by sin and evil. However, this work posits that God himself is the origin of his suffering. As noted above, God is not obligated to suffer with human beings but chooses in his sovereign freedom and goodness to suffer in response to human sin and suffering before the existence of sin and suffering of the world. In this way, God's suffering is the result of a free, righteous use of his goodness.

Lee's argument is helpful at this point in understanding the distinction between God's suffering and human suffering. General or human suffering is occasioned by and effected by an evil and can be an evil. However, redemptive or divine suffering is occasioned by an evil but is not effected by it. God's suffering is effected by his empathy for his creatures afflicted by evil, but is itself "intrinsically good, because its purpose is to overcome the evil."[55] Specifically, God chooses suffering as a mode to

---

51. Weinandy, *Does God Suffer?*, 160.

52. Randles, *Blessed God*, 29, emphasis original. Randles similarly confirms the evil nature of suffering, though he acknowledges that suffering can be imposed for benevolent reasons and can bring forth positive results: "The pain may be made to serve a good purpose; yet in itself it is evil, and not desirable *per se*."

53. Bray, *Doctrine of God*, 99–100; Geisler, *Systematic Theology*, 112–24; Wright, Ferguson, and Packer, eds., "God," 27.

54. Weinandy, *Does God Suffer?*, 153.

55. Lee, *God Suffers for Us*, 42.

manifest his love for sinners and to atone for and save them from their transgressions and wickedness. H. Hughes offers support for this differentiated view of evil: "It is very doubtful whether every kind of suffering is to be described as evil. Certainly, that is not how we are wont to regard spontaneous and joyous self-sacrifice, or the passions of souls."[56] God's passibility is not structured on the imperfection and sinfulness of human beings, even though it might ultimately relate to it, because if human sin did not exist in the world, God would not have chosen to suffer with the world. Still, if God uses suffering as the means for a greater good in these cases, God is the ultimate cause and origin of his suffering, and his suffering is thus not evil in nature but results from his eternal goodness and counsel.

Turning to Moltmann's understanding of the relationship between divine suffering and human sin, a problem is immediately encountered: for Moltmann, the event of the cross that is the focal point of the divine suffering is focused on God's solidarity with the suffering of the world and is not primarily related to sin. Moltmann writes, "The incarnation of God's Son is not an answer to sin. It is the fulfilment of God's eternal longing to become man and to make of every man a god out of grace."[57] In Moltmann's theology of the cross, therefore, it seems that even without the existence of sin, the incarnation, suffering, and death of the Son on the cross would have to occur. For Moltmann, the cross is the fulfillment of the eternal desire of God, because the divine suffering becomes a necessary means to complete the divine being.

However, a first problem with Moltmann's view is that Scripture testifies that the cross is essentially God's response to and victory over the sins of the world and over sin's effects on human beings (Isa 53:4–5). Peter Brake points out the weakness of Moltmann's theology of the cross: "That God suffers with humanity seems to be more the point for Moltmann than that the sins of the world are forgiven in the suffering, death, and resurrection of the Son."[58]

The mediating position of this work contends that God's love and suffering is not based on any act that completes and benefits the triune God, for he is already fully sufficient and actualized within himself. Instead, God's love and suffering for the world is an expression of his

---

56. Hughes, *What Is the Atonement?*, 91.
57. Moltmann, *Trinity and the Kingdom*, 46.
58. Vande Brake, "Divine Passibility," 195.

creative, redemptive, and sanctifying love that completes and actualizes human beings. To see the event of the cross as *not* resolving the issue of sin is, in Lister's words, "to misunderstand the biblically conceived aim of redemptive history, thus cheapening the biblical notions of sin and grace."[59] The victory of the cross over human sins and suffering must be a crucial part of the doctrine of the passibility of God.

A further problem with Moltmann's description of the divine suffering as belonging to the eternal being of God is that it tends to minimize the "gratuitous" character of God's suffering. His notion of God's eternal and necessary suffering leads to God having no sovereign freedom so that God cannot not love human beings and cannot not suffer with them. Yet, since all the movements of God *ad extra* have the characteristic of freedom, the triune God is free to love and suffer for the world, and the Scripture calls this "grace" (Eph 2:8).

God is not obligated to love and suffer for non-divine beings. As Frame insists, "The very idea of grace is that God is not required to give it. If God is required, even by his own nature, to give grace to us, then we have a certain claim on him. But grace excludes such claims."[60] Besides, the notion of God's unconditional love that is toward sinners who do not deserve his love is neglected in Moltmann's work. God must love them regardless of their sinful conditions, as if they deserve and have earned the right to receive divine love. On the contrary, even though God foreknew the disobedience and opposition of human beings, he still chose to love them unconditionally and freely and to undergo suffering and to invite them to participate in his goodness and love.

Nonetheless, Moltmann insists that God's love and suffering remain free acts. For Moltmann, both love and suffering are the eternal nature of God, so that his solidarity with the suffering of the world is a demonstration that God is being entirely himself.[61] Moltmann suggests that God's trinitarian freedom "consists of the mutual and common participation in life, and a communication in which there is neither lordship nor servitude,"[62] and draws on this model to insist that God suffers freely.

However, in Moltmann's system of thought, there is no option for God not to suffer with the world, since divine suffering is necessary to

---

59. Lister, *God Is Impassible*, 245.
60. Frame, *Doctrine of God*, 235.
61. Moltmann, *Trinity and the Kingdom*, 54–55.
62. Moltmann, *Trinity and the Kingdom*, 56.

demonstrate and constitute the eternal love and suffering of the triune persons. His model of divine passibility thus minimizes the value and meaning of the grace of God's passibility. Don Schweitzer agrees that in this view divine suffering "ceases to be an excellence or virtue . . . [or] something God freely undertakes, and becomes instead a fate to which God is subject," and adds that "God's suffering is not really voluntary if God needs the world to experience fulfilment."[63]

Moreover, the model of freedom with which Moltmann operates has no biblical background, for Scripture describes God's relationship with his people as that of a Lord with his servants, with the Lord exercising his sovereign freedom over them.[64] Kantzer Komline argues that in contrast with Moltmann's view, "God's freedom not to love *ad extra* . . . makes God's decision to love the world more intentionally loving, not more arbitrarily so."[65] In his grace and sovereignty, God chooses to suffer with the world freely and unconditionally.

The aim of this section was to consider God's passibility in relation to human sin in the context of his redemptive history. God freely chooses to respond to the emergence of human sin in the divine economy through his suffering and to suffer in his endeavor to save sinners, above all on the cross. When the consummation of the kingdom of God arrives, God will no longer suffer with his loved ones. Therefore, God's passibility is a temporary experience that he chooses to bear freely and belongs firmly but solely in the domain of his redemptive operations. As impassibilists point out, it is true that all types of suffering are related to human transgression, for without the existence of transgression, neither God nor human beings would have suffered. Yet against the impassibilists, God also suffers in response to human transgressions, as the passibilists have always insisted, and is the origin of his passibility. However, against the passibilists, God only suffers in his economic operations, freely and voluntarily, and not in his eternal and immanent being. This in turn suggests that even where the cause of divine suffering is sin and evil, the divine suffering itself is a holy and good event.

---

63. Schweitzer, "Aspects of God's Relationship," 13.

64. God declares that Israelites are his servants and that he is their LORD (Lev 25:42–55). Paul calls himself a servant of God (Rom 1:1; 2 Cor 6:4; Gal 1:10) and explains that as clay has no voice to protest against the potter, God is free to use some for special purposes and others for common purposes (Rom 9:21–24).

65. Komline, "Friendship and Being," 5.

God's Active and Passive Emotions

As noted in the second chapter, one of the points of contention between the impassibility and passibility group is the subject of how to interpret God's emotions. The impassibility theologians stress the active dimension of God's emotions—that they are unmoved, immutable, foreknown, and free. The passibility theologians affirm the passive dimension of God's emotions—that they are moved from outside, mutable and temporal—and emphasize the eternal and necessary aspects of divine suffering.

By contrast, some mediating theologians, such as Strong, Clarke, and Pinnock, hold that God is eternally blessed without any suffering *in se* but chooses to suffer with the world and therefore experiences emotions in a passive way. Other mediating theologians, such as Frame, affirm both the active and the passive aspects of the emotions of the God who is impassible *in se*; on such accounts, the divine emotions are unmoved, chosen, foreknown, and free, yet also moved, mutable, and temporal.

In what follows, this section first briefly delineates the kinds of emotions that God experiences in his relationship with the world. Next, drawing on the theme of the self-movement of the economic Trinity, i.e., the way in which God moves himself to move the world and to be moved by it freely, this section explores God's emotions and suffering as both active and passive.[66] Third, both these dimensions of his emotions are construed as transitive and relative emotions that relate to his interactions with human beings, emotions that he does not express or experience *in se*.

A vast range of emotions is ascribed to God in Scripture, including anger, joy, suffering, jealousy, and hatred. Anger is expressed in response to the violators and violations of his righteousness (Deut 9:18; 1 Kgs 14:9; Ezek 8:17). Joy is the expression of his bliss in respect of the obedience and faithfulness of his people (Deut 28:63; Isa 62:5; Zeph 3:7). Suffering is the illustration of his love for the world in relation to human beings who oppose his holy covenant and who themselves are undergoing various pain and hardships (Ps 78:40; Isa 63:7–9; Eph 4:30). Jealousy is the demonstration of God's burning desire for his glory and honor with reference

---

66. As noted above, the concept of suffering contains too much theological depth and complexity to be categorized simply as emotions, and certain other emotions of God may be no less significant than suffering. Nevertheless, God's suffering is explored here by a way of example in order to explore the different proposals regarding the mode of God's personal interaction with his creatures.

to individuals who do not give him the worship and praise that he deserves (Exod 20:5; Deut 4:23–24; Ezek 36:21–23). Hatred is the response of God in opposition to sin and evil, the very objects of God's eternal punishments (Ps 97:10; Amos 5:15; Jude 23; Rev 2:6). And beyond these varied emotions, God also expresses repentance (Gen 6:6; 1 Sam 15:11), love (Ps 103:17; Lam 3:31–33), and compassion (Ps 103:8; Jer 3:12).

This present work proposes that each of these divine emotions has active and passive dimensions. Turning first to the active dimension of the divine emotions, two further considerations that are closely connected with each other arise. First, as God moves himself to move the world, he chooses the mode of his emotional responses to human beings' reactions. In his foreknowledge of the future events and choices of human beings, God chooses his own emotional responses and even sets the scope of the influence of these emotions upon himself. His emotions do not burst out of himself as random incidents or involuntary impulses. Along these lines, Lister holds that God not only foreknows and ordains the acts of his creatures but also decrees his own emotional response to their reactions. In this way, God's emotions respond to human acts without being moved by them. As Geisler explains, God "has feelings in an active sense but not in a passive sense. He does not undergo feelings (as being acted upon by another), but as actively expressing them himself."[67] Frame similarly classifies divine emotions under the category of God's eternal decree in order to contend that God first chooses his own emotional response without being conditioned by the world.[68] God's chosen emotions imply that they are the most fitting way for God to respond to the conducts of human beings, because he chooses emotionally what he already knows according to his exhaustive foreknowledge. God himself is thus the origin of his emotions in time.

Second, the triune God who chooses his emotional responses to human beings foreknows his emotions perfectly. He does not learn of his emotions gradually through a historic process of interacting with the world. Frame observes that God "gains his knowledge only from himself (his nature and his plan) and serves as his own criterion of truth."[69] God cannot stop himself from foreknowing his own emotional responses. This contrasts with the position of open theists, who assert that divine

---

67. Geisler and House, *Battle for God*, 186.
68. Frame, *Doctrine of God*, 610.
69. Frame, *Doctrine of God*, 602.

foreknowledge is limited with regard to knowledge of the future choices of human beings as they occur in history.[70]

Without knowledge of the exact timing of human events and choices, so open theism argues, the divine affections occur in an unpredictable and involuntary manner. Thus, Sanders comments that it was only when human beings disobeyed God that God learned "what it is to experience grief."[71] By contrast, for this work, God himself is the ground of the knowledge of his emotions and expresses his emotions in no way that he does not know already. Helm correspondingly construes divine emotions as "his attitudes to what he knows."[72] Following the same trajectory of thought, Geisler avers, "His emotional response is not a reaction to new knowledge."[73] God knows himself completely: He cannot not foreknow his own emotional responses. Thus, he is not overwhelmed by his own emotions and does not lose control of himself as he engages in his economic operations. The danger of the open theist position is that it mistakenly portrays God's emotions in too close a parallel with human emotions, without careful consideration of the major differences: the former are chosen, foreknown, and controlled; the latter are involuntary, unknown, and uncontrolled.

Turning to the passive aspect of God's emotions, two further considerations arise. First, there is the voluntary nature of God experiencing passive emotions. It has been noted above that as God moves himself to be moved by the world, he moves himself to experience the passive aspect of emotions. Pinnock asserts that God "is moved by what happens and reacts accordingly. God is a subject and events arouse in him joy and sorrow, pleasure and anger."[74] As John Peckham affirms, this ability is rooted in the divine freedom: God has freely opened himself to "be emotionally affected by, and responsive to, the actions of creatures."[75] Bloesch concurs, observing that in God's sovereign freedom, he who is eternally and immutable joyous *in se* "allows himself to be moved by the cries and anguish of his people."[76] God, who is capable of emotions and suffering, is

---

70. Rice, *Openness of God*, 21–22.
71. Sanders, *God Who Risks*, 48.
72. Helm, "Warfield on Divine Passion," 101.
73. Geisler and House, *Battle for God*, 186.
74. Pinnock, *Most Moved Mover*, 88.
75. Peckham, "Qualified Possibility," 98.
76. Bloesch, *God the Almighty*, 47.

moved by human beings and experiences various emotions and pain, as recorded in Scripture in his personal relationship with them. Unless God first moves himself to be moved by the world, God who is impassible *in se* cannot experience passive emotions, and he moves himself passively without giving up his inner impassibility.[77] Therefore, God is impassible *in se*.

Correspondingly, God is not obligated to be moved by the world. He is a self-moving God who determines his own course of path and is free to move himself actively and passively. Arthur Mason remarks that "God is capable of grief and joy, of anger and of gratification; though there is nothing which can force such states of feeling upon him without his being willing to undergo them."[78] No attribute of God, such as love, can force him to respond necessarily to the needs of the world. God is not a prisoner of his own attributes.

At the same time, if the self-moving God is not able to move himself in such a way that he can be moved by the world freely and passively, God's glorious freedom would seem to be compromised rather than enhanced and would be considered "a defect in him, not a perfection."[79] God's voluntary passion does not undermine the divine and total otherness of the Creator but, rather, confirms the divine and total otherness of the Creator. Indeed, Alvin Plantinga argues that God's capacity for suffering demonstrates God's greatness.[80] God's passive emotions demonstrate the greatness of his capacity for both active and passive movements and are not the direct effect of any non-divine cause but the direct effect of the divine cause, the free external movement executed—and thus experienced—by the triune God.

Second, it should be emphasized that God's passive emotions are nothing other than his own active emotions experienced in passive form. Affirming God's freely chosen passion does not imply that passion is assigned to God's immutable nature *in se*. Lister observes in this connection that "God is responsive [in his relationship to the world], but never passive [in his eternal nature]."[81] As noted above, God only experiences in passive form those active emotions that he has chosen and foreknown

77. Brasnett, *Suffering of the Impassible*, 12.
78. Mason, *Faith of the Gospel*, 32–33.
79. Mason, *Faith of the Gospel*, 33.
80. Plantinga, "Self-Profile," 36.
81. Lister, *God Is Impassible*, 230.

in passive form. Erickson agrees, "Those actions and feelings [God's passive emotions] are actually the result of his choices and plan, which is now being worked out within history."[82] And thus D. Simon posits that "even when he [God] lets us act on him, it is still a self-determination."[83]

In the view of this work, God chooses his own emotional responses actively and experiences passively his chosen expressions of those emotions. Frame concludes that "God responds (both transcendently and immanently) only to what he has himself ordained."[84] That is, God's active and passive emotions can be viewed as his transcendent and immanent emotions. The passive emotions that God chose to experience are real, personal, and reciprocal responses. In this way, the emotions that God experiences passively in his interaction with creation are not chosen in such a way that they are without genuine divine experience in time, nor are they necessary responses that are somehow essential to the nature of God.

Considering God's active and passive emotions together, two final points of significance arise. First, God's active and passive emotional responses to the world should be viewed as relative and transitive emotions that he does not express and experience *in se*. His emotional responses are transitive because they only relate to objects outside of God, and his emotional responses are relative only because they occur in God's relationship with the world. The existence of these emotions is completely dependent on his intended relationship to and lordship over the world. Just as God does not need the world to be God, he does not need to express and experience these emotions to be a God who is already satisfied within himself eternally. He was aware of his own emotions even before creation, for he is not ignorant of his own self. Still, it is with reference to the event of creation that God for the first time expresses his emotions actively in the foreordination of new events and experiences them passively in relationship with his creatures. In this way, the active expression and passive experience in time of God's emotions are both relative and transitive.

Second, both the active and the passive emotions of God are equally divine and valuable. To respond to human creatures, God chooses his emotional responses actively and to experience them passively. As active

---

82. Erickson, *God the Father Almighty*, 161.
83. Simon, *Reconciliation by Incarnation*, 149.
84. Frame, *Doctrine of God*, 610.

and passive emotions are connected to the world only, they do not belong to God's life *in se*. Although God first chooses and foreknows his emotions before experiencing them passively, this chronological order does not render the active emotions superior to the passive emotions.

Both aspects of God's emotions are the outcome of his sovereign freedom to move the world actively and to be moved by it passively. There is no hierarchy in these active and passive activities of God. Though they may be transitive, relative, and new, God's passive emotions do not have to be considered imperfect to be associated directly with God *pro nobis* and *ad extra* and indirectly with God *in se*. Both the active and the passive emotions of God are of equal majesty.

The active emotions of God indicate that God chooses and foreknows his own emotional responses to the conditions and choices of human beings. God's active emotions are thus clearly distinguished from the way human beings experience emotions and suffering. God's passive emotions indicate that God experiences various emotions by being moved by the world and by experiencing his chosen and foreknown emotions passively. God's active and passive emotions both relate only to his relationship with the world and are his freely chosen emotional responses to humanity as the outcome of his sovereign freedom. Therefore, the active and passive emotions of the triune God are equally and perfectly divine.

God's Suffering and Immutability

Impassibilists such as Weinandy affirm a strong form of the immutability of God to the effect that both *in se* and *ad extra* God cannot be changed at all, while passibilists such as Moltmann uphold that the God of love is truly mutable in his reciprocal interaction in time with his covenant community. In agreement with mediating theologians, this present work advances the position that God is immutable *in se* and mutable *ad extra*. This work argues that the immanent Trinity is immutably and eternally impassible, and the economic Trinity is mutably and temporally passible, without collapsing the immanent and economic distinction.

This argument is developed across the following four discussions. The first discussion explores how God can adapt to various changes resulting from the decisions and conditions of human beings without compromising his immutability. The second discussion outlines the ways in which the triune God is both immutable *in se* and mutable *ad extra*. The third discussion focuses on God's mutability with reference to time and explores how God's lordship of eternity and time enables him to be eternal and temporal simultaneously. The fourth discussion presents two modes of the existences and of experiences of the triune God: The immanent Trinity is immutable and eternally impassible, and the economic Trinity is mutably and temporally passible.

God is inexhaustibly versatile in his freedom to respond and adjust himself to events in creation, without compromising his inner being in order to accomplish the immutable purpose that he has for his creatures.[85] As Clarke argues, God "must act in a thousand ways, varying his action with the occasion for action, while he himself changes never."[86] Correspondingly, as Strong insists, "God's immutability itself renders it certain that his love will adapt itself to every varying mood and condition of his children."[87] The immutability of God thus sustains a variety of divine actions and reactions, and freely moves him continuously and unchangingly to have a personal relationship with his beloved creatures in order to accomplish his eternal purpose. In this line of thinking, as Strong notes, God's immutability is "consistent with constant activity and perfect freedom."[88] God is able to adapt to external changes in the divine economy without becoming a limited and temporal being, and his flexible and versatile freedom is the demonstration rather than the contradiction of his infinite and unchanging perfection and glory. Therefore, God can adapt to various changes resulting from the decisions and conditions of human beings without compromising his immutability.

The premise of this work that the triune God is both impassible and passible leads to a corresponding position in respect of divine (im)mutability: God is immutable *in se* and mutable *ad extra*. Each of these will be explored in turn in what follows. God's internal immutability can be explained in the following ways.

---

85. Concurring with this view, Mason writes, "However infinite the variety of His action, it is but the manifestation, in varying circumstances, of one and the self-same character and will." Mason, *Faith of the Gospel*, 26.

86. Clarke, *Outline of Christian Theology*, 89.

87. Strong, *Systematic Theology*, 1:257.

88. Strong, *Systematic Theology*, 1:258. Similarly, Clarke argues that God's immutable will to save and love his creatures "includes all the adaptations and responses necessary to carry this intention through in personal dialogue with us." Clarke, *Philosophical Approach to God*, 108.

First, God's inner being and his immanent or absolute attributes are immutable. These attributes are connected with God's inner being and his relation to himself, independent from the existence of the world, and they include his omnipotence, omniscience, omnipresence, eternity, sovereignty, love, holiness, and self-existence. They are necessary for God to be divine; therefore, they cannot be altered by anything.

Second, as the triune God exists in timeless eternity, his inner life is immune from any temporal change. In timeless eternity, there is no time, no beginning or end, and no before or after caused by succession of time. No change can occur in this timeless eternity. As Helm posits, "Whatever is timelessly eternal is unchangeable."[89]

Third, the dynamic of the fellowship of love of the inner trinitarian persons is immutable. The Father, Son, and Holy Spirit exist in their perichoretic fellowship necessarily and freely and will continue in this communion of love ceaselessly and eternally.

Fourth, the impassibility of the immanent Trinity is immutable Only the three divine persons can move themselves and can be moved by the other divine persons.

Finally, the blessedness of the inner trinitarian persons will remain the same eternally. Given that the divine attributes and fellowship of the three persons of the immanent Trinity, which are the foundation of divine blessedness, are immutable, the blessedness of their emotional life cannot be intensified or reduced in any way and is therefore immutable. As Katherine Rogers explains, "God is infinitely happy and we can do nothing to lessen it, nor can we (even logically) add to infinity."[90]

While God remains immutable *in se*, he does change in his relationship with the world. First, there is a change in the objects of God's love in the context of creation. The Father, Son, and Holy Spirit did not in actuality love disobedient and limited beings before the creation of the world. In this way, the divine three persons have new objects of love.

Second, there is a change in the mission and purpose of the triune God with reference to creation. He never engaged in the economic operations as the Creator, Redeemer, and Sanctifier before human beings existed. The creation of the world involves new activities that the three divine persons of the economic Trinity choose to undertake and undergo to share their eternal blessedness with their creatures.

---

89. Helm, "Impossibility of Divine Passibility," 119.

90. Rogers, *Perfect Being Theology*, 51.

Third, the triune God experiences transitive and relative emotions and suffering in his relationship with human creatures. Though God always foreknew the emotions he would undergo in his relation with his creatures, he only expresses actively his feelings to human beings and experiences them passively in actuality when they begin to exist.

Fourth, God engages reciprocally with the world in a temporal way. Being immutable and timelessly eternal within himself, he had never before engaged in temporal relationships until the advent of creatures who reside in time and are temporal ontologically. In this way, God experiences mutability in a temporal framework.

Having outlined the ways in which God is immutable *in se* and mutable *ad extra*, the notion of his temporal mutability will now be discussed to establish how God can be both timelessly eternal and temporal simultaneously, and to explain divine passibility as his temporal and mutable experience. God exists in timeless eternity without beginning or end, duration, or before or after caused by succession of time. God who is timelessly eternal *in se* is the Lord over time. That is, timeless eternity is an attribute of God.[91] However, this timeless God created time for his creatures and also to use time for his glory and plans in the temporal domain.

Correspondingly, time is designed to be suitable not only for human beings to exist with one another but also for the Creator to accomplish his purposes, including interacting with and responding to his creatures. To be and act in time means that God himself changes, for this capacity was not present or involved in respect of God's inner, timeless life, that is, without reference to the creation of the world.

This change occurs not in his immutable and eternal nature but in his relationship with the temporal world, which is itself constantly in a process of change. As Grudem writes, "What God is in his own being (he exists without beginning, end, or succession of moments)" must be distinguished "from what God does outside of himself (he creates in time and acts in time in other ways)."[92] In this way, God does not have to be perceived as either atemporal or temporal; instead, he can fruitfully be considered to be both atemporal and temporal.[93]

91. A similar argument is made by Erickson when he writes that God "is atemporal/aspatial in his fundamental nature, or is ontologically atemporal/aspatial." Erickson, *God the Father Almighty*, 139.

92. Grudem, *Systematic Theology*, 172.

93. Ware notes, "God's relation to time" can be considered "as comprising both

The point of transition for God between being only eternal and being eternal and temporal is the event of creation. It is at the moment of the creation, Ware writes, that "God became both omnipresent and omnitemporal, while remaining, in himself and apart from creation, fully nonspatial and timelessly eternal."[94] God now remains in eternity, yet acts simultaneously in time, demonstrating that his transcendence does not limit him from having an intimate and temporal relationship with his creatures and does not have to be abandoned to affirm God's temporal and mutable interaction with his creatures in time. In this trajectory of thought, God chooses freely to interact with his creatures in time and to experience temporal mutability, including in such forms as suffering.

Frame explains that it is God's temporal interaction with the world that permits him to engage in reciprocal relationships with his creatures:

> God, like a temporalist God, can know (and assert) temporally indexed expressions like "the sun is rising now." He can feel with human beings the flow of time from one moment to the next. He can react to events in a significant sense (events which, to be sure, he has foreordained). He can mourn one moment and rejoice the next. He can hear and respond to prayer in time. Since God dwells in time, therefore, there is give-and-take between him and human beings.[95]

At the same time, it is crucial to remember that time is not a limitation to God. He who made time and who made his creatures to be restrained by and influenced within temporal sequences is not himself limited by time.[96] As Erickson argues, God "is not inferior, but vastly superior, to time."[97] God as the Creator and Lord of time is in complete control of the way in which he moves and is moved by time and interacts with his created beings, and at no point does God abandon his divinity and eternity. Being fully capable of being operative in both eternity and time simultaneously, God continues to be both ontologically eternal, and temporally engaged in the world, engaging with temporal beings in reciprocal relationships that involve God's emotions and suffering.

---

his atemporal existence in himself *(in se)* apart from creation, and his 'omnitemporal' existence in relation to the created order he has made *(in re)*." Ware, "Modified Calvinist Doctrine," 88.

94. Ware, "Modified Calvinist Doctrine," 88–89.
95. Frame, *Doctrine of God*, 557–58.
96. Erickson, *God the Father Almighty*, 277.
97. Erickson, *God the Father Almighty*, 274.

As the triune God is both immutable and eternal *in se* and mutable and temporal *ad extra*, he exists in two modes of existence. Since the triune God exists in the eternal life *in se*, he enters into a new, temporal mode of existence with his created beings. The three divine persons of the immanent Trinity continue to be in an eternal and immutable communion of love, fully satisfied and joyous; their communion of life is therefore a mode of existence that is not altered with the advent of creation. The Father, Son, and Holy Spirit remain constant in this eternal and immutable fellowship of love while they extend their actions externally and engage in new and temporal relationships with non-divine beings. Grenz describes this dual existence of the triune God in these terms: "[God] is that reality who is present and active within the world process. Yet he is not simply to be equated with it, for he is at the same time self-sufficient and 'beyond' the universe."[98] The triune God, having full control over time, can simultaneously relate in different ways to different individuals located in different times and places. For instance, God will respond simultaneously to faithfulness with his goodness and favor and to unfaithfulness with his anger and punishment. However, this temporal experience cannot be assigned to the eternal experience of the immanent Trinity, for otherwise it would imply that the eternal life of the immanent Trinity is impacted by the historical process. Instead, as the Father, Son, and Holy Spirit in the eternal bond of their unity take on the economic roles of Creator, Redeemer, and Sanctifier, they engage in temporal operations simultaneously without abandoning their eternal and immutable identities and communion of love.

Affirmation of these two modes of the existence of the triune God is the foundation of the argument of this work: the immanent Trinity is immutably and eternally joyous, and the economic Trinity is mutably and temporally passible. In the exercise of his sovereign and flexible freedom, the triune God who exists in eternity and blessedness chooses to extend his eternal existence to exist in a temporal mode and to experience temporal and mutable forms of suffering without himself becoming a mutable and temporal Being. Lister describes these two modes of God's life as "his *in se* impassibility and his *in re* impassionedness."[99] Martensen likewise affirms this twofold asymmetric existence of the triune God, writing that God has "a life in himself of unclouded peace and

---

98. Grenz, *Community of God*, 81.
99. Lister, *God Is Impassible*, 229.

self-satisfaction, and a life in and with his creation, in which He not only submits to the conditions of finitude, but even allows His power to be limited by the sinful will of man . . . [I]n the outer chambers is sadness, but in the inner ones unmixed joy."[100]

Divine suffering is one of God's free, mutable experiences that he decides to undergo in a temporal continuum without compromising the immanent attributes or eternal joy of the inner life of the triune persons. These asymmetric modes of existence of the immanent Trinity and economic Trinity are authentic reality. Frame urges that "we should not say that his atemporal, changeless existence is more real than his changing existence in time. . . . Both are real. Neither form of existence contradicts the other."[101] This distinction is sustained by the lordship and freedom of the triune persons, who can be eternal and immutable within their communion of love and blessedness and simultaneously temporal and mutable in their economic relations.

The immanent Trinity is immutably and eternally joyous, and the economic Trinity is mutably and temporally passible, without the economy Trinity being transmuted into the immanent Trinity. God's versatile and flexible freedom and God's lordship over eternity and time enable him to exist in both eternal and temporal realms and to be eternally joyous while simultaneously experiencing the passive dimension of emotions and suffering. In this way, the distinction between God's life *in se* and *ad extra* is maintained without either violating God's blessed and glorious life or rejecting God's suffering in the economy as a negative and imperfect experience of God.

God's Suffering on the Cross

As observed in the second chapter, the traditionalist understanding of the impassibility and immutability of the triune persons does not allow

---

100. Martensen, *Christian Dogmatics*, 101. By categorizing suffering as temporal experience only, Storr likewise holds both God's eternal peace and his temporal suffering: "God suffers with His world. Can we not hold that, and at the same time hold that He is a centre of peace? Strife and struggle belong to time, not to eternity. God dwells in eternity. . . . I think we can hold both thoughts of God without making either of them unreal. We can assert that He really suffers, and at the same time sees the time process as a whole which moves towards the perfection which belongs to His transcendent life." Storr, *Problem of the Cross*, 126.

101. Frame, *Doctrine of God*, 571.

the Son as divine to suffer on the cross and the Father and Holy Spirit to be moved by the plight of Jesus and thus to undergo suffering.[102] For passibilists, meanwhile, it is affirmed that all three divine persons suffer in the event of the cross in their fellowship.[103] As discussed previously, mediating theologians such as Frame affirm the suffering of the Son and Father in the event of the cross, and Pinnock further indicates the pain of the Holy Spirit.[104] In this way, the argument advanced here is closer to the positions of the passibilists and Pinnock and is differentiated from the positions of Frame and Lister.

There are two ways in which applying the dynamic reciprocity model deepens this presentation of the suffering of the divine persons of the economic Trinity. The first is that it allows an exploration of the way in which the Father, Son, and Holy Spirit freely determine their particular operations on the event of the cross. The second is that it further illuminates how each divine person's suffering is connected to the unique redemptive functions of the other divine persons on the cross and how these particular experiences of suffering move them and the other divine persons in the unity of their fellowship of love. These two results of drawing on dynamic reciprocity model differentiate the position adopted in this work from that of other mediating theologians, and in what follows each will be explored in turn.

First, the three divine persons of the economic Trinity freely determine and accomplish their redemptive operations together. The salvation history that reaches its climax on the cross is not simply the individual activity and history of the Son but embraces the distinct and unified activities and histories of all three divine persons. Torrance explains this dynamic in this way: "The whole undivided Trinity is involved in our salvation, and thus in the central atoning passion of Christ, God the Father and God the Spirit, as well as God the Son, in their different but

---

102. Weinandy, *Does God Suffer?*, 226. Weinandy, in rejecting the suffering of the Father argues, "Since the persons of the Trinity can never be deprived of their divine perfection, they never experience any inner angst over their own state of being which would cause them to suffer."

103. Moltmann, *Crucified God*, 245. Moltmann discusses the suffering of the Father and Son extensively. He also stresses the suffering of the Holy Spirit in *The Spirit of Life*, 62. Lee argues that the suffering of the Son is the suffering of the Father and Holy Spirit, for the triune persons participate in the experiences of one another. Lee, *God Suffers for Us*, 75.

104. Frame, *Doctrine of God*, 613-14; Pinnock, *Most Moved Mover*, 58.

coordinated ways."[105] Each person plays his own role in the economy as the crucifixion unfolds, for it is not the Father who suffers and dies on the cross, nor the Son who pours down his wrath and curse upon the Father. Their respective responsibilities on Golgotha might be depicted in this way: The Holy Spirit leads the Son to the hill of Golgotha; the Father forsakes the Son; the Son dies on the cross. Still, regardless of their distinct, functional roles, they are all completely involved in each of these operations, working together economically without ever ceasing to be in eternity the Father, Son, and Holy Spirit who are deeply unified in their fellowship of love.[106]

The three divine persons freely move themselves actively and are moved passively in their accomplishment of the distinct roles they assume in the event of the cross. The Son wills himself to suffer and die on the cross and is simultaneously moved by the wills of the Father and Holy Spirit, who in turn both will the Son to be the sacrifice on the cross. The Father voluntarily effects the crucifixion of the Son and is simultaneously moved by the wills of the Son and Holy Spirit to take on this function; they in turn are moved by the Father's will in their own operations. The Holy Spirit wills to lead the Son to Golgotha and is simultaneously moved by the Father and the Son to do so; they in turn will the Holy Spirit to lead the Son this way.

The three divine persons foreknow the heavy burden of their respective missions, yet still will freely, in their own individual ways, to work to accomplish the purpose of the cross. The cross is their cross, and they will to bear the burden of the cross together as the means to accomplish their end—to share their eternal blessedness and glory with creatures with whom they have personal and reciprocal relationships. Even though they willed to engage in this redemptive drama for the world and foreknew the glory and victory that would result on Good Friday, there is no denying the fact that the cross and the events of the Friday remain a terrible and dreadful drama in the experience of the persons of the economic Trinity.

Second, the particular suffering of each of the divine persons in the economy in relation to the event of the cross is related to their distinct economic responsibilities. To begin with the Son: the heavy burden of

---

105. Torrance, *Christian Doctrine of God*, 252.

106. Horton, "'Lord and Giver of Life,'" 48. Horton's comment is helpful in understanding the interplay of the external works of the economic Trinity: "It is not that the divine persons perform different works but that they are engaged differently in every work."

the Son was to suffer in his divine and human natures and to die in the flesh on the cross, and thereby to undergo the salvific suffering required to save sinners from the consequences of their sinful deeds.[107]

Many biblical references explain the saving nature of the suffering and death of the Son of God and point to the way he gave himself to atone for the iniquities of sinners and to reconcile them to God.[108] As Strong argues, the experiences of the suffering of the Christ on Golgotha "are substitutionary, since his divinity and his sinlessness enable him to do for us what we could never do for ourselves."[109] Torrance similarly observes that the suffering of the Son is "the vicarious act of God himself in order to bring about our salvation," the "atoning sacrifice for the sin of the world and its redemption of mankind from the antagonistic powers of darkness."[110] The Son specifically took on himself the suffering and judgment of human beings "to redeem mankind from suffering and redeem suffering in mankind."[111]

In the case of the Father, his experience of passibility involves suffering the pain of forsaking the Son. The Father, fully knowing the divinity and righteousness of the Son, forsakes the Son as he hangs on the cross as a cursed criminal. The Father's role in effecting the crucifixion was foreknown and chosen by all three persons of the economic Trinity. However, it is the Father specifically who suffers the pain of delivering up the Son to crucifixion and seeing him executed.

Barth offers a helpful observation that highlights the Father's suffering in relation to his active role in the event of the cross:

> It is not at all the case that God has no part in the suffering of Jesus Christ even in his mode of being as the Father ... [P]rimarily it is God the Father who suffers in the *offering and sending of his Son in his abasement*. ... This fatherly fellow-suffering of

---

107. As indicated in chapter 1, this book's account of the doctrine of divine (im)passibility starts from the doctrine of God, and not from the revelation of the economic Trinity or from the theology of the cross. The detailed discussion of the Son's suffering on the cross has been intentionally excluded in the previous chapters. This work affirms the suffering of the Son in his divine and human natures without exploring the nature of the hypostatic union of the Son's human and divine natures and the associated doctrines.

108. Matt 20:28; Mark 10:45; John 3:16; Rom 4:25; 5:6; 8:32; 14:9; 1 Cor 8:11; 15:3; 2 Cor 5:14–15; Gal 1:4; 2:20–21; Eph 5:2; Titus 2:14; 1 Thess 5:10; 1 Pet 3:18.

109. Strong, *Systematic Theology*, 2:715.

110. Torrance, *Christian Doctrine of God*, 247, 252.

111. Torrance, *Christian Doctrine of God*, 248.

> God is the mystery, the basis, of the humiliation of his Son; the
> truth of that which takes place historically in his crucifixion.[112]

Even though the triune persons freely determine the crucifixion of the Son as the means of the salvation of all sinners, this does not alleviate the weight of the cross that the Son bore and the gravity of the Father's sorrow in forsaking the Son on the cross.

Mason offers here the analogy of earthly parents to portray the suffering of the Father, and concludes that "the suffering and grief of the Father, in delivering up His Son for us all, was even greater than what He would have endured if He could have borne it all in His own Person."[113] The sorrow of the Father is thus not reduced to the aloof and passionless heart of an executioner,[114] for it is simply not possible to "think of Him as watching Jesus suffer with calm, indifferent eyes."[115]

As for the Holy Spirit, his experience of passibility involves the suffering of having to lead the Son to the cross. The role of the Holy Spirit is to guide and effect the Son taking the path to Golgotha by accompanying him throughout his earthly life and messianic ministry. Having intimate fellowship with the Son, the Holy Spirit was with the Son when he was born in the manger, tempted in the desert by the devil, moved by the suffering and sickness of his people, and betrayed by his own covenant community.

Throughout his earthly life, Jesus experienced various types of travail and suffering associated with the world's sins.[116] Correspondingly, the Holy Spirit also experienced these travails: being always with the Son, the Holy Spirit suffered with the Son, including in the event of the cross.

---

112. Barth, *Church Dogmatics*, IV/2, 357, emphasis added.

113. Mason, *Faith of the Gospel*, 181. He continues, "A pious cottager on hearing the text, 'God so loved the world,' exclaimed, 'Ah! that *was* love! I could have given myself, but I could never have given my son.' If this be true, we may read in the Crucifixion not only the indignation and pain of the Father at men's sin, but the intensity of His love for the sinners, which made Him willing to endure such anguish, a thousandfold more acute for being inflicted, not on Him, but on One dearer than Himself." Mason, *Faith of the Gospel*, 181, emphasis original.

114. Barth, *Church Dogmatics*, IV/3, 414.

115. Storr, *Problem of the Cross*, 113–14. Lee affirms the intimate relationship of the triune persons such that the Father and the Spirit share in the suffering of the Son. Indeed, he writes, to deny "the suffering of the Father in spite of the suffering of His Son is also the denial of the intimate relationship between the Father and the Son through the Holy Spirit." Lee, *God Suffers for Us*, 75.

116. Martensen, *Christian Dogmatics*, 308.

Moltmann argues that the Holy Spirit not only leads Jesus throughout his life but also accompanies him even in his travails, becoming "his *companion* in suffering."[117] As the Son and Holy Spirit are united in carrying out their respective operations in the economy, so "the story of the suffering of the messianic Son of God is the story of the suffering of God's Spirit too."[118] It is the task of the Holy Spirit to guide the Son on the path that completes their economic mission to save God's people, and this includes experiencing the grief of leading the Son to crucifixion and witnessing the event of the cross itself.

Having explored the suffering of each of the three divine persons in relation to the cross, it is important to consider the way in which these distinct experiences of suffering are related. The Father, Son, and Holy Spirit not only foreknow the particular forms of suffering that will accompany their specific responsibilities on the cross, but also every aspect of the travails that the other divine persons must endure to accomplish their respective roles on Good Friday.

Instead of ignoring the afflictions of the other divine persons, they move themselves to participate in and to experience the sufferings of the other divine persons in the event of the cross. That is, as this chapter has argued, the divine suffering on the cross has both active and passive dimensions that are chosen and experienced in the freedom of the triune persons who move themselves towards the world and are moved by it freely.

As the divine persons move themselves and are moved by the other divine persons freely, the Father and Holy Spirit experience and are moved by the salvific and substitutionary suffering of the Son that he endures for the sins and suffering of the world, and share in the pain of the Son. The Father and Son experience and are moved by the Holy Spirit's co-suffering with the Son throughout his life and the Holy Spirit's sorrow at leading the Son to Golgotha. And the Son and Holy Spirit experience and are moved by the suffering of the Father, who forsakes the Son for the purpose of redemption.

If the divine persons are not moved by the experience of suffering of the other divine persons, that would be, according to Mason, "a Tritheistic idea" that "ignores the necessary relations of the Blessed Persons," for they cannot have been unaffected by the suffering experiences of the

---

117. Moltmann, *Spirit of Life*, 62, emphasis original.
118. Moltmann, *Spirit of Life*, 64.

divine others.[119] Thus, all divine three persons experience the burden and suffering not only of carrying out their own roles in respect of the event of the cross, but also that of the other divine persons.

In their unbreakable communion of love, the Father, Son, and Holy Spirit are moved both by bearing of their own suffering and by sharing the painful experience of the other divine persons. The trinitarian event of the cross is a paradox: there is at the same time an event of abandonment of the Son by the Father and also a maintaining of the triune fellowship of love. The three persons of the economic Trinity who are present in and moved by the event of the cross are in a communion of love, so that even when they seem most divided and estranged, they are always unified in the unbreakable unity of the triune love. It is within the context of the Father's great and unbreakable love for the Son that he suffers the pain of the crucifixion of the Son.[120]

It is as the Holy Spirit witnesses the relationship of forsakenness between the Father and the Son at the end of the road to Golgotha that he continues perfectly to love both. It is as the Son continues to love the Father and Holy Spirit with the filial love that is demonstrated on the cross that he experiences the excruciating pain of being abandoned by the Father.[121] In this way, the cross and its associated suffering are the ultimate demonstration of the depth of the fellowship of love that exists between the divine persons in the economy. This unbreakable communion of the divine love *ad extra* is in turn grounded in the eternal and loving communion of God *in se*, in which the triune persons love themselves and are loved by one another, and in which they originally freely determine that they will suffer in the economy in their respective roles on the cross.

Drawing on the self-movement of the economic Trinity and on the dynamic reciprocity model, this section has focused on considering how the three divine persons choose to move themselves actively and passively as they assume different roles in the redemptive event of the cross.

---

119. Mason, *Faith of the Gospel*, 181.

120. Moltmann sustains this dynamic of love and forsaking relationship between the Father and Son: "The Son suffers in his love being forsaken by the Father as he dies. The Father suffers in his love the grief of the death of the Son." Moltmann, *Crucified God*, 245.

121. Even though Weinandy does not support the suffering of the divine nature of the Son, he correctly explains that the suffering of the Son "was an act of sacrificial love offered to the Father, for in love the Son offered his own life to the Father to atone for and so offset or, literally, counteract all humankind's ungodly sinful acts." Weinandy, *Does God Suffer?*, 223.

It has indicated that the divine persons experience not only the distinct sufferings entailed in their own roles but also the suffering experienced by the other divine persons. Being moved by the suffering experience of the other divine persons, all three persons suffer both actively and passively. Nonetheless, within the context of these divine sufferings, the trinitarian persons remain unbreakably bound together in their fellowship of love, both in time and in eternity.

7

Concluding Thoughts on God's (Im)Passibility

The guiding question of this publication has been whether God can be associated with suffering and be moved by the world and, more specifically, whether the triune God, who is both almighty and love, can respond to the iniquities and pain of his beloved creatures, creatures who were made in his likeness and yet violated his holiness, through his suffering.

The conclusion is that the impassible God, who is not moved by the world and who is eternally joyous *in se*, moves himself in the economy both to move towards the world and to be moved by it voluntarily. As a result, he is able to respond to human sin and suffering through the active and passive dimensions of his suffering and emotions without jeopardizing his inner perfections, blessedness, and triune fellowship. In this sense, this work advances a mediating position that the triune God is both impassible and passible: the immanent Trinity is impassible but is also passible when acting for the benefit of world in the economy.

Answering Mozley's Six Necessary Questions

At the conclusion of Mozley's book *The Impassibility of God*, he proposed "six necessary questions" that he believed were crucial to answer if a theologically balanced doctrine of the passibility of God were to be constructed. Replying to these questions will function as a summary of the argument of this constructive mediating position on the (im)passibility of God and demonstrate that the argument of this book can be entertained as a theologically balanced and acceptable account of divine (im)passibility.

CONCLUDING THOUGHTS ON GOD'S (IM)PASSIBILITY

The first question that Mozley asks is concerned with God's absolute and personal nature: "What do you imply by the term 'God'?"[1] The triune God is both absolute and personal. God is absolute as he is self-sufficient and self-determined and has perfect attributes such as eternity, omnipotence, omniscience, immutability, sovereignty, omnipresence, love, holiness, and aseity. Simultaneously, God is personal, for he exists necessarily and freely in the reciprocity of love of the three divine persons of the Father, Son, and Holy Spirit. The three divine persons both move themselves and are moved by one another. In this way, the triune God, who is absolute and personal, is impassible *in se*: he is not moved by the world for only he can move himself and exists in eternal blessedness for his perfect attributes and triune fellowship determine the degree of his emotional life.

The second question is, "What is the true doctrine of God's relationship to the world, and, especially, with reference to creation?"[2] The self-moving, triune God is not *in se* moved by the world; but he is free to move towards the world and to be moved by it. The three triune persons of the economic Trinity move themselves actively and are moved by the other divine persons passively to be the Creator, Redeemer, and Sanctifier and thereby to engage in creative, redemptive, and sanctifying relationships with human creatures. The distinctive characteristics of the immanent Trinity, which are freedom and necessity, are distinct from the characteristics of God's relationships with human beings, which are his freedom and his love for the world. The three divine persons of the economic Trinity freely chosen to suffer with human creatures as the expression of their love for sinners and to participate in reciprocal relationships with them that entail mutable and temporal emotions and suffering. In this way, the economic Trinity is passible freely.

Third, "Can the life of God be essentially blessed and happy, as being that eternal life which cannot, as such, be in any way affected by the time-series and its contents, and yet also a life in which suffering finds a place, in so far as the life of God enters into the time-series and works within it?"[3] Since the triune God is immutable and eternal *in se* and is mutable and temporal *ad extra*, he exists in two modes of life. The immanent Trinity exists in the reciprocity of love of the three divine persons and in eternal blessedness, remaining the same immutably.

1. Mozley, *Impassibility of God*, 178.
2. Mozley, *Impassibility of God*, 178.
3. Mozley, *Impassibility of God*, 179.

Simultaneously, in the economy, the three divine persons interact with human beings in time and undergo suffering as a temporal and mutable experience. This is possible for the triune God for two reasons. One, he is immutable within himself and mutable only in his relationship with the world. He is flexible and versatile and thus able to adapt to the various conditions and choices of human creatures without being changed in himself. Two, God is Lord of eternity and time. Time is a limitation to human beings, and they cannot but change within it; however, such a limitation does not apply to the God who is above time, has created time and chosen all temporal changes. Divine passibility is the way that God chooses to demonstrate his love for the world and to respond to human sin and suffering; it is a part of the economic operations of the Trinity, which does not impact the fellowship of love, joy, and glory of the eternal triune persons.

Fourth, "How is feeling in God related to feeling in men? And is there a particular kind of feeling properly describable as suffering, and experienced as suffering by God?"[4] Two answers can be offered. God's emotion is radically different from human emotion. God chooses to express and to experience his emotional responses (including suffering) both actively and passively. Foreknowing and predetermining his emotional responses, he is never surprised by the future events of the world and future choices of human beings or overwhelmed by his emotions and suffering. In this sense, divine emotions are radically different from the emotions of human beings, who only experience the passive dimension of emotions.

In addition, divine emotions and human emotions are similar— they are both experienced passively. Even though God's passive emotions and human emotions are similar in so far as they occur in temporal and mutable form, there are also important differences. The divine emotional responses do not affect God's nature *in se*, because they represent the various manifestations of his immutable will, truth, love, and purpose. Moreover, the divine emotions are different because God's feelings are grounded in divine perfection and holy love, while human feelings arise out of and are inalienably linked to the limitations and sinful conditions of human beings.

Mozley's fifth question is focused on whether divine passibility or impassibility has any religious value: "Is a real religious value secured in

---

4. Mozley, *Impassibility of God*, 180.

the thought of the passibility of God?"⁵ The answer to this question has two aspects. First, the value of the doctrine of the impassibility of God is that it functions as an apophatic qualifier, demonstrating the infinite distinction between the Creator and his creation. This infinite distinction cannot be collapsed, and it cannot be truly comprehended by finite and limited human beings. In addition, God's eternal blessedness, which perdures without a hint of suffering or mutability, serves as the ultimate hope for human beings who are trapped in the apparently unbreakable cycle of sin, evil, and suffering. In his perfect felicity and sufficiency, the triune God invites his creatures to enjoy him and dwell with him eternally. Only a God who is impassible in this way has the capacity to save transgressors, and thus he is the only hope of humanity.

At the same time, the value of the doctrine of the passibility of God is that it reveals the depth of God's love for the world. The most beautiful and glorious God inflicted suffering on himself, experiencing suffering along with his beloved human creatures. Suffering was inflicted on created beings by God for their iniquities but was self-inflicted by the Creator out of his love for them. Still, it is only in the light of the impassible God that the free and gracious character of this love and suffering can truly shine forth. The point is that the triune God, who is fully sufficient within himself and is not moved by human beings, *chooses* to be moved by the conditions and choices of human beings and *chooses* to redeem their sins through his own sacrifice. Only through the passibility of God can human beings grasp and believe the unconditional love for the world that underlies this divine choice.

The sixth and final question Mozley poses is, "What is the relationship of the Cross as the historic means of God's redemption of the world to that eternal background of God's love out of which the Cross is given?"⁶ The historical cross on Golgotha is the freely chosen expression of God's holy love for his creatures and does not serve as a direct revelation of the life of the immanent Trinity. If the cross on Golgotha was the temporal expression of an eternal cross that was somehow in the heart of God, the event of the cross would be a necessary event for God to fulfill his eternal nature, not a free event of grace. This would in turn collapse the distinction between the economic and immanent Trinity and jeopardize the self-identity of the triune God. All three divine persons of the economic

---

5. Mozley, *Impassibility of God*, 181.
6. Mozley, *Impassibility of God*, 182.

Trinity are involved in the event of the cross, and each person has its own role: the Holy Spirit leads the Son to the hill of Golgotha; the Father crucifies the Son; the Son dies on the cross. All three divine persons in the economy suffer on the cross and are moved by the suffering of the other divine persons.

This publication enhances the discussion of the doctrine of the (im)passibility of God in three ways. First, making a distinction between the active and passive dimensions of God's emotions and suffering clarifies the contending points between the impassibilists and passibilists. Second, this work demonstrated that divine passibility can be explored and constructed with a view to the domain of theology proper and that divine passibility can be sustained without limiting God's infinite perfections. Third, a mediating theology can be a helpful tool to develop a balanced form of theology of suffering that can serve people around the world going through various types of suffering to explore and search their unanswered theological questions.

This work enriches the discussion of the dynamics of the self-movement and reciprocal relations of the three persons of the immanent and economic Trinity in the following ways. First, the concept of the self-moving God, who moves himself and is moved by himself, and applied this conception of divine being to each of the persons of the Trinity, has been used to explore how the triune God moves himself actively and passively *ad intra* in order to provide an analogue for how he is moved by the world and how he moves it actively and passively *ad extra*.

Second, the dynamic reciprocity model was introduced as a new way of thinking about the relations between and functions of the eternal actions and passions of God. The model suggests that it is permissible to consider eternal passions as being prior to eternal action, as well as vice versa, in such a way that it can be suggested that eternal actions and eternal passions mutually condition each other in the eternal life of the immanent Trinity.

On this basis, third, this work has explored in detail the way in which the three divine persons share their love, blessedness, and glory with one another *ad intra*. On this foundation, it has considered in depth how the three divine persons engage together in the redemptive operations of salvation history *ad extra*, with particular reference to the event of the cross and the pinnacle of suffering that the trinitarian persons undergo there.

To conclude this book with answering the above guiding question, God can be associated with suffering and be moved by the world. The triune God who is both almighty and all-loving can respond to his image bearers implicated by sin and suffering through his own suffering. The triune God does not go through any suffering within himself but experiences both active and passive dimensions of suffering in his relationship with his beloved human beings, as a means to demonstrate his special love for them. Only the almighty and all-loving God can save human beings from their suffering and sin.

Bibliography

Anselm. "Proslogium." In *St. Anselm: Basic Writings: Proslogium, Monologium, Gaunilon's: In Behalf of the Fool, Cur Deus Homo*, translated by S. W. Deane, 49–80. 2nd ed. La Salle, IL: Open Court, 1962.
Aquinas, Thomas. *Summa Theologica*. Translated by Fathers of the English Dominican Province. Vol. 1. Rev. ed. Chicago: William Benton, 1923.
Arnold, Bill T. "Genesis." In *New Cambridge Bible Commentary*, edited by Ben Witherington III. New York: Cambridge University Press, 2009.
Augustine. "Concerning the Nature of God, Against the Manichaeans." In *A Select Library of the Nicene and Post-Nicene Fathers*, vol. 4, edited by P. Schaff, translated by Albert H. Newman, 351–65. Buffalo, NY: Christian Literature, 1887.
Aune, David E. *Revelation 6–16*. Word Biblical Commentary 52b. Dallas: Word, 1998.
Baik, Chug-Hyun. *The Holy Trinity: God for God and God for Us*. Eugene, OR: Pickwick, 2011.
Bartel, T. W. "Could There Be More Than One Lord?" *Faith and Philosophy: Journal of the Society of Philosophers* 11.3, (July 1, 1994) 357–78.
Barth, Karl. *Church Dogmatics*. Translated by G. W. Bromiley and Thomas F. Torrance. 14 vols. Peabody, MA: Hendrickson, 2010.
Barrett, John K. "Does Inclusivist Theology Undermine Evangelism?" *Evangelical Quarterly* 70.3 (1998) 219–45.
Basinger, David. *The Case for Freewill Theism: A Philosophical Assessment*. Downers Grove, IL: InterVarsity, 1996.
Bauckham, Richard. "In Defence of the Crucified God." In *The Power and Weakness of God: Impassibility and Orthodoxy*, edited by Nigel M. de S. Cameron, 93–118. Papers presented at the Third Edinburgh Conference in Christian Dogmatics, 1989. Edinburgh: Rutherford House, 1990.
———. "'Only the Suffering God Can Help': Divine Passibility in Modern Theology." *Themelios* 9 (1984) 6–12.
Bavinck, Herman. *The Doctrine of God*. Translated by William Hendriksen. 1951. Reprint: Carlisle, PA: The Banner of Truth Trust, 1977.
Beck, James R., and Bruce Demarest. *The Human Person in Theology and Psychology: A Biblical Anthropology for the Twenty-First Century*. Grand Rapids: Kregel, 2005.
Beilby, James K., and Paul R. Eddy. *Divine Foreknowledge: Four Views*. Downers Grove, IL: InterVarsity, 2001.
Berdyaev, Nikolai. *The Meaning of History*. London: Geoffrey Bles, 1936.
Berkhof, Lewis. *Systematic Theology*. 1939. Reprint, London: The Banner of Truth Trust, 1963.

Bloesch, Donald G. *Essentials of Evangelical Theology.* San Francisco: Harper & Row, 1978.
———. *God the Almighty: Power, Wisdom, Holiness, Love.* Christian Foundations. Downers Grove, IL: InterVarsity, 1995.
Blount, Brian K. *Revelation: A Commentary.* The New Testament Library. Louisville: Westminster John Knox, 2009.
Boff, Leonardo. *Trinity and Society.* Translated by Paul Burns. 1988. Reprint: Eugene, OR: Wipf and Stock, 2005.
Bonhoeffer, Dietrich. *The Cost of Discipleship.* New York: Macmillan, 1949.
Boyd, Gregory A. *God of the Possible.* Grand Rapids: Baker, 2000.
———. *Is God to Blame? Beyond Pat Answers to the Problem of Suffering.* Downers Grove, IL: InterVarsity, 2003.
Brasnett, Bertrand. *The Suffering of the Impassible God.* London: Macmillan, 1928.
Bray, Gerald L. *The Doctrine of God.* Downers Grove, IL: InterVarsity, 1993.
———. "Has the Christian Doctrine of God Been Corrupted by Greek Philosophy?" In *God Under Fire: Modern Scholarship Reinvents God,* edited by Douglas S. Huffman and Eric L. Johnson, 105–17. Grand Rapids: Zondervan, 2002.
Brent, Charles H. *The Mount of Vision.* London: Longmans, 1918.
Brierley, Michael. "Introducing the Early British Passibilists." *Zeitschrift Für Neuere Theologiegeschichte* 8.2 (2001) 218–33.
Brown, William. "The Theology of William Newton Clarke." *Harvard Theological Review* 3.1 (1910) 167–80.
Brunner, Emil. *The Christian Doctrine of God.* Vol. 1. Louisville: Westminster, 1950.
Bushnell, Horace. *The Vicarious Sacrifice: Grounded in Principles Interpreted by Human Analogies.* New York: Charles Scribner, 1871.
Caird, John. *The Fundamental Ideas of Christianity.* Vol. 2. Glasgow: James MacLehose and Sons, 1899.
Callen, Barry L. "Clark H. Pinnock: His Life and Work." In *Semper Reformandum: Studies in Honour of Clark H. Pinnock,* edited by Stanley E. Porter and Anthony R. Cross, 1–15. Carlisle, PA: Paternoster, 2003.
———. *Clark H. Pinnock: Journey Toward Renewal, an Intellectual Biography.* Nappanee, IN: Evangel, 2000.
Calvin, John. *Institutes of the Christian Religion.* Edited by John T. McNeill. Translated by Ford Lewis Battles. Library of Christian Classics 20–21. Philadelphia: Westminster, 1967.
Campbell, John M. *The Nature of the Atonement and its Relation to Remission of Sins and Eternal Life.* London: Macmillan, 1906.
Carson, D. A. *The Difficult Doctrine of the Love of God.* Wheaton, IL: Crossway, 2000.
———. *The Gagging of God: Christianity Confronts Pluralism.* Grand Rapids: Zondervan, 1996.
Castelo, Daniel. *The Apathetic God: Exploring the Contemporary Relevance of Divine Impassibility.* Paternoster Theological Monographs. Eugene, OR: Wipf and Stock, 2009.
———. "Qualified Impassibility." In *Divine Impassibility: Four Views,* edited by Robert J. Matz and A. Chadwick Thornhill, 53–86. Downers Grove, IL: IVP Academic, 2019.
Cauthen, Kenneth. *The Impact of American Religious Liberalism.* New York: Harper & Row, 1962.

Charles, R. H. "A Critical and Exegetical Commentary on the Revelation of St. John." In *The International Critical Commentary*, vol. 1. Edinburgh: T & T Clark, 1920.

Charnock, Stephen. *The Existence and Attributes of God*. Grand Rapids: Kregel, 1985.

Christian, Timothy K. "The Experiential Theology of Augustus Hopkins Strong after a Century." *Southwestern Journal of Theology* 50.2 (2008) 183–206.

Clarke, William N. *Can I Believe in God the Father?* New York: Charles Scribner's Son, 1899.

———. *The Christian Doctrine of God*. The International Theological Library. New York: Charles Scribner's Son, 1909.

———. *An Outline of Christian Theology*. 1919. Reprint: Piscataway, NJ: Gorgias, 2010.

———. *The Use of the Scriptures in Theology*. New York: Charles Scribner's Sons, 1905.

Clarke, W. Norris. "A New Look at the Immutability of God." In *God, Knowable and Unknowable*, edited by Robert J. Roth, 43–72. New York: Fordham University Press, 1973.

———. *The Philosophical Approach to God*. Winston-Salem, NC: Wake Forest University Press, 1979.

Clement of Alexandria. "Book Two." In *Clement of Alexandria: Stromateis, Books One to Three*, translated by John Ferguson, 157–255. Fathers of the Church. Washington, DC: Catholic University of America Press, 1991.

Cobb, John B., Jr. *God and the World*. Philadelphia: Westminster, 1969.

Coburn, Robert C. "Professor Malcolm on God." *Australasian Journal of Philosophy* 41.2 (1963) 143–62.

Cohn-Sherbok, Lavinia. "Marten, Hans Lassen (1808–1884)." In *Who's Who in Christianity*. The Routledge Who's Who Series. London: Routledge, 1998.

Cone, James. *God of the Oppressed*. Rev. ed. Maryknoll, NY: Orbis, 1997.

Cooper, John. *Panentheism: The Other God of the Philosophers. From Plato to the Present*. Grand Rapids: Baker, 2006.

Coppedge, Allan. *The God Who Is Triune*. Downers Grove, IL: InterVarsity, 2007.

Cottrell, Jack W. "Conditional Election." In *Grace Unlimited*, edited by Clark H. Pinnock, 51–73. Minneapolis: Bethany Fellowship, 1975.

———. *What the Bible Says about God the Redeemer*. Joplin, MO: College, 1987.

Creel, Richard E. *Divine Impassibility: An Essay in Philosophical Theology*. 1986. Reprint: Eugene, OR: Wipf and Stock, 2005.

Crerar, Douglas. "Hermeneutics of Augusus Hopkins Strong: God and Shakespeare in Rochester." *Foundations* 21.1 (January 1978) 71–76.

Cross, Frank L., and E. A. Livingstone, eds. "The Impassibility of God." In *The Oxford Dictionary of the Christian Church*, 828–38. 3rd ed. New York: Oxford University Press, 2005.

Dabney, Robert L. *Systematic Theology*. 1878. Reprint: Carlisle, PA: The Banner of Truth Trust, 1985.

Davis, Stephen T. *Logic and the Nature of God*. Library of Philosophy and Religion. Grand Rapids: Eerdmans, 1983.

Dinsmore, Charles A. *Atonement in Literature and Life*. Boston: Houghton Mifflin, 1906.

Dodds, Michael J. *The Unchanging God of Love: Thomas Aquinas and Contemporary Theology on Divine Immutability*. Washington, DC: Catholic University of America Press, 2008.

Dolezal, James E. "Still Impossible: Confessing God Without Passions." *Journal of the Institute of Reformed Baptist Studies* 1 (2014) 125–51.

———. "Strong Impassibility." In *Divine Impassibility: Four Views of God's Emotions and Suffering*, edited by Robert J. Matz and A. Chadwick Thornhill, 13–52. Downers Grove, IL: IVP Academic, 2019.

Dorner, Isaak August. *Divine Immutability: A Critical Reconsideration*. Translated by Robert R. Williams and Claude Welch. Fortress Texts in Modern Theology. Minneapolis: Fortress, 1994.

Dorrien, Gary. *The Remaking of Evangelical Theology*. Louisville: Westminster John Knox, 1998.

Duby, Steven J. *Divine Simplicity: A Dogmatic Account*. T & T Clark Studies in Systematic Theology. London: T & T Clark, 2018.

Edwards, Jonathan. *Works of Jonathan Edwards*. Edited by Sang Hyun Lee. Vols. 1–26. New Haven: Yale University Press, 1957-2008.

Edwards, Rem B. "The Pagan Dogma of the Absolute Unchangeableness of God." *Religious Studies* 14 (1978) 305–13.

Emery, Giles. "The Immutability of the God of Love and the Problem of Language Concerning the 'Suffering of God.'" In *Divine Impassibility and the Mystery of Human Suffering*, edited by James F. Keating and Thomas Joseph White, 27–76. Grand Rapids: Eerdmans, 2009.

———. *The Trinitarian Theology of Saint Thomas Aquinas*. Translated by Francesca Aran Murphy. Oxford: Oxford University Press, 2010.

Erickson, Millard J. *God in Three Persons: A Contemporary Interpretation of the Trinity*. Grand Rapids: Baker, 1995.

———. *God the Father Almighty: A Contemporary Exploration of the Divine Attributes*. Grand Rapids: Baker, 1998.

Fairbairn, Andrew M. *The Place of Christ in Modern Theology*. New York: Charles Scribner's Sons, 1893.

Feinberg, John S. *No One Like Him*. Wheaton, IL: Crossway, 2001.

Feser, Edward. *Five Proofs of the Existence of God*. San Francisco: Ignatius, 2017.

Fiddes, Paul S. *The Creative Suffering of God*. Oxford: Clarendon, 1988.

Frame, John M. "Backgrounds to My Thought." In *Speaking the Truth in Love: The Theology of John Frame*, edited by John Hughes, 9–30. Phillipsburg, NJ: P&R, 2009.

———. *The Doctrine of God: A Theology of Lordship*. Phillipsburg, NJ: P&R, 2002.

———. "Introduction to the Reformed Faith." In *The Works of John Frame & Vern Poythress*. June 4, 2012. https://frame-poythress.org/introduction-to-the-reformed-faith/.

———. "Machen's Warrior Children." In *Alister E. McGrath and Evangelical Theology: A Dynamic Engagement*, edited by Sung Wook Chung, 113–46. Carlisle, PA: Paternoster; Grand Rapids: Baker Academic, 2003.

———. "My Books: Their Genesis and Main Ideas." In *Speaking the Truth in Love: The Theology of John Frame*, edited by John Hughes, 3–8. Phillipsburg, NJ: P&R, 2009.

———. *No Other God: A Response to Open Theism*. Phillipsburg, NJ: P&R, 2001.

———. "A Primer on Perspectivalism." In *The Works of John Frame & Vern Poythress*. Rev. ed. June 4, 2012. https://frame-poythress.org/a-primer-on-perspectivalism/.

———. "Reply to Mark W. Karlberg." *Mid-America Journal of Theology* 9.2 (1993) 297–308.

Fretheim, Terence E. *The Suffering of God: An Old Testament Perspective.* Overtures to Biblical Theology. Minneapolis: Fortress, 1984.

Fritsch, Charles T. *The Anti-Anthropomorphisms of the Greek Pentateuch.* Princeton: Princeton University Press, 1943.

Gale, Richard. "Omniscience-Immutability Arguments." *American Philosophical Quarterly* 23.4 (1986) 319–35.

Gamble, Richard C. "The Relationship between Biblical Theology and Systematic Theology." In *Always Reforming: Explorations in Systematic Theology*, edited by A. T. B. McGowan, 211–39. Downers Grove, IL: InterVarsity, 2006.

Garcia, Mark A. "The Word Made Applicable: Frame on Biblical Theology among the Disciplines." In *Speaking the Truth in Love: The Theology of John Frame*, edited by John Hughes, 233–47. Phillipsburg, NJ: P&R, 2009.

Gavrilyuk, Paul L. *The Suffering of the Impassible God: The Dialectics of Patristic Thought.* The Oxford Early Christian Studies. New York: Oxford University Press, 2004.

Geisler, Norman L. *Creating God in the Image of Man?* Minneapolis: Bethany House, 1997.

———. *Systematic Theology.* Minneapolis: Bethany House, 2011.

Geisler, Norman L., and H. Wayne House. *The Battle for God: Responding to the Challenge of Neotheism.* Grand Rapids: Kregel, 2001.

Gess, Wolfgang F. *Die Lehre von der Person Christi.* Basel: Bahnmaiers Buchhandlung (C. Detlof), 1856.

Goetz, Ronald. "The Suffering of God: The Rise of a New Orthodoxy." *The Christian Century* 103 (1986) 385–89.

Goldingay, John. *Old Testament Theology: Israel's Gospel.* Vol. 1. Downers Grove, IL: InterVarsity, 2015.

Grant, Colin. "Possibilities for Divine Passibility." *Toronto Journal of Theology* 4 (1988) 3–18.

Gregory of Nazianzus, Saint. "Third Theological Oration." In *On God and Christ: The Five Theological Orations and Two Letters to Cledonius*, translated by Frederick Williams and Lionel R. Wickham, 69–93. St. Vladimir's Seminary Press Popular Patristics Series 23. Crestwood, NY: St. Vladimir's Seminary Press, 2002.

Grenz, Stanley J. *Rediscovering the Triune God: The Trinity in Contemporary Theology.* Minneapolis: Fortress, 2004.

———. *Renewing the Center: Evangelical Theology in a Post Theological Era.* 2nd ed. Grand Rapids: Baker, 2006.

———. *Theology for the Community of God.* Grand Rapids: Eerdmans, 2000.

Grenz, Stanley J., and Roger E. Olson. *Twentieth-Century Theology: God and the World in a Transitional Age.* Downers Grove, IL: InterVarsity, 1992.

Gresham, John L. Jr. "The Social Model of the Trinity and Its Critics." *Scottish Journal of Theology* 46 (1993) 325–43.

Grillmeier, Aloys. *Christ in Christian Tradition.* Vol. 1. 2nd ed. Translated by John Bowden. Atlanta: John Knox, 1975.

Grudem, Wayne A. *Systematic Theology.* Grand Rapids: Zondervan, 1994.

Gunton, Colin E. *The Promise of Trinitarian Theology.* 2nd ed. London: T & T Clark, 2003.

Hall, Douglas John. *God & Human Suffering: An Exercise in the Theology of the Cross.* Minneapolis: Augsburg, 1986.

Handy, Robert T., ed. *The Social Gospel in America, 1870–1920*. Library of Protestant Thought. New York: Oxford University Press, 1966.

Harrington, Wilfrid. *The Tears of God, Our Benevolent Creator and Human Suffering*. Collegeville, MN: Liturgical, 1992.

Harris, Samuel. *God the Creator and Lord of All*. Vol. 1. New York: Charles Scribner's Sons, 1896.

Hart, David B. *The Beauty of the Infinite: The Aesthetics of Christian Truth*. Grand Rapids: Eerdmans, 2003.

———. "No Shadow of Turning: On Divine Impassibility." *Pro Ecclesia* 11.2 (2002) 184–206.

Hartshorne, Charles. *Man's Vision of God and the Logic of Theism*. Hamden, CT: Archon, 1964.

Hasker, William. "An Adequate God." In *Searching for An Adequate God: A Dialogue Between Process and Free Will Theists*, edited by John B. Cobb Jr., and Clark H. Pinnock, 215–45. Grand Rapids: Eerdmans, 2000.

———. *Metaphysics and the Tri-Personal God*. Oxford: Oxford University Press, 2013.

———. *Providence, Evil and the Openness of God*. Routledge Studies in the Philosophy of Religion 3. London: Routledge, 2004.

Hastings, James, ed. *Encyclopedia of Religion and Ethics*. Vol. 7. New York: Charles Scribner's Sons, 1964.

Helm, Paul. "B. B. Warfield on Divine Passion." *Westminster Theological Journal* 69.1 (2007) 94–104.

———. *Eternal God: A Study of God without Time*. Oxford: Clarendon, 1988.

———. "The Impossibility of Divine Passibility." In *The Power and Weakness of God: Impassibility and Orthodoxy*, edited by Nigel M. de S. Cameron, 119–40. Papers presented at the Third Edinburgh Conference in Christian Dogmatics, 1989. Edinburgh: Rutherford House, 1990.

Henry, Carl F. H. *God, Revelation and Authority*. Vol. 5 of *God Who Stands and Stays: Part One*. Waco, TX: Word, 1979.

———. *Personal Idealism and Strong's Theology*. Wheaton, IL: Van Kampen, 1951.

Henry, Martin. *On Not Understanding God*. Maynoot Bicentenary Series. Dublin, Ireland: Columba, 1997.

Heschel, Abraham J. *The Prophets*. 1962. Reprint: New York: Perennial, 2001.

Highfield, Ron. *Great Is the Lord: Theology for the Praise of God*. Grand Rapids: Eerdmans, 2008.

Hodge, Archibald A. *Outlines of Theology*. Vol. 1. Carlisle, PA: The Banner of Truth Trust, 1972.

Hodge, Charles. *Systematic Theology*. Vol. 1. Peabody, MA: Hendrickson, 2001.

Holmes, Stephen R. "Three versus One? Some Problems of Social Trinitarianism." *Journal of Reformed Theology* 3 (2009) 77–89.

Hopkins, Charles Howard. *The Rise of the Social Gospel in American Protestantism 1865–1915*. New Haven, CT: Yale University Press, 1940.

Horton, Michael S. *The Christian Faith: A Systematic Theology for Pilgrims on the Way*. Grand Rapids: Zondervan, 2011.

———. "'Lord and Giver of Life': The Holy Spirit in Redemptive History." *Journal of the Evangelical Theological Society* 62.1 (2019) 47–63.

———. *Lord and Servant: A Covenant Christology*. Louisville: Westminster John Knox, 2005.

House, Francis H. "The Barrier of Impassibility." *Theology* 83 (1980) 409–15.
Howe, Claude L., Jr. *The Theology of William Newton Clarke*. The Baptist Tradition. New York: Arno, 1980.
Hughes, H. Maldwyn. *What Is the Atonement? A Study in the Passion of God in Christ*. London: James Clarke, 1924.
Jantzen, Grace. *God's World, God's Body*. Philadelphia: Westminster John Knox, 1984.
Jenkins, David E. *The Glory of Man*. Bampton Lectures for 1966. London: SCM, 1967.
Jüngel, Eberhard. *God as the Mystery of the World: On the Foundation of the Theology of the Crucified One in the Dispute between Theism and Atheism*. Translated by Darrell L. Guder. 1983. Reprint: Eugene, OR: Wipf and Stock, 2009.
Justin Martyr. "The First Apology." In *St. Justin Martyr: The First and Second Apologies*, translated and edited by Leslie William Barnard, 23–114. Ancient Christian Writers. New York: Paulist, 1997.
Kärkkäinen, Veli-Matti. *Trinity Global Perspective*. Louisville: Westminster John Knox, 2007.
Karlberg, Mark W. "On the Theological Correlation of Divine and Human Language: A Review Article." *Journal of the Evangelical Theological Society* 32.1 (March 1989) 99–105.
Kearsley, Roy. "Faith and Philosophy in the Early Church." *Themelios* 15 (1990) 81–86.
Keating, James F., and Thomas Joseph White. "Introduction: Divine Impassibility in Contemporary Theology." In *Divine Impassibility and the Mystery of Human Suffering*, edited by James F. Keating and Thomas Joseph White, 1–26. Grand Rapids: Eerdmans, 2009.
Kelly, J. N. D. *Early Christian Doctrines*. Rev. ed. San Francisco: Harper Collins, 1978.
Kennedy, G. A. Studdert. *The Hardest Part*. London: Hodder and Stoughton, 1919.
Kenny, Anthony. *The God of the Philosophers*. Oxford: Clarendon, 1977.
Kitamori, Kazoh. *Theology of the Pain of God: The First Original Theology from Japan*. 1965. Reprint: Eugene, OR: Wipf and Stock, 2005.
Komline, Han-luen Kantzer. "Friendship and Being: Election and Trinitarian Freedom in Moltmann and Barth." *Modern Theology* 29.1 (2013) 1–17.
Kuyper, Lester J. "The Suffering and the Repentance of God." *Scottish Journal of Theology* 22.3 (1969) 257–77.
LaCugna, Catherine Mowry. *God for Us: The Trinity and Christian Life*. 1973. Reprint: San Francisco: Harper San Francisco, 1991.
Lavinia, Cohn-Sherbok. "Martensen, Hans Lassen (1808–1884)." In *Who's Who in Christianity*. The Routledge Who's Who Series. London: Routledge, 1998.
Lee, Jung Young. *God Suffers for Us: A Systematic Inquiry into a Concept of Divine Passibility*. The Hague: Martinus Nijhoff, 1974.
Leigh, Edward. *A Treatise of Divinity*. Vol. 2. London: William Lee, 1646.
Lewis, Gordon, and Bruce Demarest. *Integrative Theology*. Vol. 1. Grand Rapids: Zondervan, 1987.
Lister, Rob. *God Is Impassible and Impassioned: Toward a Theology of Divine Emotion*. Wheaton, IL: Crossway, 2012.
Long, D. Stephen. "Aquinas on God's Sovereignty." In *The Sovereignty of God Debate*, edited by D. Stephen Long and George Kalantzis, 42–60. Eugene, OR: Cascade, 2009.
Lossky, Vladimir. *The Mystical Theology of the Eastern Church*. Crestwood, NY: St. Vladimir's Seminary Press, 1976.

Luther, Martin. *Word and Sacrament III*. Edited by Robert H. Fischer. *Luther's Works* 37. Minneapolis: Fortress, 1976.

Mackintosh, Robert. *Historic Theories of Atonement*. London: Hodder & Stoughton, 1920.

Marshall, Bruce D. "The Dereliction of Christ and the Impassibility of God." In *Divine Impassibility and the Mystery of Human Suffering*, edited by James F. Keating and Thomas Joseph White, 246–98. Grand Rapids: Eerdmans, 2009.

Martensen, Hans L. *Christian Dogmatics: A Compendium of the Doctrines of Christianity*. Translated by William Urwick. Edinburgh: T & T Clark, 1866.

Mason, Arthur James. *Faith of the Gospel: A Manual of Christian Doctrine*. 2nd ed. London: Rivingtons, 1889.

Mathews, Shailer. "In Memoriam: William Newton Clarke." *The American Journal of Theology* 16.3 (1912) 444–48.

Matz, Robert J., and A. Chadwick Thornhill, eds. *Divine Impassibility: Four Views of God's Emotions and Suffering*. Downers Grove, IL: IVP Academic, 2019.

McCabe, Lorenzo Dow. *Divine Nescience of Future Contingencies a Necessity: Being an Introduction to "The Foreknowledge of God, and Cognate Themes."* New York: Phillips & Hunt, 1882.

McCall, Thomas H. *Which Trinity? Whose Monotheism? Philosophical and Systematic Theologians of Trinitarian Theology*. Grand Rapid: Eerdmans, 2010.

McFague, Sallie. *The Body of God: An Ecological Theology*. Minneapolis: Augsburg Fortress, 1993.

McGiffert, Arthur C. "Immanence." In *Encyclopedia of Religion and Ethics*, vol. 7, edited by James Hastings, 167–72. New York: Charles Scribner's Sons, 1951.

Meerson, Michael Aksionov. *The Trinity of Love in Modern Russian Theology: The Love Paradigm and the Retrieval of Western Medieval Love Mysticism in Modern Russian Trinitarian Thought (from Solovyov to Bulgakov)*. Quincy, IL: Franciscan, 1998.

Molnar, Paul D. *Faith, Freedom and the Spirit: The Economic Trinity in Barth, Torrance and Contemporary Theology*. Downers Grove, IL: IVP Academic, 2015.

Moltmann, Jürgen. *The Crucified God: The Cross of Christ as the Foundation and Criticism of Christian Theology*. Translated by R. A. Wilson and John Bowden. New York: Harper & Row, 1974.

———. *God in Creation: A New Theology of Creation and the Spirit of God*. Gifford Lectures 1984–1985. Minneapolis: Fortress, 1993.

———. "God's Kenosis in the Creation and Consummation of the World." In *The Work of Love: Creation as Kenosis*, edited by John Polkinghorne, 137–51. Grand Rapids: Eerdmans, 2001.

———. *The Spirit of Life: A Universal Affirmation*. Translated by Margaret Kohl. Minneapolis: Fortress, 1992.

———. *The Trinity and the Kingdom: The Doctrine of God*. Translated by Margaret Kohl. Minneapolis: Fortress, 1993.

Moore, LeRoy, Jr. "Academic Freedom: A Chapter in the History of the Colgate Rochester Divinity School." *Foundations* 10.1 (January 1967) 64–79.

Morgan, G. Campbell. *The Bible and the Cross*. New York: Fleming H. Revell, 1909.

Morris, Thomas V. *Our Idea of God*. Downers Grove, IL: InterVarsity, 1991.

Mosser, Carl. "Fully Social Trinitarianism." In *Philosophical and Theological Essays on the Trinity*, edited by Thomas McCall and Michael C. Rae, 131–50. Oxford: Oxford University Press, 2009.

Mozley, J. K. *The Doctrine of the Atonement.* New York: Charles Scribner's Sons, 1916.

———. *The Impassibility of God: A Survey of Christian Thought.* 1926. Reprint: Cambridge: Cambridge University Press, 2014.

Müller, Julius. *The Christian Doctrine of Sin.* Translated by William Urwick. Vol. 2. Edinburgh: T & T Clark, 1885.

Muller, Richard A. *The Divine Essence and Attributes.* Vol. 3 of *Post-Reformation Reformed Dogmatics: The Rise and Development of Reformed Orthodoxy, ca. 1520 to ca. 1725.* 2nd ed. Grand Rapids: Baker Academic, 2003.

Mullins, R. T. *The End of the Timeless God.* Oxford Studies in Analytic Theology. New York: Oxford University Press, 2015.

Nash, Ronald H. *The Concept of God: An Exploration of Contemporary Difficulties with the Attributes of God.* Grand Rapids: Zondervan, 1983.

Ngien, Dennis. "The God Who Suffers." *Christianity Today* 41.2 (1997) 38–42.

Oden, Thomas C. *Systematic Theology: The Living God.* Vol. 1. San Francisco: Harper & Row, 1987.

Ohlrich, Charles. *The Suffering God: Hope and Comfort for Those Who Hurt.* Downers Grove, IL: InterVarsity, 1982.

Olson, Roger E. *The Journey of Modern Theology: From Reconstruction to Deconstruction.* Downers Grove, IL: InterVarsity, 2013.

———. "Post Conservative Evangelical Theology and the Theological Pilgrimage of Clark Pinnock." In *Semper Reformandum: Studies in Honour of Clark H. Pinnock*, edited by Stanley E. Porter and Anthony R. Cross, 16–37. Carlisle, PA: Paternoster, 2003.

Oord, Thomas J. *Defining Love: A Philosophical, Scientific, and Theological Engagement.* Grand Rapids: Brazos, 2010.

———. "Strong Passibility." In *Divine Impassibility: Four Views of God's Emotions and Suffering*, edited by Robert J. Matz and A. Chadwick Thornhill, 129–66. Downers Grove, IL: IVP Academic, 2019.

Origen. "Homily 6." In *Homilies 1–14 on Ezekiel*, translated by Thomas P. Scheck, 86–98. Ancient Christian Writers: The Works of the Fathers in Translation 62. New York: Newman, 2010.

Owen, H. P. *Concepts of Deity.* Philosophy and Religion Series. London: Palgrave Macmillan, 1971.

Packer, J. I. "Theism for Our Time." In *God Who Is Rich in Mercy*, edited by Peter T. O'Brien and David G. Peterson, 1–23. Grand Rapids: Baker, 1986.

Pannenberg, Wolfhart. *Basic Questions in Theology.* Translated by George H. Kehm. Vol. 2. 1971. Reprint: Philadelphia: Westminster, 1983.

Peckham, John C. *The Doctrine of God: Introducing the Big Questions.* London: T & T Clark, 2019.

———. "Qualified Passibility." In *Divine Impassibility: Four Views*, edited by Robert Matz and A. Chadwick Thornhill, 87–128. Downers Grove, IL: IVP Academic, 2019.

Pelikan, Jaroslav. *Christian Doctrine and Modern Culture (since 1700).* Vol. 5 of *The Christian Tradition: A History of the Development of Doctrine.* Chicago: University of Chicago Press, 1989.

Pike, Nelson. *God and Timelessness.* London: Routledge & Kegan Paul, 1970.

Pinnock, Clark H. *Flame of Love: A Theology of the Holy Spirit.* Downers Grove, IL: InterVarsity, 1996.

———. *The Grace of God, the Will of Man: A Case for Arminianism*. Grand Rapids: Zondervan, 1989.

———. *Most Moved Mover: A Theology of God's Openness*. Grand Rapids: Baker Academic, 2001.

———. "Systematic Theology." In *The Openness of God: A Biblical Challenge to the Traditional Understanding of God*, 101–25. Downers Grove, IL: InterVarsity, 1994.

Pinnock, Clark, Richard Rice, John Sanders, William Hasker, and David Basinger. *The Openness of God: A Biblical Challenge to the Traditional Understand of God*. Downers Grove, IL: InterVarsity, 1994.

Piper, John. *A Godward Life: Seeing the Supremacy of God in All of Life*. Rev. ed. Colorado Springs: Multnomah, 2015.

Plantinga, Alvin. "Self-Profile." In *Alvin Plantinga*, edited by James E. Tomberlin and Peter van Inwagen, 3–97. Dordrecht: D. Riedel, 1985.

Placher, William C. *Narratives of a Vulnerable God: Christ, Theology, and Scripture*. Louisville: Westminster John Knox, 1994.

Pollard, T. E. "Impassibility of God." *Scottish Journal of Theology* 8 (1955) 353–64.

Pool, Jeff. *God's Wounds: Hermeneutic of the Christian Symbol of Divine Suffering*. Vol. 1 of *Divine Vulnerability and Creation*. Princeton Theological Monograph Series. Cambridge: James Clarke, 2009.

Powell, Samuel M. *The Impassioned Life: Reason and Emotion in the Christian Tradition*. Minneapolis: Fortress, 2016.

Rahner, Karl. *The Trinity*. 1970. Reprint: New York: Crossroad, 2005.

Randles, Marshall. *The Blessed God: Impassibility*. London: C. H. Kelly, 1900.

Reist, Irwin W. "Augustus Hopkins Strong and William Newton Clarke: A Study in Nineteenth Century Evolutionary and Eschatological Thought." *Foundations* 13.1 (January 1970) 26–43.

———. "William Newton Clarke: Nineteenth-Century Evolutionary and Eschatological Immanentism." *Foundations* 18.1 (January 1975) 5–25.

Renihan, Samuel. *God Without Passions: A Reader*. Palmdale, CA: Reformed Baptist Academic, 2015.

Rice, Richard. "Biblical Support for a New Perspective." In *The Openness of God: A Biblical Challenge to the Traditional Understanding of God*, 11–58. Downers Grove, IL: InterVarsity, 1994.

———. "Does Open Theism Limit God?" *Wesleyan Theological Journal* 48.2 (2013) 30–43.

———. *The Openness of God: The Relationship of Divine Foreknowledge and Human Free Will (Horizon)*. Nashville: Review and Herald, 1980.

Richard of Saint Victor. *On the Trinity: English Translation and Commentary*. Translated by Ruben Angelici. Cambridge: James Clarke, 2012.

Richardson, Cyril C. *The Doctrine of the Trinity*. Nashville: Abingdon, 1958.

Richardson, Kurt A. "Augustus Hopkins Strong." In *Baptist Theologians*, edited by Timothy George and David S. Dockery, 289–306. Nashville: Broadman, 1990.

Roberts, Robert C. *Emotions: An Essay in Aid of Moral Psychology*. Cambridge: Cambridge University Press, 2003.

Robinson, Henry W. *Suffering: Human and Divine*. New York: Macmillan, 1939.

Rogers, Katherine A. *Perfect Being Theology*. Edinburgh: Edinburgh University Press, 2000.

Rowe, William L. *Philosophy of Religion*. Encino, CA: Dickenson, 1978.

Rubenstein, Richard L. *After Auschwitz*. 2nd ed. Baltimore: Johns Hopkins University Press, 1992.
Sanders, Fred. "Entangled in the Trinity: Economic and Immanent Trinity in Recent Theology." *Dialog* 40.3 (2001) 175–82.
Sanders, John. *The God Who Risks: A Theology of Divine Providence*. 2nd ed. Downers Grove, IL: InterVarsity, 2007.
———. "Historical Considerations." In *The Openness of God: A Biblical Challenge to the Traditional Understanding of God*, 59–100. Downers Grove, IL: InterVarsity, 1994.
Sarot, Marcel. "Auschwitz, Morality and the Suffering of God." *Modern Theology* 7.2 (January 1991) 135–52.
———. *God, Passibility and Corporeality*. Kampen: Kok Pharos, 1992.
———. "Patripassianism, Theopaschitism and the Suffering of God. Some Historical and Systematic Considerations." *Religious Studies* 26 (1990) 363–75.
———. "Suffering of Christ, Suffering of God?" *Theology* 95 (1992) 113–18.
Schilling, S. Paul. *God and Human Anguish*. Nashville: Abingdon, 1977.
Schiørring, J. H. "Martensen." In *Kierkegaard's Teachers*, edited by Niels Thulstrup and Marie Mikulová Thulstrup, 177–207. Bibliotheca Kierkegaardiana 10. Copenhagen: C. A. Reitzels Forlag, 1982.
Schleiermacher, Friedrich D. E. *The Christian Faith*. Edinburgh: T & T Clark, 1928.
Schweitzer, Don. "Aspects of God's Relationship to the World in the Theologies of Jürgen Moltmann, Bonaventure and Jonathan Edwards." *Religious Studies and Theology* 26.1 (2007) 5–24.
Scrutton, Anastasia Philippa. *Thinking Through Feeling: God, Emotion and Passibility*. Continuum Studies in Philosophy of Religion. New York: Continuum International, 2011.
Shedd, William G. T. *Dogmatic Theology*. Vol. 1. New York: Charles Scribner's Sons, 1888.
Simon, D. W. *Reconciliation by Incarnation: The Reconciliation of God and Man by the Incarnation of the Divine Word*. Edinburgh: T & T Clark, 1898.
Smyth, Egbert Coffin. *Progressive Orthodoxy: A Contribution to the Christian Interpretation of Christian Doctrines*. Boston: Houghton Mifflin, 1892.
Sonderegger, Katherine. *Systematic Theology*. Vol. 1. Minneapolis: Fortress, 2015.
Sproul, R. C. *Willing to Believe: The Controversy over Free Will*. Grand Rapids: Baker, 1997.
Steen, Marc. "The Theme of the 'Suffering' God: An Exploration." In *God and Human Suffering*, edited Jan Lambrecht and Raymond F. Collins, 69–94. Louvain Theological & Pastoral Monographs 3. Louvain, Belgium: Peeters, 1990.
Stevens, George Barker. *The Christian Doctrine of Salvation*. International Theological Library. New York: Charles Scribner's Sons, 1905.
Stewart, Jon. "Kierkegaard and Hegelianism in Golden Age Denmark." In *Kierkegaard and His Contemporaries: The Culture of Golden Age Denmark*, edited by Jon Steward, 106–48. Kierkegaard Studies Monograph Series 10. Berlin: Walter De Gruyter, 2003.
Storr, Vernon F. *The Problem of the Cross*. London: John Murray, 1919.
Strong, Augustus H. *Christ in Creation and Ethical Monism*. Philadelphia: Roger Williams, 1899.
———. *Systematic Theology*. 1907. Reprint: Old Tappan, NJ: Fleming H. Revell, 1969.
Sturch, R. L. "The Problem of Divine Eternity." *Religious Studies* 10.4 (1974) 487–93.

Surin, Kenneth. "The Impassibility of God and the Problem of Evil." *Scottish Journal of Theology* 35 (1982) 97–115.

Swinburne, Richard. *The Coherence of Theism*. Oxford: Oxford University Press, 1977.

Taliaferro, Charles. "The Passibility of God." *Religious Studies* 25.2 (1989) 217–24.

Tertullian. *Tertullian's Treatise Against Praxeas: The Text Edited, with an Introduction, Translation, and Commentary*. Edited and translated by Ernest Evans. London: SPCK, 1948.

Thaumaturgus, Gregory, Saint. *St. Gregory Thaumaturgus: Life and Works*. Translated by Michael Slusser. The Fathers of the Church. Washington, DC: Catholic University of America Press, 1998.

Thomas, Derek. "Frame on the Attributes of God." In *Speaking the Truth in Love: The Theology of John Frame*, edited by John Hughes, 351–68. Phillipsburg, NJ: P&R, 2009.

Thompson, Curtis L. *Following the Cultured Public's Chosen One: Why Martensen Mattered to Kierkegaard*. Danish Golden Age Studies 4. Copenhagen: Museum Tusculanum, 2008.

Torrance, Thomas F. *The Christian Doctrine of God: One Being, Three Persons*. Edinburgh: T & T Clark, 1996.

Trumper, Tim J. R. "John Frame's Methodology: A Case Study in Constructive Calvinism." In *Speaking the Truth in Love: The Theology of John Frame*, edited by John Hughes, 145–72. Phillipsburg, NJ: P&R, 2009.

Turretin, Francis. *Institutes of Elenctic Theology*. Vol. 1. Edited by James T. Dennison Jr. Translated by George Musgrave Giger. Phillipsburg: P&R, 1992.

Tymms, T. Vincent. *The Christian Idea of Atonement*. New York: Macmillan, 1904.

Unamuno, Miguel de. *Tragic Sense of Life*. Translated by J. E. Crawford Flitch. New York: Dover, 1954.

Van den Brink, Gijsbert. "Social Trinitarianism: A Discussion of Some Recent Theological Criticisms." *International Journal of Systematic Theology* 16 (2014) 331–50.

Van Dusen, Henry P. *The Vindication of Liberal Theology*. New York: Scriber, 1963.

Vande Brake, Peter H. "Divine Passibility." PhD diss., Calvin Theological Seminary, 2001.

Vanhoozer, Kevin J. *Remythologizing Theology: Divine Action, Passion, and Authorship*. New York: Cambridge University Press, 2010.

von Harnack, Adolf. *History of Dogma*. Vol. 1. Translated by Neil Buchanan. New York: Russell & Russell, 1958.

Ware, Bruce A. "An Evangelical Reexamination of the Doctrine of the Immutability of God." PhD diss., Fuller Theological Seminary, 1984.

———. "An Evangelical Reformulation of the Doctrine of the Immutability of God." *Journal of the Evangelical Theological Society* 29 (1986) 431–36.

———. *God's Greater Glory: The Exalted God of Scripture and the Christian Faith*. Wheaton, IL: Crossway, 2004.

———. *God's Lesser Glory: The Diminished God of Open Theism*. Wheaton, IL: Crossway, 2000.

———. "How Shall We Think About the Trinity?" In *God Under Fire: Modern Scholarship Reinvents God*, edited by Douglas S. Huffman and Eric L. Johnson, 253–78. Grand Rapids: Zondervan, 2002.

———. "A Modified Calvinist Doctrine of God." In *Perspectives on the Doctrine of God: Four Views*, edited by Bruce Ware, 76-120. Nashville: Broadman and Holman, 2008.
Webster, John. *God without Measure: Working Papers in Christian Theology*. Vol. 1. London: T & T Clark, 2016.
Weinandy, Thomas G. *Does God Suffer?* Notre Dame: University of Notre Dame Press, 2000.
Welch, Claude. *God and Incarnation in Mid-Nineteenth Century German Theology: G. Thomasius, I. A. Dorner, A. E. Beidermann*. New York: Oxford University Press, 1965.
———. *In This Name: The Doctrine of the Trinity in Contemporary Theology*. New York: Charles Scribner's Sons, 1952.
White, Andrew Dickson. *A History of the Warfare of Science with Theology in Christendom*. Vol. 2. New York: Appleton, 1896.
White, Douglas. *Forgiveness and Suffering: A Study of Christian Belief*. Cambridge: Cambridge University Press, 1913.
Whitehead, Alfred North. *Process and Reality: An Essay in Cosmology*. Gifford Lectures delivered at the University of Edinburgh during the Session 1927-28. Edited by David Ray Griffin and Donald W. Sherburne. New York: Free Press, 1978.
Wiles, Maurice. "Some Reflections on the Origins of the Doctrine of the Trinity." *Journal of Theological Studies* 8 (1957) 92-106.
Williams, Daniel Day. "Suffering and Being in Empirical Theology." In *The Future of Empirical Theology*, edited by B. L. Meland, 175-94. Essays in Divinity. Chicago: University of Chicago Press, 1969.
Williams, Thomas. "Introduction to Classical Theism." In *Models of God and Alternative Ultimate Realities*, edited by Jeanine Diller and Asa Kasher, 95-100. New York: Springer, 2013.
Wolterstorff, Nicholas. "God Everlasting." In *Contemporary Philosophy of Religion*, edited by Sven M. Cahn and David Shatz, 181-203. New York: Oxford University Press, 1982.
Wright, David F., Sinclair Ferguson, and J. I. Packer, eds. "God." In *New Dictionary of Theology*, 274-77. Downers Grove, IL: InterVarsity, 1988.
Wright, R. K. McGregor. *No Place for Sovereignty: What's Wrong with Freewill Theism*. Downers Grove, IL: InterVarsity, 1996.
Wuellner, Bernard. "Passion." In *Dictionary of Scholastic Philosophy*, 88-89. Milwaukee: Bruce, 1956.
Young, Frances M. "Incarnation and Atonement: God Suffered and Died." In *Incarnation and Myth: The Debate Continued*, edited by Michael Goulder, 101-3. London: SCM, 1979.
Zizioulas, John D. *Being as Communion: Studies in Personhood and the Church*. Contemporary Greek Theologians 4. Crestwood, NY: St. Vladimir's Seminary Press, 1993.

www.ingramcontent.com/pod-product-compliance
Lightning Source LLC
Chambersburg PA
CBHW022015220426
43663CB00007B/1088